Strategies for Active Learning

James E. Twining
Community College of Rhode Island

Allyn and Bacon
BOSTON LONDON TORONTO SYDNEY TOKYO SINGAPORE

To my wife,
Kathleen Ann

Executive Editor: Joseph Opiela
Series Editorial Assistant: Amy Capute
Production Administrator: Rowena Dores
Editorial-Production Service: Editorial Inc.
Cover Administrator: Linda Dickinson
Composition and Manufacturing Buyer: Louise Richardson

Library of Congress Cataloging-in-Publication Data

Twining, James E.
Strategies for active learning / James E. Twining.
p. cm.
Includes index.
ISBN 0-205-13070-4
1. Study, Method of. 2. Self-culture. 3. Adult learning.
I. Title.
LB2395.T88 1991
371.3'028'1—dc20

90-23621
CIP

This textbook is printed on recycled, acid-free paper.

CREDITS

Chapter 6, note 8, from *Power and Politics in America,* 5th ed., by L. Freedman and R. A. Riske, copyright © 1987 by Brooks/Cole Publishing Company, a division of Wadsworth, Inc. Reprinted by permission.

Credits continued page 381, which constitutes an extension of the copyright page.

Printed in the United States of America
10 9 8 7 6 5 4 3 2 1 95 94 93 92 91 90

Contents

Preface xi

CHAPTER 1 The Importance of Self-awareness **1**

Self-awareness 2
Self-awareness and College Resources 3
Self-awareness and Problem Solving 4
Understand the Situation 4 ▫ Examine Your Strengths and Weaknesses 6 ▫ Plan a Response 7 ▫ Apply Your Plan 8 ▫ Evaluate the Results 8
Self-assessment 10
The Self-assessment Questionnaire 10 ▫ Analyzing the Assessment 15
Maintaining a Positive Attitude 18
Chapter Review 19

CHAPTER 2 Active Learning **23**

Taking Responsibility 24
How People Learn 24

Preparation for Learning 26
Know Yourself 26 □ Critical Tasks 27 □ The Nature of the Material 27 □ Learning Strategies 28
Monitoring Your Efforts 29
Monitoring Comprehension 30
Evaluating Learning 32
Self-testing 32 □ Type of Information 33 □ Review and Memory 33
Summary 35
Chapter Review 37

CHAPTER 3 Managing Time Effectively 40

Clearly Established Goals 41
Be Specific 43 □ Goals for the Present 43 □ Immediate Goals 44
Careful Planning 45
A Term/Semester Schedule 45 □ Weekly Schedules 46 □ A Typical Week 46 □ The Immediate Situation 51
Monitoring Your Activities 55
Questions for Self-monitoring 55
Problem Solving 58
The Situation 59 □ The Response 59 □ The Result 59
Evaluation 60
A Strategy for Time Management 61
Chapter Review 62

CHAPTER 4 Purposeful Study 65

A Positive Self-concept 66
Positive Self-talk 66
Planning Purposeful Study 67
Preparing Psychologically 68 □ Creating a Study Environment 70 □ Establishing Goals 71 □ Organizing a Schedule 73 □ Choosing Organizational Strategies 74

Monitoring Your Progress in Study 76
Monitoring with a Checklist 77 □ Problem Solving and Strategy Revision 78 □ A Think-aloud Strategy 79 □ Cooperative Learning 80
Evaluating the Study Process 81
Flexibility 82 □ Seeking Additional Help 82 □ A Final Point 83
Summary 84
Chapter Review 84

CHAPTER 5 Taking Lecture Notes 87

Active Listening 88
Purpose in Listening 89 □ Listening to Lectures 89 □ Asking Questions 90 □ Following the Organization 91
Techniques for Taking Lecture Notes 92
A Format for Note-taking 94 □ Organizing Notes 94 □ Sample Notes 96
Revising and Reviewing 100
Revision 101 □ Periodic Review 101
Self-monitoring Checklist 107
Summary 108
Chapter Review 108

CHAPTER 6 Reading Textbooks 112

Informational Text 113
A Typical Chapter 114 □ The Content of a Chapter 114 □ The Reading Process 120
A Systematic Approach to Reading 121
Preview 121 □ Reading Textbooks 124 □ Self-testing 133 □ The Review Process 135
Monitoring Textbook Reading 142
Summary 143
Chapter Review 144

CHAPTER 7 Marking Texts and Taking Notes 147

Active Involvement 148
Marking Text 148
A Marking Technique 149 ▫ A Closer Look 150
Taking Notes 154
Sentence Summaries 154 ▫ To Clarify a Point 154
Using Paraphrase 160
An Example 160
Periodic Information Summaries 163
An Example 163
Graphic Techniques 166
Mapping Information 166 ▫ An Example 168 ▫ Flowcharting Information 173 ▫ A Practical Look 174
Self-monitoring 176
A Final Note 177
Chapter Review 178

CHAPTER 8 Vocabulary and Concept Development 181

Distinguishing Words 182
Examining Concepts 184
A Strategy for Learning 187
Intent to Learn 187 ▫ Prior Knowledge 188 ▫ A Common Approach to Unfamiliar Words 188 ▫ Elaboration and Integration 192 ▫ Rehearsal and Reinforcement 198 ▫ Self-monitoring 200 ▫ Evaluation 201
Integration with Active Learning 203
Value the Incidental 203
Chapter Review 204

CHAPTER 9 Memory 207

Memory as a Process 208

Sensory Register 208 □ Short-Term Memory 209 □ Long-Term Memory 209
Improving Memory 210
The Encoding Process 210 □ The Storage Process 212 □ The Retrieval Process 220
A Strategy for Remembering 225
Know Your Task 226 □ Plan Your Approach 226 □ Be Flexible 226 □ Self-monitor 227 □ Evaluate Your Success 227
Self-monitoring 228
Summary 228
Chapter Review 229

CHAPTER 10 Taking Tests **232**

Predicting Test Questions 233
Sources of Information 233 □ Practice Questions 234
Overcoming Test Anxiety 237
Progressive Relaxation 238
A Strategy for Taking Tests 240
Follow Directions 240 □ Preview the Exam 241 □ Plan Your Approach 242 □ Put the Plan into Action 243 □ Briefly Review the Exam 246 □ Evaluate the Results 247
Monitoring the Test-taking Process 248
Summary 250
Chapter Review 250

CHAPTER 11 Studying Science and Math **253**

Studying Textbooks 254
Chapter Previews and Graphic Overviews 254 □ Following the Organization 257 □ Use of Illustration 259
Learning Concepts 260
Solving Problems 265
Remembering Information 269
Self-monitoring 272
Summary 273
Chapter Review 274

CHAPTER 12 Reading Literature 277

Elements of Fiction 278
Character 278 □ Setting 279 □ Plot 280 □ Theme 281
Strategies for Reading 282
Dividing the Text 282 □ Asking Questions 283 □ Visualizing Characters and Events 285 □ Personal Involvement 288
Organizing Strategies 289
Summarize Plot 289 □ Describe Character 289 □ Identify Setting 289 □ State Theme 289
Monitoring Questions 291
Evaluating Your Success 304
Chapter Review 305

CHAPTER 13 Writing Papers 308

Planning a Paper 309
Selecting a Topic 309 □ Making a List 311 □ Planning an Outline 312
Drafting a Paper 314
Introduction 314 □ Development 315 □ Conclusion 316
Revising 317
Resources 318
Self-monitoring 320
Summary 321
Chapter Review 322

CHAPTER 14 Using the Library 325

Investigating the Library 326
Primary Sources 328
Card Catalog 328 □ Periodicals 331 □ Academic Index 334
Libraries and Learning 336
Monitoring the Library Experience 338
Summary 339
Chapter Review 339

Post-assessment Questionnaire 342

Appendixes
Appendix to Chapter 5 350
Appendix to Chapter 6 356
Appendix to Chapter 7 360
Appendix to Chapter 8 366
Appendix to Chapter 10 368
Appendix to Chapter 11 370
Appendix to Chapter 12 372

Index 376

Preface

Higher education once again finds itself at a crossroads. On the one hand, changing demographics and a less-than-excellent secondary education system present colleges and universities with fewer and somewhat less prepared traditional students. At the same time, increasing numbers of older adults with limited academic experience and younger educationally disadvantaged students—so-called nontraditional students—are entering postsecondary institutions. On the other hand, public attitudes and economic circumstances demand not only that students' lack of academic preparation be resolved by postsecondary institutions but also that greater numbers graduate with a higher quality of education. One response to this situation is *Strategies for Active Learning.*

Strategies for Active Learning is designed to introduce students to a systematic approach to learning that will enhance any student's potential for success. In one sense, this book is part of a long tradition in education of providing students with the study skills necessary for academic success. But it is more than that because *Strategies for Active Learning* is concerned with an active approach to learning how to learn. This approach does not simply tell students what they ought to know; rather, it promotes the view that individual responsibility and a strategic awareness of the learning process comprise the primary path to success. Furthermore, *Strategies for Active Learning* incorporates recent developments in cognitive psychology and learning theory—schema theory, metacognitive processes, and training studies—that offer new promise for the total realm of developmental education.

The specific rationale for this work grows from a desire to promote student success by combining schema theory and a metacognitive approach to active learning, and by articulating strategies used by fluent readers and supported by current educational research. Schema theory suggests that fluent readers acquire a systematic approach to learning as a consequence of their education and experience. A metacognitive approach to learning suggests that certain strategies dominate the learning process. In the most fundamental sense, these dominant strategies involve a process of planning, monitoring, and evaluating. Specific learning strategies such as note-taking and concept mapping or visual imagery and think-aloud activities can be incorporated into this larger framework, thereby drawing upon the insight of research with specific techniques or procedures. The end result is that students develop an awareness of how to approach such problems as taking lecture notes, reading textbooks, or studying science by following a general routine. At the same time, they make individual decisions about how to handle specific problems, such as organizing a study schedule, mastering a complex reading assignment, or preparing for a comprehensive examination. Most important, students learn how to monitor their own learning activities, to track their progress with a particular task, and to make knowledgeable decisions regarding the success of their efforts.

Underlying the text's design is the link between increasing students' awareness of the learning process and promoting their control of that process. The material presents a systematic approach to active learning based on a metacognitive approach. For instance, Chapter 1 introduces students to "self-awareness" in learning and provides a detailed "self-assessment" of study habits as the starting point for change. This foundation links self-awareness with a problem-solving process for mastering new situations, thereby creating a framework for individual initiative. Chapter 2 presents an overview of the metacognitive approach to "active learning," the basics of which underlie the total design of the text. Students are thereby presented with an overview of an integrated schemata for learning that has a very practical application, concluding with a self-interrogation strategy for evaluating the study process. This chapter foreshadows many of the strategies presented throughout the text.

Each subsequent chapter presents a strategy or strategies for resolving problems associated with various aspects of the learning process. A range of subjects from time management to reading textbooks, from purposeful study to improving memory, and from studying science to reading literature are the feature topics of individual chapters. The focus of each is on learning a systematic procedure for accomplishing certain tasks and on monitoring those learning activities to determine progress with each step in the task or to take any necessary corrective action.

One of the primary reasons for creating strategies rather than simply discussing skills or techniques is that strategies help to promote a way of thinking, a way of approaching a learning task or similar problematic situations. Current research indicates that various instructional strategies actually create a cognitive framework for independent efforts. Integrated throughout the presentation are brief exercises that further sensitize students to a given problem or require some application of the strategies studied. The text concludes with a post-assessment of study habits that offers students an opportunity to reassess, or evaluate, their progress and to decide which areas may require additional attention.

There are sample learning activities throughout the text and a variety of specific exercises are offered to give students practical experience with the strategy being presented. The focus of these activities is on modeling strategies through the application of systematic procedures, including such important areas as comprehension monitoring, semantic mapping, visual imagery, and cooperative learning. Specific exercises are incorporated into the text, and the material used is mostly excerpted from college texts so that it presents examples of connected discourse of reasonable length. The use of naturalistic examples of text is crucial to a student's transfer of learning strategies to the academic environment. In addition, considerable emphasis is placed on going beyond the text to the required learning activities of academic life.

Each chapter also integrates a structured model for reading, so students follow a systematic strategy for effective reading while studying new strategies for learning. The model includes beginning the chapter with preview exercises; establishing a purpose for reading; using questions based on the central features of the chapter to guide the reading process, to periodically summarize and predict the content, and to review the chapter; and finishing with a chapter review incorporating true-false, multiple choice, short essay, application, and synthesis questions. In this manner, reading and thinking are systematically integrated with the presentation of specific strategies for improving the learning process.

Graphic or visual representations of the information under discussion are also integrated throughout the text. The emphasis on the visual is a further effort to link self-awareness and learning strategies through images. Visual imagery plays an important role in both problem-solving and memory; therefore, graphic images further enhance the concept and strategic elements of the text.

As for presentation, every attempt is made to present material in a conversational style without over-simplifying issues or speaking down to the reader. In some places the text attempts to counsel and guide students and is rather informal; in other places, the text is clearly instructional and is, therefore, somewhat more formal. To some extent, the narrative itself helps to promote a schemata for learning in the sense that the narrative is a way of thinking. In general, the style provides a level of readability compatible with its prospective audience, college students.

Strategies for Active Learning is designed to be used in a number of settings from reading and study skills programs to the student development programs. It can be used in a traditional classroom setting, in an individually oriented learning lab, or as an independent self-help book. In addition, it can be used sequentially, following the chapter development design, or in a more varied fashion based on student needs as identified by the self-assessment in Chapter 1. The text displays the same versatility that the active learning process demands. With thoughtful planning, systematic self-monitoring, and periodic evaluation, active learning is the path to academic success.

Acknowledgments

The making of a textbook is no simple task. Influential teachers and scholars, long-remembered students, and a multitude of experiences establish the foundation for the project. Quite obviously, many individuals contribute to the making of a successful text; however, a few require special note because their contributions to this book were direct and significant. Foremost among these individuals is my wife, Kathleen Ann, who is an important source of intellectual and emotional support, and a valuable critic of innumerable drafts. She has my deepest appreciation. I must also thank my editor at Allyn and Bacon, Joseph Opiela, who deserves credit for providing support and guidance to a project that must blend the various needs and desires of students, professors, and the author into an effective learning text. And my thanks also to his assistant, Rebecca Dudley, who helped refine the writing process. Finally, I would like to acknowledge the helpful advice and valuable suggestions of the many reviewers of my early drafts:

Joanne Carter-Wells, California State University at Fullerton
Suzette Cohen, Cleveland State University

Thomas Deschaine, Grand Rapids Junior College
Helen Gilbart, St. Petersburg Junior College
Paul Kazmierski, Rochester Institute of Technology
Kathleen T. McWhorter, Niagara County Community College
Clyde Moneyhun, University of Texas at Arlington.

1

The Importance of Self-awareness

Preview Exercise

To begin this chapter, take a few moments to read the introduction, the conclusion, and each of the topic subheadings. Also look at the illustrations and exercises. Use that information as a guide to the content of the chapter. Then give yourself a purpose for reading. Your purpose might be: To understand how self-awareness can improve my learning ability. Another purpose might be: To identify my strengths and weaknesses in studying.

PURPOSE FOR READING: ______________________________

____

____

College is a challenge in self-awareness. It is a unique opportunity for growth—personal, social, and academic. College is also a time of transition from one stage in life to another. It is the beginning of an exciting future.

Yet college may also be a time of confusion and anxiety. People tend to be creatures of habit, and college requires change—serious change. Such change invokes both excitement and apprehension. And going to college changes people's lives.

A former student recently recalled her initiation to this change. Her involvement came in stages. At first she could not decide whether or not to go to college. Her marriage, her children, and her responsibilities at home required most of her time. She felt confused. After she made the decision to register for classes, she felt a great deal of anxiety: Would there be time for both school and family? She became apprehensive, wondering if she had made the right choice. Could she be wife, mother, and student all at the same time? Would she succeed? College was a new experience that she approached hesitantly. Yet once she was *in* the college environment—meeting students, attending classes, learning new ideas—she was excited by the experience. She knew, of course, that she would meet certain difficulties as she proceeded, but her newfound self-awareness—the confidence that she could attend college and still have enough time for her family—would guide her as she continued her education.

Guiding Questions

As you read this chapter, think about the following questions and read to find answers:

1. How can self-awareness contribute to your college success?
2. Why do self-awareness and problem solving play such important roles in active learning?
3. How can a self-assessment of your strengths and weaknesses help you master the learning process?
4. What benefits are there to approaching new and perhaps frightening situations with a positive attitude?

SELF-AWARENESS

Diversity defines the college experience. College campuses are incredibly active places. For students, daily academic activities may range from history lectures to biology labs, from public speaking to writing research reports. And then there is that wide world beyond the classroom, with young men and women rushing from dining hall to dance club and from library to football stadium. For many students today, there's a full-time job as well as never-ending family responsibilities, and late evening classes. Many demands fill the lives of college students. Meeting them requires a sound sense of self-awareness—the knowledge of who you are, where you are, what your purpose is, how you can accomplish each new task, and how you can ultimately achieve success. Such awareness provides a sense of purpose and the inner resources to master new situations.

Self-awareness and College Resources

If diversity defines the college experience, so does the feeling of being overwhelmed. How often do students find themselves having to choose between going out on a date or studying the next chapter for psychology, between having dinner with the family or finishing a library assignment? Always there is the question of what to do first, what has priority. This is partially a question of time management, a topic considered in a later chapter. But it is also a question of using college resources to make wise decisions and become a more effective student.

Mastering the diversity of the college environment requires an awareness of resources. One of the first resources you need in order to plan a course of study leading to a degree is the college catalog. There you will find a variety of information, from sample programs to specific course descriptions, from general degree requirements to specific program requirements. In addition, for more direct guidance in planning a course of study, there is the advising and counseling center. Such centers provide guidance to help students with a variety of problems from program planning to personal counseling, so your awareness of such a resource is one way to begin mastering difficult situations.

Recognizing the difficulties inherent in the college experience, colleges and universities have created numerous resources to help students—from advising and counseling centers to student health centers, from the campus ministry to the learning assistance center, from the office of financial assistance to the computer resource center. Become familiar with these and other college services and you'll find your college adventure less frustrating and more rewarding.

A Brief Exercise

Becoming familiar with campus resources is crucial to your college success. Most institutions offer new students an orientation, but no orientation answers *all* your questions. As you walk around the campus, therefore, visit the various offices. Find out when counseling and learning assistance services are available, where the library and the health center are located, and how to use each of these resources. Identify those services that can benefit you specifically and plan to make use of them. For now, use your notebook to make a list of resources you want to find out more about.

Summary and Prediction Questions

1. To summarize the previous discussion, answer this question: In what way will awareness of college resources contribute to your college success?
2. To focus your attention on the next stage of the discussion, read to answer this question: What is the value of a problem-solving approach?

SELF-AWARENESS AND PROBLEM SOLVING

Many students feel overwhelmed by the time-consuming demands of their courses. How efficient and effective are your methods for planning and organizing your studies? How well do you meet the demands of studying textbooks, completing assignments, thinking critically, writing papers, preparing for exams—trying to attain academic success?

Self-awareness can help you tackle the conflicting demands of college life if you use a problem-solving approach. Each new situation, each conflicting demand, can be viewed as a problem to be solved. Figure 1.1 is a diagram of a step-by-step approach that is helpful for resolving problems and studying effectively.

Understand the Situation

Each new learning experience—listening to a lecture, studying a textbook, or writing a paper—requires understanding. Imagine yourself in some new situation, a biology laboratory perhaps. To figure out what's going on, you will need to observe the situation, listen carefully, and ask certain critical questions. For instance, when you first enter the lab, you begin to observe it; you are probably trying to determine how things are organized and whether any of the equipment looks familiar. You are com-

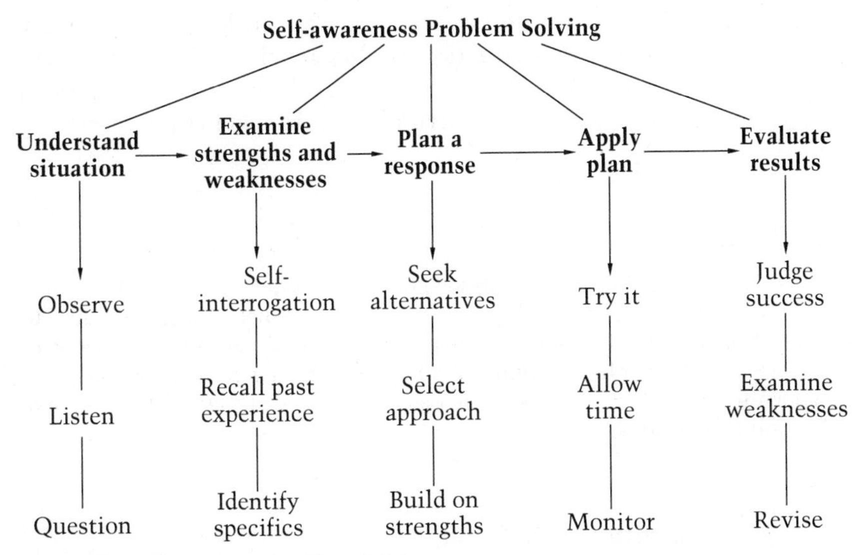

Figure 1.1. Self-awareness Problem Solving

paring the present (this college biology lab) with the past (your high school biology lab) to decide how new and different this experience might be for you. You know that laboratory courses are designed to demonstrate the application of new information, so that careful observation is a critical learning tool.

Tied closely to observation is careful listening. On the one hand, the introduction and explanation of new material, a laboratory procedure for instance, often proceeds very rapidly; most instructors expect students to adapt readily to new situations. Therefore, alertness to new information and careful listening become critical. On the other hand, additional insight about learning can be gained by listening to other students in the same situation, because their prior experience and perspectives may differ from yours. Fellow students who completed a similar exercise in another course may help you better understand the lab procedure that the instructor explained so quickly.

Insights gained from both observation and listening in any situation can be further explored by asking pertinent questions. Such questions frequently help you focus your attention on the important information. Even general questions such as, "What's going on here?" help you focus on the important facts or procedures. Then, to better understand the situation, ask yourself more specific questions such as, "What are the requirements for this activity?" "Do I have any previous experience with this sort of situation?" "What can I do to prepare myself further?" "How do my learning skills apply in this situation?" "How much time must I allot to this program?" and so forth. Thinking through these and other questions also helps you decide what you need to know or do next in the situation.

A Brief Exercise

Take the opportunity to apply this idea of understanding a situation by visiting your college library. Take a look at the facilities. See what's available. Listen to what's going on; listen for useful tips on how to use the library. And ask questions. Librarians can be your best resource. Find out something new that you might use to your advantage. Then, on a separate piece of paper, write a brief description of what you have learned.

Examine Your Strengths and Weaknesses

New learning situations also involve new tasks. To gauge your ability to meet new tasks, ask questions, examine your prior experience, and identify your special strengths. Imagine that you are taking a course in American history. Because history courses usually require a great deal of reading, you might begin your assessment with the question, "How effective are my study-reading habits?" Since history courses also involve regular lectures and frequent library research, you might also ask yourself, "Do I listen carefully and take well-organized lecture notes?" and "What does my previous experience with library research suggest I need to do to fulfill the requirements for this course?"

Such questions also lead to specific consideration of prior experience. How you judge your ability to study a history assignment is probably influenced by your past experience in history courses. It may be useful to recall your experience with high school history courses. What does that experience tell you about your current needs? What appeared to be your strengths and weaknesses at that point? What have you learned in the meantime? Have you investigated any new approaches for this type of study?

If you did a decent job with history courses in the past and enjoy reading history, your study practices are probably sufficient for the current course. However, your self-assessment may suggest, instead, that you need some outside assistance. For instance, if you think you lack the research skills necessary for writing a history paper, it may be useful to take advantage of the library orientation program if your school offers one.

You might also consider meeting with your instructor to discuss a solution to the problem.

Identifying your strengths and weaknesses will allow you to use your strengths more effectively while, at the same time, take action to overcome any specific weaknesses.

Plan a Response

Assessing your abilities puts you in a good position to plan a response to new or difficult academic situations. Most of your daily affairs revolve around plans; you plan what to wear, where to go, what to buy, when to eat. Yet you may fail to make firm plans when it comes to learning. Once you have identified the strengths and weaknesses in your study skills, you are in a good position to consider alternative strategies for learning.

Friends are frequently an initial source of assistance. It is reasonable to ask, "What do other students do to avoid these problems?" "Are there strategies they use about which I am unaware?" and so forth. Visiting a learning assistance center is another way to find help. Many colleges have centers designed to aid students with reading, writing, and general study problems. Study groups are another way to cope with the problems of certain classes. Members of study groups not only provide social support in difficult courses but also provide a form of peer tutoring, helping one another learn *how* to learn. Another resource is the personal tutor; some schools have tutoring programs in which tutors work one-on-one with individual students, helping them to master particular courses.

There are various strategies for resolving learning problems. Some strategies involve making plans and seeking assistance. If you suspect a specific learning disability, a thorough diagnosis may be in order. In this case, the assistance of an advising and counseling center is a reasonable first step. Other strategies involve selecting a plan designed to accomplish some task, such as improving time management, taking notes efficiently, or avoiding exam panic. Reading this book is one path toward becoming more proficient in each of these areas.

Once you become aware of the strategies available, you can select the ones most appropriate to your needs. Meanwhile, since serious change requires time and practice, be sure to choose a plan of action that builds on your strengths while working to eliminate any weaknesses.

A Brief Exercise

Take a few minutes to look through this book. Pay special attention to chapters like "Purposeful Study" and "Reading Textbooks." Think about how you might use the strategies in this book to become a more active learner. Where might you begin to improve your ability as an active learner?

Apply Your Plan

Once you decide on a plan of action to resolve a particular problem—such as a plan to overcome difficulty in note-taking—you are ready to try it out. Imagine that you have a problem taking lecture notes and that you have decided (1) to reorganize your note-taking approach, (2) to revise the notes after class, and (3) to consult with classmates about their notes.

This plan involves three different changes—notebook, revision, classmates—that will require careful attention and take some time to accomplish. The new form of notebook organization, clearly distinguishing between main points and supporting details, for instance, may be put into effect quickly, but the revision after class may require more time and involve some change in how you manage your time. Perhaps your classmates cannot give the help you had hoped for, since they also have difficulty taking notes. Nonetheless, their experience may help you refine your approach to revising notes. Judging the success of your new strategy by the results of your next examination requires waiting until exam time. So don't expect miracles. Instead of waiting until the exam, learn to monitor your progress as you go along.

Questions are a useful approach to monitoring, as they are to any assessment. In self-monitoring it is useful to consider questions like these: "Do I feel comfortable with the plan I've selected?" "Is the amount of work planned reasonable?" "Does the plan build on my strengths while working to overcome current weaknesses?" "Is the plan working as expected or does it have some unexpected consequences?" Such questions are critical for judging the effectiveness and application of any study plan. Furthermore, your ability to change study strategies requires conscious control of the learning process, and careful monitoring is one step in that process.

Evaluate the Results

Evaluating the results of your efforts is directly linked to monitoring your own progress because the success of any plan must be judged both in its application and with its final results. Consider note-taking again. Ideally, the new organization of your notes helped make the classroom lectures more meaningful. You are now able to distinguish important information more readily. And while fellow students weren't as helpful as expected, because they have their own note-taking problems, the new emphasis on after-class revision helped eliminate earlier problems with missing information. One indication of a successful change is the quality of the notes themselves—clear organization, complete ideas, supporting details, useful revisions, and so forth.

Further evaluation comes with the results of the next class examination. Compare test questions missed with the lecture notes in order to find out why your answers were wrong. Then ask yourself: "Is this new study approach a practical one?" "Does it effectively resolve the current problem?" "Does it introduce any new problems?" "Do the results suggest revisions needed?" "Can I make the strategy more efficient?"

Such questions help you to accurately evaluate strategies and determine any needed revision. If the evaluation suggests that the problem is not quite resolved, continue refining the strategy until you receive satisfactory results.

Developing self-awareness, especially with regard to identifying your strengths and weaknesses in the learning process, is crucial to academic achievement and personal success. Tying self-awareness to problem solving is one way to take control of problematic situations and to strive for success. Such control is simply a matter of (1) understanding the situation, (2) examining strengths and weaknesses, (3) planning a response, (4) applying the plan, and (5) evaluating the results.

A Brief Exercise

On a separate sheet of paper, list the five steps in the problem-solving strategy, and explain how each can help you become more aware of how you learn and how you can improve your learning. Finally, describe your reaction to this strategy.

Since one key element in achieving success involves identifying your specific strengths and weaknesses, such an assessment is now in order.

Summary and Prediction Questions

1. To summarize the discussion on self-awareness, answer the following question: Why does self-awareness and problem solving play such an important role in learning?
2. To focus your attention on the next stage of the discussion, read to answer this question: How can self-assessment help me master the learning process?

SELF-ASSESSMENT

A useful approach to solving problems is to identify the source of a problem quickly and then take some appropriate action to resolve it. Self-assessment provides valuable insight into any activity and is especially useful in the learning process. The general question is simple: "What are my strengths and weaknesses?"

College studies make numerous demands on students, and achieving success in college requires the student to know and apply an array of learning strategies. Preparing for and taking exams, for instance, is one such demand. Assessing appropriate strategies is a response. The answer to an assessment question such as, "How should I study for an essay exam?" leads to a new sense of self-awareness. And self-awareness offers direction for future efforts.

Now look at a more formal approach to self-assessment.

The Self-assessment Questionnaire

The following questionnaire is designed to help you assess your own study behavior. The questionnaire is divided into categories, such as "Managing Time Effectively" and "Reading Textbooks." These categories reflect common student concerns and the topic organization of this book. Within each category are five statements, each requiring a numeric response. For instance, in response to the statement "In order to remember details, I rehearse the information by talking to myself," you circle the number representing the word that best characterizes your behavior: Always = 5, Frequently = 4, Sometimes = 3, Rarely = 2, or Never = 1. Following the questionnaire are instructions on how to judge your responses and determine the strengths and weaknesses of your study skills.

Remember, this is an assessment of your study habits, so be honest with yourself. If you know that you should avoid daydreaming while listening to lectures, but you frequently drift off, identify daydreaming as a problem so that you can do something about it. Don't avoid reality. Now complete the questionnaire.

SELF-ASSESSMENT FORM

Directions: For each of the statements below, circle the number most closely reflecting your behavior. Answer all statements and be honest about what you do, even if you know you should use a different approach. Try to gain an accurate understanding of your actual study habits.

1 = Never
2 = Rarely
3 = Sometimes
4 = Frequently
5 = Always

Active Learning

1. I regularly prepare a plan of action to successfully complete my course requirements.	1	2	3	4	5
2. When preparing for any assignment, I have a clear purpose in mind.	1	2	3	4	5
3. I frequently summarize important information as I study.	1	2	3	4	5
4. I keep track of my progress of my studying by asking and answering questions about the material.	1	2	3	4	5
5. Continuous review is a regular part of my study schedule.	1	2	3	4	5

Managing Time Effectively

1. I prepare a general schedule of activities at the beginning of each semester.	1	2	3	4	5
2. As each assignment is given, I make a plan for completing the assignment and integrate it into my general schedule.	1	2	3	4	5
3. When I set up a study schedule, I also take into account my need for rest and relaxation.	1	2	3	4	5
4. As I plan a schedule, I allow enough flexibility to deal with unexpected events.	1	2	3	4	5
5. Whenever I organize a schedule, I keep in mind that some activities take priority over others.	1	2	3	4	5

Purposeful Study

1. I make sure I have a quiet place to work before I try to study.	1	2	3	4	5
2. I space my study periods to that I don't overload myself.	1	2	3	4	5
3. I establish goals for studying so that I know what I have to do and when I've completed the task.	1	2	3	4	5
4. I organize my time, place, and methods of study to make studying a habit.	1	2	3	4	5
5. Before I begin studying, I relax and clear my mind in order to concentrate on the task at hand.	1	2	3	4	5

Taking Lecture Notes

1. When I go to class, I make sure to take my notebook and a couple of pens or pencils.	1	2	3	4	5
2. As I listen to lectures, I pay close attention to the presentation and avoid daydreaming.	1	2	3	4	5
3. As I listen to lectures, I record important information as accurately as possible.	1	2	3	4	5
4. If necessary, I ask questions to fill any gaps that appear in my notes.	1	2	3	4	5
5. I review my notes as soon as possible after class and add anything I may have left out.	1	2	3	4	5

Reading Textbooks

1. Before reading a chapter, I take time to preview the material to prepare myself for reading.	1	2	3	4	5
2. As I read a chapter, I ask myself questions about the material and then read to answer those questions.	1	2	3	4	5
3. If the chapter is fairly long or contains a lot of new information, I divide it into manageable "chunks" in order to study it efficiently.	1	2	3	4	5
4. While reading I pay close attention to any charts, graphs, and illustrations that are presented.	1	2	3	4	5
5. I periodically review chapters until I am sure I know the information.	1	2	3	4	5

Marking Texts and Taking Notes

1. I underline important information as I read so that I can keep track of major points.	1	2	3	4	5

2. I use different methods for marking different types of information, such as underlining important points and numbering supporting examples.	1	2	3	4	5
3. I make note of important information as I read by writing the ideas in my own words.	1	2	3	4	5
4. I periodically summarize important information while reading, especially following major subdivisions within a chapter.	1	2	3	4	5
5. I use text notes to organize a visual, or graphic, overview of my reading assignments, especially for chapter review.	1	2	3	4	5

Vocabulary and Concept Development

1. I actively seek the meaning of new words that I encounter.	1	2	3	4	5
2. If I encounter an unknown word while reading, I use the context of the word and my knowledge of word parts to determine its meaning.	1	2	3	4	5
3. Because unfamiliar words in textbooks frequently represent new concepts, I read carefully for definitions and explanations.	1	2	3	4	5
4. I regularly devote extra attention to new concepts while studying, using special techniques—such as semantic mapping—when necessary.	1	2	3	4	5
5. I incorporate new words and concepts into my vocabulary by using them in my thinking, speaking, and writing.	1	2	3	4	5

Memory

1. With new information, I visualize the information mentally in order to remember it.	1	2	3	4	5
2. When I have a lot of information to memorize, I space the practice so I'm not trying to cover too much at one time.	1	2	3	4	5
3. In order to remember details, I rehearse the information by talking to myself.	1	2	3	4	5
4. I use mnemonic techniques (such as NATO = North Atlantic Treaty Organization) to aid my recall of information.	1	2	3	4	5

5. I organize information graphically in order to store it in my memory. 1 2 3 4 5

Taking Tests

1. As I prepare for exams, I make up sample questions based on the material I am studying. 1 2 3 4 5
2. When I begin a test, I read the directions twice and then survey the exam to make sure I know what to do. 1 2 3 4 5
3. When taking an essay test, I briefly outline my answer before I begin writing the essay. 1 2 3 4 5
4. Before answering any exam question, I read it carefully and completely. 1 2 3 4 5
5. On multiple-choice and true-or-false tests I pay special attention to the exact wording of the question. 1 2 3 4 5

Studying Science and Math

1. I pay close attention to the pattern of organization used to present scientific information. 1 2 3 4 5
2. I regularly use the illustrations, graphs, and charts to better understand scientific explanations. 1 2 3 4 5
3. I apply a systematic approach to problem solving that emphasizes working practice problems. 1 2 3 4 5
4. I regularly use either the chapter's "discussion questions" or my own question-and-answer techniques to monitor my understanding of a textbook chapter. 1 2 3 4 5
5. I typically sketch drawings and graphs as a method for studying scientific information. 1 2 3 4 5

Reading Literature

1. When I read literature, I give special attention to plot, setting, character, and theme. 1 2 3 4 5
2. To read actively, I continually ask questions about things like plot and character, and I read for answers. 1 2 3 4 5
3. After reading, I summarize the plot to gain an overview of events. 1 2 3 4 5
4. I mentally visualize characters and events in order to understand and remember them. 1 2 3 4 5
5. While reading I continually analyze situations to infer the meaning or theme of the story. 1 2 3 4 5

Writing Papers

1. When preparing a report or paper, I develop a plan before I begin writing the first draft.	1	2	3	4	5
2. Before any writing I make sure I have done enough research and have enough information.	1	2	3	4	5
3. I use an outline to organize the information for my paper.	1	2	3	4	5
4. After writing the first draft, I revise as necessary according to the purpose of my paper and the needs of the intended audience.	1	2	3	4	5
5. I proofread my final draft for any errors in spelling or sentence structure.	1	2	3	4	5

Using the Library

1. I use the library as an important source of information.	1	2	3	4	5
2. I start with the card catalog or a computer index when doing library research.	1	2	3	4	5
3. I use the *Reader's Guide to Periodical Literature* or similar guides when preparing research papers.	1	2	3	4	5
4. When in doubt about how to locate some specific type of information, I ask a librarian.	1	2	3	4	5
5. I visit the library to read periodicals relevant to my course work.	1	2	3	4	5

Analyzing the Assessment

Once you have finished the questionnaire, you need to analyze your responses for an overall assessment. Notice that each statement is presented positively. In fact, each item indicates an effective approach to each subject. So one way to judge your strengths and weaknesses is to see how often you do these things. If you do some things quite frequently, that suggests you're on the right track. If you do other things less frequently, there's room for improvement. This approach to the questionnaire offers specific information.

Next notice that each response is followed by the numbers 1 2 3 4 5. These numbers allow you to rate your responses. "Always" gives you a high score of 5, and "Never" yields a low score of 1. Now for each category of five statements, you should add your scores together. For instance, perhaps you circled 4 ("Frequently") for a statement in a category. Then if your response to the next three statements was "Sometimes," the score is

	Active learning	Managing time effectively	Purposeful study	Taking lecture notes	Reading textbooks	Marking texts and taking notes	Vocabulary and con-cept development	Memory	Taking tests	Studying science and math	Reading literature	Writing papers	Using the library
25													
24													
23													
22													
21													
20				X									
19													
18	X												
17													
16													
15													
14		X											
13													
12													
11			X										
10													
9													
8													
7													
6													
5													
4													
3													
2													
1													

Figure 1.2. Sample Assessment Chart

3 for each. And one "Never" equals 1. The total score for those five statements is 14. Next, mark the score of 14 on the chart, as shown in Figure 1.2. Simply locate the study skill area and put an X on the chart according to the score received. The score numbers across the top of the chart will guide the placement of your score.

Once your scores are plotted on the chart, you can make a graph of the scores by connecting the X's with a line as shown in Figure 1.2. For example, a score of 18 for Active Learning, 14 for Managing Time Effectively, 11 for Purposeful Study, and 20 for Taking Lecture Notes give you the graph shown in the figure. The completed graph gives you a clear visual

	Active learning	Managing time effectively	Purposeful study	Taking lecture notes	Reading textbooks	Marking texts and taking notes	Vocabulary and concept development	Memory	Taking tests	Studying science and math	Reading literature	Writing papers	Using the library
25													
24													
23													
22													
21													
20													
19													
18													
17													
16													
15													
14													
13													
12													
11													
10													
9													
8													
7													
6													
5													
4													
3													
2													
1													

Figure 1.3. Self-assessment Chart.

image of your scores. The finished graph then is one way for you to see the strengths and weaknesses in your study techniques. You can plot your own scores on the blank chart provided as Figure 1.3.

As you study the graph, look at where your scores are generally high. These are areas of strength. If you wish to continue improving these areas, you have a good start. Notice where your scores seem lower. Here your self-assessment alerts you to problems. You realize certain areas need attention. Your new awareness of these gaps is the first step toward resolving the problem.

Perhaps you have scores that tend to fall in the "Sometimes" category, around midpoint on the graph. What does that mean? Well, it may mean you should be more systematic in your approach to learning. Sometimes you employ effective techniques; sometimes you don't. Or it may mean you are not sure how to approach these study situations. In either case, the "Sometimes" response probably means you need greater awareness of the topic and a more systematic approach to improvement.

Each category of the Self-assessment Form is examined in a separate chapter in this book. Each subject is discussed in depth, and techniques or strategies for improvement are presented. You can study this material in a variety of ways. One way is simply to work through the chapters in sequence, seeking general improvement. Another is to first review the chapters that discuss areas of strength and then devote full attention to areas of weakness. Or you may decide to attack a couple of major problems first and then work through the chapters in sequence. Whatever you decide, make sure you have a purpose in mind, a plan to follow, and a goal to reach.

One additional note regarding your use of the book: Difficulties in learning are more easily overcome if you have a clear sense of how learning takes place. So before you start reading any of the chapters based on your self-assessment, read Chapter 2, on active learning. Combined with self-awareness, active learning is a good strategy for achieving success.

Summary and Prediction Questions

1. To summarize the study habits assessment, answer this question: What did I learn from my self-assessment that will help me in the future?
2. To focus your attention on the next stage of the discussion, read to answer this question: What are the benefits of approaching new situations with a positive attitude?

MAINTAINING A POSITIVE ATTITUDE

Maintaining a positive attitude is essential to success in college, or in any other aspect of life for that matter. Much of the college experience is new; therefore, much of the experience, at least initially, tends to be confusing. It takes time to understand and succeed in new circumstances. At times you may find yourself saying, "I can't do this." Beware of this simple phrase. It can become an obstacle to your success.

Psychologists and counselors point out that when people say, "I can't," they frequently mean, "I won't." Confronting the initial confusion of new situations provokes anxiety and fear, perhaps a fear of failure. Rather than try something new and fail, the response is "I can't do this." Taking such a position not only prevents failure, it also prevents success. Moreover, don't imagine that this is purposeful behavior. In fact, once a student is gripped by the anxiety and fear of a situation, "I can't" becomes an unconscious, yet natural, response.

As you approach any new situation, try taking a positive attitude. Realize that your past success has led you to this stage in life and that the future is in your hands. Self-awareness gives you direction in new situations. A positive attitude gives you motivation and self-assurance. Of course problems may arise, but with the right attitude you can guide yourself through each problem, regarding it as a challenge and rewarding yourself for a job well done.

Success comes in steps. If you find yourself afraid—and you will sometimes—confront that fear. Imagine yourself facing the problem and resolving it. But be realistic: A positive attitude alone doesn't guarantee success. Serious problems require a well-planned response. However, if you believe in yourself, understand the importance of taking appropriate action, and are willing to make the effort to act, success can be yours. Each step in the right direction is a step toward success.

Review Questions

Review your understanding of the chapter by answering each of these questions:

1. How can self-awareness contribute to college success?
2. Why are self-awareness and problem solving so important to active learning?
3. How can a self-assessment of your strengths and weaknesses help you master the learning process?
4. What benefits are there to approaching new, and perhaps frightening, situations with a positive attitude?

CHAPTER REVIEW

To complete this chapter, answer the following questions. When you have finished, review the chapter to check your answers.

1. True or False: It is natural for people to experience anxiety in new situations.

2. True or False: A negative attitude seems to guarantee failure because it causes many to approach a challenge with an "I can't!" attitude.
3. True or False: Self-awareness is a first step toward mastering new situations.
4. True or False: If you take time to become familiar with a variety of college resources, the knowledge you gain becomes one of your strengths.
5. Which of the following is *not* an effective way to approach a new learning situation?
   a. Examine your strengths and weaknesses.
   b. Avoid the roadblock of negative attitudes.
   c. Look for new methods only when you fail.
   d. Understand the reality of new situations.
6. Which of the following is not a benefit of self-assessment?
   a. It offers motivation.
   b. It identifies problems.
   c. It creates a framework for change.
   d. It indicates current skills.
7. Briefly explain how self-awareness can help you achieve success in college. Write your explanation in the space provided:

   ____

   ____

   ____

   ____

8. Select one of your courses and apply the five-step approach to self-awareness and problem solving.
   a. First, understand the situation: Summarize the course description, the type of assignments required (including reading, exams, and papers), and your goals for the course.

      ____

      ____

____

____

b. Now examine the strengths and weaknesses of your study skills as they relate to the course. Perhaps the exams will not be a problem, but you worry about the amount of writing. What are your strengths and weaknesses in this case?

____

____

____

____

c. Third, plan a response. How can you use your strengths? What will you do to overcome any weaknesses?

____

____

____

____

d. Now apply your plan. Begin monitoring your work. After you've started acting on your plan, ask yourself, "Am I comfortable with my plan? Does it use my strengths? Are things working for me?" and so on. Note any problems.

____

____

____

____

e. Finally, evaluate your progress from time to time. Judge the success of your efforts. How are things going? Describe the results of your efforts.

Learn to monitor your progress regularly and take action to solve any problems.

9. Make a list of college resources that you believe will be most valuable to your success. Then use them.

10. Describe your reaction to this chapter, what you think about self-awareness and problem solving, what you learned from the self-assessment, and how you feel about your potential for success.

2

Active Learning

Preview Exercise

Take a few moments to carefully preview this chapter.[1] Read the introductory paragraphs and the chapter summary. Try to determine what the chapter is about. Then look over the various subheadings and examine the illustrations. Think about how the chapter is organized and which topics are covered in the study of active learning.

Now establish a purpose for reading the chapter. One purpose is to find out how learning takes place.

PURPOSE FOR READING: ____________________

____

____

How people learn is an intriguing subject. Ask a group of students what they do when given a reading assignment, and most will respond, quite logically, "I read it." If you then ask, "How do you know when you've completed the assignment?" the answer is typically, "I've completed it when I'm finished reading." Neither response says much about how learning takes place.

TAKING RESPONSIBILITY

Knowing when an assignment is complete is at the heart of the learning process. It suggests that the purpose of the assignment is clearly understood and that the activities necessary to complete the work are also known. More important, this knowledge suggests that each of us is responsible for our own learning, for taking charge of the learning process. Think about what that means.

Studies done by psychologists and others show that active learners—those who take charge of their learning—are successful learners. One result their research demonstrates is that students who use appropriate study methods, such as underlining key ideas and taking notes, remember more from a study period than those who do not. Furthermore, the research shows that those students who search for ways to improve their methods of study and who further develop their skills are much more likely to become successful learners. But most of all, these studies show that active and successful learners are aware of *how to think* about a learning situation, such as studying a textbook chapter in preparing for an exam, and *how to regulate* the learning process, such as making specific plans to pass a test successfully.

How People Learn

As people grow, they learn many things that are quite difficult to grasp at first but eventually become so familiar that they are done automatically. Learning to ride a bicycle is one of these tasks. Think of how many rules riding a bike requires us to know: Keep the wheel straight, keep pedaling, hold your balance, watch where you're going, and so on. Yet, once bike riding is learned, you do it automatically. You don't think about holding your balance; you just do it, naturally.

Learning how to learn is a bit like learning how to ride a bike. It is not always easy, it is sometimes confusing, and it doesn't guarantee success, particularly in the beginning. But knowing how to learn, how to use specific strategies, and to make good study habits a routine practice improves the likelihood of success.

Learning is also like problem solving. Each course assignment is essentially a problem to be solved. Your job is to get from point X, an assignment to learn a subject about which you have little or no knowledge, to point Y, a thorough understanding of the material and the increased potential for success on an examination. But to get from point X to point Y, to solve the problem, means moving in steps—doing things first, second, and so forth until completion. And because of the many steps to learning, it is useful to think about grouping them in three major stages: planning, monitoring, and evaluating.

Active learners plan how they will accomplish a task. They monitor their work carefully to make sure things are working as they had planned. And they evaluate their results to be sure they have accomplished the task, to be sure that they are now successful learners. That's why you need to look closely at how this learning process works.

A Brief Exercise

Before continuing with this chapter, take a few minutes to think about how you normally approach a learning task such as studying a reading assignment to prepare for an exam. Identify what you do first, second, and so on; how you keep track of necessary information; how you prepare for the exam; and how you judge the results of your efforts. Compare your approach with the major stages—planning, monitoring, and evaluating. Then as you continue reading this chapter, compare your approach with the specific steps presented in the discussion. Consider your strengths and weaknesses in successfully learning the assigned material.

One cautionary note: The purpose of this chapter is to survey the learning process. Many of the ideas introduced are not explained in detail until subsequent chapters. So read this chapter as a guide to learning, and examine each of the other chapters for more detailed information.

Guiding Questions

As you read this chapter, think about the following questions and try to find answers for them:

1. How do active learners plan for successful learning?
2. How do active learners monitor their study activities?
3. How can the results of an activity be evaluated?

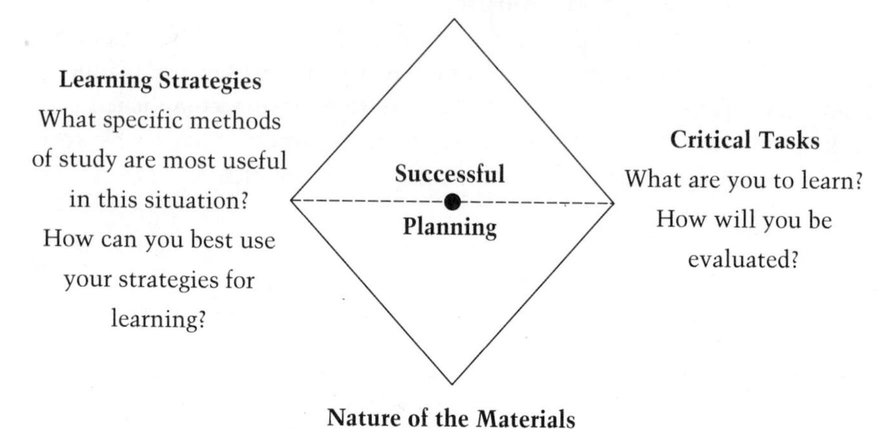

Figure 2.1. A Model for Making Plans

PREPARATION FOR LEARNING

Planning is the first step in successful learning. Planning is, in fact, an integral part of everyday life. People make plans to go out. They make plans to see friends. They make plans for the weekend. It seems quite reasonable, therefore, that people also make plans for learning.

One approach to planning[2] is presented in Figure 2.1. Notice that this approach considers four types of information: the characteristics of the learner, the critical tasks or specific assignments, the nature of the materials, and the learning strategies necessary to complete the task.

Know Yourself

Good planning requires first that you know yourself, know your characteristics as a learner. This is the primary subject of Chapter 1. The more aware you are of how you learn, of your strengths and weaknesses, and of how you can build your strengths, the more successful you are likely to be in learning how to learn. That's what this book is about.

Do you take good notes, or should you learn how to take better notes? Are you able to retain much that you study, or should you learn more efficient memory techniques? These are the issues of self-awareness. To accomplish any task, you must be aware of how best to guide your learning.

Critical Tasks

You must also plan with purpose. What is the critical task, the specific assignment to be completed? How will you be evaluated? What method of testing will the instructor use? How will you know before the exam whether your efforts are succeeding?

Imagine, for instance, that your assignment is to read a chapter in your sociology text on socialization (how people become a part of their community) and to prepare for a quiz on the difference between socialization in highly developed urban communities and in more traditional rural communities. The assignment is the critical task; it creates the purpose for your study: (1) what you need to do—read the chapter on socialization; (2) what you need to know—the differences between the two communities; and (3) how to judge when you are done—to test your knowledge of the differences. You fulfill your purpose, and you are done when you know those differences.

The Nature of the Material

Next, consider the nature of the study material. What type of material is it? Is it typical of a textbook chapter or a magazine article? How is it organized? Differences, for example, are frequently presented with comparison and contrast patterns. Is there a plan of action most appropriate to this type of material? These questions suggest a couple of important points.

On the one hand, you need to be aware of how different reading materials are organized. Recognize, for instance, the difference between the organization of textbook chapters, which are very explicit (new ideas are both explained and illustrated) and the organization of short stories, which are less explicit (new ideas are introduced via the interaction of character, plot, and setting). These differences influence your choice of method to study the material.

On the other hand, different types of study material present different organizational clues. Textbook authors frequently signal important parts of the text with phrases like "the key point here" and "to summarize." The clues in the short story are more general. Understand the characters—how they are presented, how they behave, what the consequences of their thoughts and actions are—and you will understand the story. Reading materials differ in their purpose and structure, and these differences determine how best to study them.

Learning Strategies

Next, good planning requires that you determine which learning strategies are most useful for the task, the material, and your strengths as a learner. What strategies will make you an efficient and effective learner? To a large extent, those strategies are the subject of this book. But for the moment, look again at the hypothetical sociology assignment.

The task is to know the differences in socialization for urban and rural communities. Because the material follows standard textbook organization, the information should be fairly explicit. As you think about your reading habits, you realize that you sometimes lose your concentration while reading textbooks and that careful underlining helps you stay alert and keep track of important facts. Imagine then that the strategy you choose may look something like this:

- My *purpose* is to know the differences in socialization between urban and rural societies.
- I will *read* the text to answer this *question*: "What is the difference between rural and urban patterns of socialization?"
- I will *underline* important ideas as I read to keep track of the information.
- Once I have completed my reading, I will *review* my underlined points to be sure I understand them and that they help answer the question.
- I will also *reread* sections I find confusing.
- To evaluate my understanding, I will give myself a written *self-test* to see if I know the differences and can explain them.
- *Reviews* and additional *self-tests* will depend on my previous successes. My success on my self-test will determine when I'm done.

This, of course, is just one example, but it does suggest how planning works. To be successful, you should consider: (1) your characteristics as a learner, (2) the critical tasks of learning, (3) the nature of the materials to be learned, and (4) the variety of learning strategies available.

A Brief Exercise

Select an assignment from another course. Then carefully assess the assignment, using Figure 2.1. Finally, consider how planning might help improve your approach to learning.

Summary and Prediction Questions

1. To summarize the discussion thus far, answer this question: What should I consider when planning my study activities?
2. To focus your attention on the next stage in the discussion, read to answer this question: How do active learners monitor their activities?

MONITORING YOUR EFFORTS

To monitor your efforts in the learning process involves keeping a check on the quality and progress of your work. Active learners know how to think about a learning situation (by planning) and they know how to regulate their learning (by self-monitoring). For an active learner, the question is: How can I best monitor, or regulate, my efforts?

As soon as you put your plan into play, begin monitoring. Start by observing your activities to see if your plan and your strategies are working successfully. Try to decide if the material you are studying makes sense, if your approach is appropriate to the assigned task, and if your progress is proceeding efficiently. Remember that learning always carries time limits.

Self-questioning

You might think of the monitoring process, at least initially, as a self-questioning procedure. You can examine your progress by asking a series of questions about your purpose, your task, and your response. You might consider checking your work with these questions:

_____ Is my purpose clear?

_____ Am I able to identify important ideas?

_____ Does my underlining and note-taking aid my comprehension?

_____ Are the questions I ask about the subject being answered by the text?

_____ Can I summarize the main points in the material I've studied?

_____ Am I using effective memory techniques to help me retain the information?

A Brief Exercise

Call to mind a couple of recent assignments. Consider what strategies you used to monitor the progress of your studies. Did you have a clear purpose in mind? How did you identify important points? What memory techniques did you use? Did you keep a schedule? How did you know when you were done? Finally, think about how a self-questioning procedure might improve your awareness of how effectively you study.

Monitoring Comprehension

Also consider the importance of monitoring your reading comprehension, because reading is such an integral part of all study. Reading is a continuous process of interpreting what is happening in the text and predicting what will happen next. To the extent you understand—comprehend—the material, you will succeed in learning it. To the extent you don't, your comprehension will break down.

For example, read the following sentence: "To determine the growth rate of a population, one would have to look at the factors that tend to *increase* the number of individuals within that population and those that tend to *decrease* the number of individuals in the population."[3] After reading the first part of the sentence, it is reasonable to predict that the authors will explain how to determine the growth rate of a population. The second part of the sentence can be interpreted to mean that factors affecting both increases and decreases must be understood if the growth rate of a population is to be determined. So reading is a process of prediction and interpretation. But for active learning even more is necessary.

Three basic strategies are generally suggested to help you monitor your comprehension in the reading for study: note-taking, questioning, and summarizing.

Note-taking

Note-taking has long been considered an effective strategy for learning because it requires the learner to pay close attention to the text and to construct, through notes, a meaningful interpretation of the text. Paraphrasing—rewriting in your own words—the important information from the text also helps clarify its meaning. Note-taking creates the opportunity for you to think about the material you are reading, thereby increasing your ability to understand and remember its most important points.

Questioning

Questioning strategies work much like note-taking strategies in that questioning also requires the learner to pay close attention to the text. Specifically, questioning helps you to identify important ideas in the text, to use those ideas to ask further questions, and to think of possible answers to those questions.

For example, thinking about the note-taking paragraph above, you might ask, "How can note-taking increase my comprehension?" Then your recall of the details of the paragraph—"Notes help me think about what I'm reading"—answers the question and checks your understanding. Furthermore, self-generated questions increase your awareness of the learning process and your potential for success because they make you a more active learner. Questioning is also used throughout this book as a strategy to keep you actively involved in the discussion.

Summarizing

Summarizing is another useful technique for monitoring comprehension. Summarizing helps organize large quantities of information into a condensed, more easily remembered version and tests your understanding. Effective summarizing aids learning by making you identify key elements of a text once again and restate, or reorganize, that information in a meaningful fashion.

Good summaries focus on the main point of a reading selection, identify major supporting points, and eliminate all unnecessary information.[4] Imagine yourself writing a summary of a short article about the negative influence of television on children's reading habits. An effective summary requires that you:

- Ignore unnecessary material. For example, exclude issues other than reading habits.
- Delete redundant, or repeated, points. For example, eliminate repeated examples or additional statements making similar points about the negative influence of television.
- Use general statements to consolidate details. For example, summarize the conclusions from different examples of television watching.
- Select important topic sentences. For example, find statements in the text that explain the negative influence of television.
- Invent topic sentences where necessary to focus on key information. For example, create a sentence that links heavy viewing and low reading scores.

Summarizing helps you to monitor your comprehension by keeping you alert to important points and it helps you to comprehend by requiring you to organize information in a meaningful way. (Refer to Chapter 6, "Reading Textbooks" and Chapter 7, "Marking Texts and Taking Notes" for more detailed discussion.)

A Brief Exercise

Take a few moments to review the strategies you currently use to monitor your comprehension. Do you make use of note-taking, questioning, and summarizing? How effective is your approach? How might you improve your efforts?

Monitoring is a continuous process of checking your work to make sure you are accomplishing your task. By alerting you to any breakdown in learning, it allows you to take corrective action before it's too late. Monitoring your progress as you go along in a course of study is crucial to evaluating the success of your efforts at learning.

Summary and Prediction Questions

1. To summarize the discussion on monitoring, answer this question: What procedure can I use to monitor my learning?
2. To focus your attention on the next stage of the discussion, read to answer this question: How do active learners evaluate their efforts?

EVALUATING LEARNING

Evaluating your success in learning means judging whether or not you have achieved your purpose and are able to retain what you have learned. In practice, it is a continuous cycle of self-testing and review. Regular self-testing promotes successful academic performance.

Self-testing

Self-testing is a natural part of learning in everyday life as in academic life. Imagine that you are having some friends over for dinner and you want to prepare something very special. You decide first to look for a fancy seafood dish in your favorite cookbook. But once you find a recipe, study it carefully, and imagine how tasty it is, you realize you have no experience with such a dish. What if the recipe is a flop with your guests?

The answer for many people is to cook the new dish ahead of time to gain practice before it's time to cook for friends. That first cooking is not simply practice; it is also a self-test. It is one way to judge your ability to handle the job ahead of the actual test. The same is true of self-tests in academic life (the cooking example is somewhat similar to the way laboratory classes promote understanding in science courses). The test provides you with an opportunity to judge your understanding of a subject prior to a formal examination. Self-testing prepares you for the actual experience.

Type of Information

Self-testing to evaluate learning should also correspond to the type of information being studied. For instance, if you are learning a number of new concepts that you are expected to define and illustrate, you could study the presentation in the text and practice the material by reciting it aloud. Then you could design a self-test to evaluate your knowledge of definitions and examples.

If you are studying biology and must learn the circulatory system, you could study the supporting illustrations in the text and practice visualizing the system—creating a mental picture of it—and labeling the appropriate parts. Then you could create practice tests with photocopies of the circulatory system, evaluating your ability to label the parts. Or, if you are studying history, you can practice explaining the historical events and then design a self-test of sample essay questions that evaluates your ability to explain their underlying causes. If, for example, you were studying the economic conditions leading to the stock market crash of 1929, a good question might be "What economic conditions preceded the market crash of 1929?"

Whatever the course, self-testing helps you judge the extent and accuracy of your learning and can be readily adapted to a variety of learning activities.

Review and Memory

Evaluation also contains a review component. All students recognize the hazardous effects of forgetting. In fact, it is not uncommon for students to find themselves staring blankly at a test question, searching for an answer they know they studied but have completely forgotten.

Why does memory fail? There are many reasons. You may, for instance, not understand the material and, therefore, not remember it. Understanding is probably the most important element of good memory. You may very well understand the material while you are reading, but the information may seem so obvious that it is merely included in your short-term memory and quickly lost as you continue reading.

Still further, you may understand the material and incorporate it into your long-term memory by noting its importance and by rereading it. Yet you may still not remember the material at some later point. The problem is that, while long-term memory can retain vast amounts of information and is apparently unlimited, if the information studied is not thoroughly understood, appropriately organized, systematically stored, and regularly reviewed, it is quite quickly forgotten.

To your benefit, a few basic study strategies will increase your memory and support your continuous review. The strategies are spaced study, active rehearsal or recitation, overlearning, and relearning.[5]

Spaced Study

Spaced study means simply: Don't try to learn everything at once. Fatigue undermines learning and remembering primarily because of a loss in concentration. To study for three or four 45-minute periods with a 5- or 10-minute break between is much better for learning than to study for three or four hours straight. Smaller units of time with clear purpose, good concentration, and effective strategies will aid learning and memory, especially if supported by follow-up reviews. A good sequence, for instance, might be to study for three 45-minute periods and then to review that material in the fourth period.

Verbal Rehearsal

Active rehearsal or recitation of material studied is an excellent technique for storing information in your long-term memory. Practicing your knowledge by thinking aloud is also a good method for regular review. You can "rehearse" material—talk it over with yourself—at any time, and then use self-tests to judge your accuracy. The point is to give yourself repeated practice through verbal rehearsal.

Overlearning

Another useful technique is "overlearning." Common sense may suggest that once you learn something, the job is complete. It is learned. Overlearning seems a waste of time. But the fact of the matter is that once you learn something, it can still be rather quickly forgotten. Therefore, it is frequently worth your time to overlearn important information. Overlearning gives you more practice, and learners who give themselves more practice remember more of what they learn. When you think you're done with analyzing or memorizing some material, practice it a few more times; you'll do much better in the long run.

Relearning

A final aid to memory is relearning—sometimes referred to as the savings technique. Simply stated, it is easier to learn—or relearn—information previously studied than it is to learn new information. That idea is probably obvious to you. It's a bit like riding a bicycle. Even if you haven't been on a bike in years, riding quickly comes back to you if you once learn how. The benefit of ease in relearning lends further support to the review process. Once something is learned, it is much easier to relearn or retain if it is reviewed from time to time. And once you have thoroughly reviewed, you can evaluate the accuracy of your knowledge through self-testing.

A Brief Exercise

Compare your current methods for evaluation with those presented in the discussion. Then identify areas where you might improve your study efforts. What specific techniques might be most useful for you? (The chapters on purposeful study, reading textbooks, memory, and taking tests all provide additional information on this subject.)

Summary Question

1. To summarize the discussion on evaluation, answer this question: What procedures can I use to evaluate my learning?

SUMMARY

Planning, monitoring, and evaluating each are critical stages in the learning process (see Figure 2.2). They are not always easy to apply and they don't guarantee success. They do give the learner a sense of direction and allow active learners to take charge of their learning. Each stage offers you the opportunity to think about your learning and to direct and control it. The goal is for you to establish habits for learning, to develop auto-

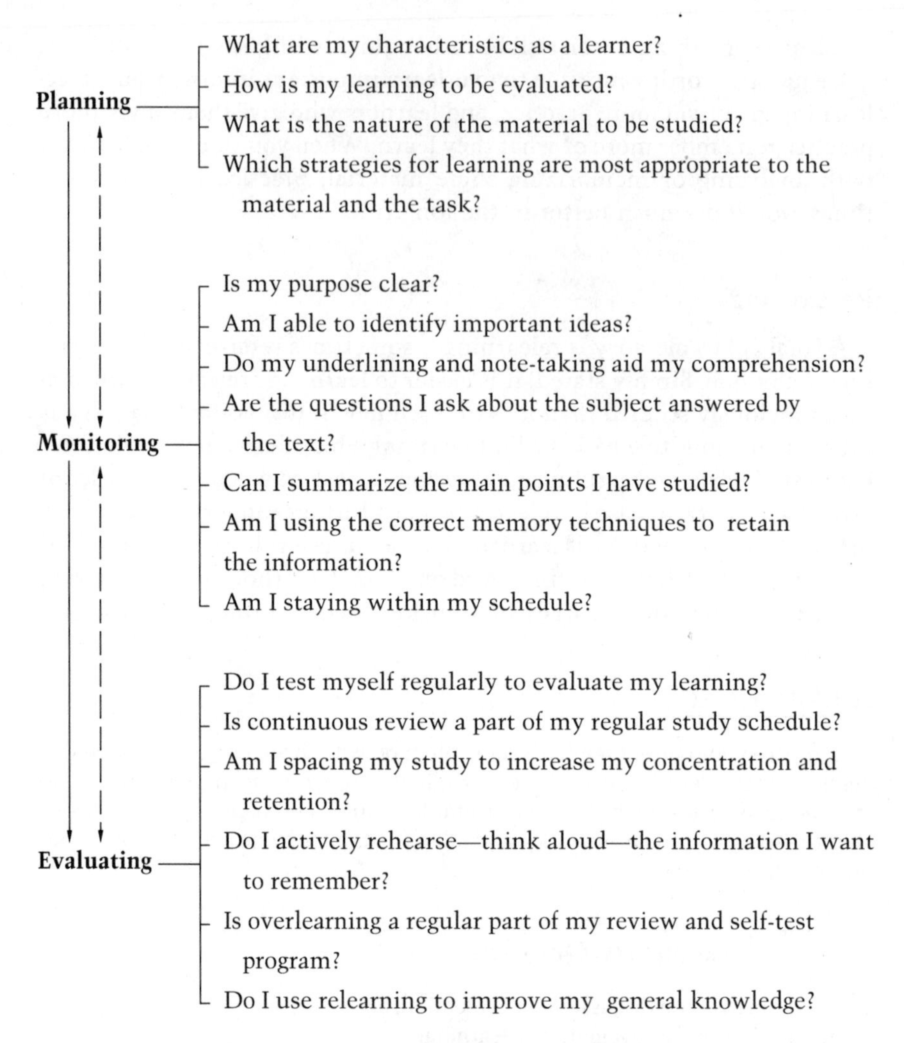

Figure 2.2. Active Learning

matic approaches to thinking about learning, approaches that allow you to decide for yourself how to get from point X to point Y most effectively, most efficiently, and most successfully.

Review Questions

Review your understanding of the chapter by answering each of the following questions:

1. How do active learners plan for successful learning?
2. How do active learners monitor their study activities?
3. How can the results of an activity be evaluated?

CHAPTER REVIEW

To complete this chapter, answer the following questions. When you are finished, review the chapter to check your answers.

1. True or False: Active learners know that the success of their efforts is based on continuous rereading.
2. True or False: The learning process may be thought of as having three major stages: planning, monitoring, and evaluating.
3. True or False: The selection of a learning strategy is much easier if the purpose of a task is clearly understood.
4. True or False: Planning a specific approach to learning is only necessary if you begin to fail a course.
5. Which of the following is not a technique for monitoring learning?
   a. summarizing
   b. library research
   c. note-taking
   d. questioning
6. Self-testing is useful for evaluation because
   a. professors regularly provide test questions ahead of time.
   b. it is an alternative to overlearning material.
   c. spaced study doesn't help with some assignments.
   d. the accuracy of learning can be judged prior to actual examination.
7. Apply the guidelines for active learning to a regular homework assignment. If the procedure overwhelms you at first, try one or two new ideas each time you study. And steadily build on your experience. Then evaluate your strengths and weaknesses in using the procedure. Continue applying the process of planning, monitoring, and evaluating until you feel comfortable with the activity.

___

___

___

8. Briefly discuss the value of spaced study for active learning.

9. List the five techniques for creating effective summaries.

10. Discuss your reaction to this discussion of active learning.

NOTES

1. The material in this chapter is heavily influenced by the following: L. Baker and A. L. Brown, "Metacognitive Skills," Technical Report 188 (Urbana:

University of Illinois, Center for Study of Reading. November 1980); A. L. Brown, J. D. Bransford, R. A. Fierra, and J. C. Campione, "Learning, Remembering, and Understanding," Technical Report 244 (Urbana: University of Illinois, Center for Study of Reading, June 1982); D. E. Rumelhart, "Schemata: The Building Blocks of Cognition," in R. J. Spiro, B. C. Bruce, and W. F. Brewer (Eds.), *Theoretical Issues in Reading Comprehension* (Hillsdale, NJ: Lawrence Erlbaum Associates, 1980).

2. This model is adapted from A. L. Brown, "Learning How to Learn from Reading," in J. A. Langer and M. Trika Smith-Burke (Eds.), *Reader Meets Author/Bridging the Gap* (Newark, DE: International Reading Association, 1982); J. J. Jenkins, "Four Points to Remember: A Tetrahedral Model and Memory Experiments," in L. S. Cermak and F. I. M. Craik (Eds.), *Levels and Processing in Human Memory* (Hillsdale, NJ: Lawrence Erlbaum Associates, 1979).

3. Charles E. Kupchella and Margaret C. Hyland, *Environmental Science: Living within the System of Nature,* 2nd ed. (Boston: Allyn and Bacon, 1989), p. 68.

4. A. C. Brown, J. C. Campione, and J. D. Day, "Learning to Learn: On Training Students to Learn from Texts," *Educational Researcher 10* (1981): 14–24.

5. Elton B. McNeil and Zick Rubin, *The Psychology of Being Human,* 2nd ed. (New York: Harper & Row, 1977).

3

Managing Time Effectively

Preview Exercise

Preview the chapter by reading the introduction, the conclusion, and the subheadings, and by examining the illustrations and exercises. Notice especially how the chapter is organized and how the process of managing time effectively is presented. Think about how your approach to time management compares with the approach the chapter suggests. Now establish a purpose for reading the chapter.

PURPOSE FOR READING: ______________________________

____

____

"May I speak with you for a moment, professor?"

"Sure, Sam. What's the problem?"

"Well, you know I got a D on last week's test, and now I'm not ready with my paper."

"Assignments are due on time, Sam; what causes you to be late?"

"I don't know. I just never have enough time to get anything done. And this isn't the only class I'm having trouble with."

Does this story sound familiar? Not enough time is a complaint frequently heard around colleges and universities. There never seems to be enough time to get the job done, and grades suffer as a consequence. But why does there seem never to be enough time?

Shortage of time has many causes. For Sam the problem may be as simple as poor planning. Sam may wait until the last minute to do assignments or not allot enough time for his work. He may not even plan a schedule for completing assignments. He may just "get to things" as the assignments come due. Whatever the case, Sam has a problem completing assignments on time. There are many reasons why students find themselves short of time: insufficient planning, lack of priorities, wasted hours, forgetfulness, overcommitment, and many more. Yet success in virtually any task demands that time be managed effectively. The question is how to do it.

Effective time management requires five basic steps: (1) establish clear goals, (2) plan carefully, (3) self-monitor progress, (4) solve problems simply, and (5) perform a final evaluation.

Guiding Questions

Use the following questions to guide your reading; look for specific answers as the ideas are discussed.

1. Have I established clear goals for attending college?
2. Do I plan carefully in order to achieve my goals?
3. How can I monitor my plan of activities to be sure I'm on the right track?
4. Is there a simple approach to solving my problems if I run into trouble?
5. How can I evaluate my use of a time management strategy?

CLEARLY ESTABLISHED GOALS

Much effort is easily wasted if the goals that guide study activities are unclear or nonexistent. Many times you may find yourself weakly committed to an activity simply if you feel the goal of the activity is someone else's. Far too often, students view assignments as an instructor's goal, not their own. Further discussion with Sam, the student short of time, for instance, may reveal that he spends a lot of time at his part-time job. And when he's not at school or work, he's active in a sports program. If Sam hasn't completed an assignment, it may be because he was busy doing something else. What Sam must do is decide what his goals are and organize his time accordingly.

You must have a strong sense of who you are, what you're about, and what your goals are in any situation, if you are to be successful. To start, ask yourself what you hope to accomplish by going to school. You may, for instance, want to gain more educational experience before you select a career, you may want to be a medical lab technician, or you may want to improve your writing ability to obtain a promotion at work. What is your purpose? Try the following exercise.

A Brief Exercise

My purposes for attending school are

1. ______________________________

2. ______________________________

3. ______________________________

4. ______________________________

5. ______________________________

There are many reasons for going to college: to become an educated person, to get a good job, or to prepare for a profession such as accountant, computer programmer, or biology teacher. Your purpose may be to earn credit in business management or labor relations for a promotion in your current job. In the past, it was common for students to attend college full time to obtain a general education. Today, more and more students attend college part-time while working full-time, so the emphasis tends to be more specific. If you feel unsure about how to respond, take some time to think about what you want from your educational experience. The important point is to make sure you have a clear goal, or set of goals, for your education (or anything else in life for that matter).

Be Specific

Try to be specific with your goals. Determine your priorities. If there is a conflict between accomplishing two different goals, which one gains first attention? Obtaining a good job, for instance, is an important goal. Even better is identifying a more specific occupational goal, such as a career in chemical technology. With a specific program goal you can quickly establish which courses are required and which are recommended. You may also have another goal such as developing an artistic talent or mechanical ability. This may be an important goal, but for now the occupational goal probably comes first. You must decide. Keep your priorities in mind. Creating a clear set of goals and priorities is simply a form of self-awareness, motivating you to complete your schoolwork before you do something else. Make sure you establish these long-term goals. It's your future.

Goals for the Present

The only disadvantage of long-term goals is that they seem distant when you are trying to organize your life in the here and now. The present, the current term or semester, for example, demands precise goals, both for meeting current situations and for reaching long-range goals. Imagine for a moment you are a chemistry major with the following schedule for the term or semester: introductory chemistry, calculus, music history, and American literature. In addition to those courses, you also plan to work part time. What then are your short-term goals?

Here's one approach to thinking about setting goals.

"Since I'm a chemistry major, I want to do best in introductory chemistry and calculus. Those subjects are critical to my degree and to a good job. They require special attention on pretty much a daily basis, and I'm after high grades in both classes.

"I've always enjoyed literature, so I can probably get a good grade there. The problem with the literature class is the amount of reading. I should set aside extra time for this one. The key is not to fall behind.

"Music isn't my best subject, but an arts elective is required for my degree, so it has to have some priority. It may also take some extra time. Maybe I can find someone in that class to study with.

"Well, I'm going to be busy this semester. I guess I should limit my work hours on my outside job. I sure want to leave some time to have fun."

This imaginary situation suggests a number of things about short-term goals. First, there is clear purpose: pass four courses, work part-time, and have some fun. Second, it establishes that certain issues have priority; a chemistry major must give special attention to courses crucial to the major and still not ignore others required for the degree. Third, while the part-time work is a clear goal, it must be limited by demanding course requirements and priorities. Finally, allowing time out for fun is recognized as realistic. It will be hard to achieve the serious educational goals without taking time out. Now you try it. Think about what you want to accomplish and what your priorities are for the term/semester.

A Brief Exercise

My goals for this term/semester are

1. ____________________

2. ____________________

3. ____________________

4. ____________________

5. ____________________

Immediate Goals

Once goals for term or semester are set, immediate goals of a weekly or daily sort follow. These goals are dictated by the immediate demands of the situation, and change more quickly than long-range or short-range goals. For instance, if one week's goal is to complete a literature assignment and Wednesday afternoon is free, then the goal for Wednesday afternoon is to finish that assignment. Weekly and daily goals are determined by the immediate situation, but they will only be accomplished if you establish the goals and plan your schedule. Immediate goals are subject to frequent change, quite obviously, but they are necessary to your success. Therefore, as you begin the week (or day), take time to establish your goals. A few moments on Sunday evening will help you organize the week.

A Brief Exercise

My goals for this week (day) are

1. ______________________________

2. ______________________________

3. ______________________________

4. ______________________________

5. ______________________________

Once you have a clear set of goals—long-term, short-term, and immediate—you are in a good position to do some serious planning.

Summary and Prediction Questions

1. To summarize the previous discussion, answer this question: How can I establish clear goals for myself?
2. To focus your attention on the next section, read to answer this question: How can I best plan for achieving my goals?

CAREFUL PLANNING

Developing a plan to meet your goals and closely monitoring your progress are the next critical issues of time management. Your long-range goals guide your general planning for seeking a good education, selecting a field of study, deciding on priorities, and so forth. Short-range goals and the requirements of the immediate situation tend to demand the most attention.

A Term/Semester Schedule

A term/semester schedule is a method commonly suggested for general planning because it presents a visual layout of the term or semester. Many college bookstores sell wall-size year or term/semester planning calendars that can be used to lay out the major events of the term or semester and, just as important, to revise as plans change. For instance, from the syllabus for each class you can note on your planning calendar the dates of major exams, the due dates for research papers or oral presentations, and the dates of special activities. This type of schedule serves as a guide to when assignments are due, when the schedule appears light, and when you are most likely to be under the pressure of deadlines. This planning then allows you to develop more specific plans, with these events as the context for further organization.

As you become more involved in the activities of the term or semester, you can add events like the sports schedule, special campus functions, school dances, and so forth. Then by comparing assignment dates with other activities, you can develop a general plan of study, setting aside certain evenings for lengthy preparation and certain days for library research. At each point in the evolution of the term/semester schedule, you increase your chance of success by managing your time more efficiently. And always remember your priorities.

Figure 3.1 is one example of a term/semester schedule; Figure 3.2 is a form you can use to plan such a schedule. Remember that these schedules are plans that provide an overview of key events, a sequence of activities that create a clear course of action. Knowing what's ahead allows you to plan realistically. Just remember that the term/semester schedule should focus on academic pursuits. More specific plans are outlined in weekly and daily schedules.

Weekly Schedules

Weekly schedules keep you aware of upcoming events, enabling you to plan more carefully. They remind you of daily events such as regular classes or labs and part-time work, and allow you to see where adjustments are possible, so you can accomplish weekly goals.

Start your weekly schedules by identifying the "givens"—when you are in class, when you regularly eat, when you work, when you are obligated to be somewhere. Also identify major events of the week such as exams, papers, dances, sports, and so forth. Most important, identify regular study periods. Take a look at Figure 3.3, which exemplifies a typical week.

A Typical Week

Notice in Figure 3.3 that classes, work, study, and various other daily activities take up large blocks of time. It's important that your weekly

MONTH September

SUN	MON	TUE	WED	THU	FRI	SAT
1	2	3	Classes Begin 4	5	6	Football Game 7
8	9	Study Q 10	Chem. Quiz 11	12	Dance 13	14
15	Study Q 16	Calc. Quiz Am. Lit. Test 17	Study Q 18	Music Test 19	20	Football Game 21
22	Speaker: Ecology 23	Study Q 24	Chem. Test 25	Study Q 26	Calc. Test Dance 27	28
Library 29	30					

MONTH November

SUN	MON	TUE	WED	THU	FRI	SAT
					1	2
Library Study 3	Oral Pres. Music 4	Student Play 5	Study Q 6	Am. Lit. Quiz 7	8	Football Game 9
Library Movie 10	Study Q 11	Music Test 12	Chem. Q 13	14	Civil Liberties Speaker 15	16
Study Q 17	Calc. Test 18	19	Study Q 20	Am. Lit. Test 21	22	Weekend Away 23
— 24	25	Study 26	Chem. Test 27	28	29	30

Figure 3.1 Sample Term/Semester Schedule

MONTH October

SUN	MON	TUE	WED	THU	FRI	SAT
		Study Q 1	Chem. Quiz 2	3	4	Music Field Trip 5
Library Study Q 6	Calc. Test Library 7	Study 8	Am. Lit. Paper 9	10	11	Football Game Dance 12
Library 13	Study Q 14	Mid-Term Chem. Study Q 15	Mid-Term Calc. 16	Study Q 17	Music Test 18	19
20	Film 21	22	Study Q 23	Am. Lit. Test 24	25	Library 26
Library 27	28	Study 29	Study 30	Chem. Paper 31		

MONTH December

SUN	MON	TUE	WED	THU	FRI	SAT
Library 1	2	Study 3	4	Lit. paper 5	6	7
Library Study 8	9	Classes End Study 10	FINAL EXAMS Study 11	Am. Lit 12	Dance 13	Study 14
EXAMS Library Study 15	Chem. Calc. 16	Study 17	Study 18	Music 19	20	21
22	23	24	25	26	27	28
29	30	31				

MONTH ______________________

SUN	MON	TUE	WED	THU	FRI	SAT

MONTH ______________________

SUN	MON	TUE	WED	THU	FRI	SAT

Figure 3.2 Term/Semester Schedule

MONTH ____________________

SUN	MON	TUE	WED	THU	FRI	SAT

MONTH ____________________

SUN	MON	TUE	WED	THU	FRI	SAT

schedules show exactly how certain times are used, including routine daily functions like eating and sleeping, which offer some flexibility. Students who are committed to a full-time job or raising a family need to be especially careful to note their full schedule of responsibilities. It is also important to note that many blocks of time are frequently left open. Schedules are flexible, not rigid. Some open blocks may not really be open or free time. You may need to go shopping, get a haircut, or go for a walk. These open blocks may offer an opportunity to complete a specific assignment for that week. Other blocks that are currently filled may be modified to fit the demands of the week. A major exam might require you to take some time off from work, for instance. Or perhaps you could reorganize the time to study on Thursday afternoon, go to a movie Thursday night, and do the laundry on Friday. Schedules allow you to decide how to use your time more effectively.

A Scheduling Exercise

Now try setting up a weekly schedule for yourself using Figure 3.4.

Once you begin working with a weekly schedule, you will have some sense of the regularity of your activities, an awareness that will help you organize your time more effectively. You will simply "know" when you are supposed to be somewhere.

It may also be true that, once you establish a regular schedule, only important events or special activities for the week need be noted in later planning. In other words, once you have a clear sense of your routine, there's no reason to create a highly detailed schedule each week. Simply note special events or deadlines. Let good judgment be your guide here.

Forgetting an appointment or assignment always is a possibility. That's where the daily schedule, or the "things to do" list comes in handy. Are you keeping a daily list of "things to do"?

The Immediate Situation

Good planning for the immediate situation keeps you in control of events. It eliminates both worry about not getting things done and actually forgetting what you're supposed to do. Good planning is simple: Start each day with a "things to do" list.

Probably the simplest way to handle a "things to do" list is to use 3″×5″ note cards, which are easily tucked into pocket or purse. Either the night before or the first thing in the morning, take a moment to jot down what

	SUN	MON	TUE	WED	THU	FRI	SAT
7 AM		Wake	Wake	Wake	Wake	Wake	Wake / Eat
8 AM		Break-fast	Break-fast	Break-fast	Break-fast	Break-fast	Work
9 AM	Wake	Prep. Chem	Am. Lit.	Am. Lit.	Am. Lit.	Prep. Chem.	Work
10 AM		Chem.	Chem.	Chem.	Chem. Exam	Chem.	Work
11 AM		Prep. Calc.	Prep. Calc.			Prep. Calc.	Work
12 PM		Calc.	Calc.			Calc.	Work
1 PM	Lunch	Lunch	Lunch	Lunch	Lunch	Lunch	Eat
2 PM	Library		Music		Music	Music	Foot-ball
3 PM	Library	Eat		Eat	Laundry		Foot-ball
4 PM	Library	Work		Work	Laundry		Foot-ball
5 PM		Work		Work			Eat
6 PM	Dinner	Work	Dinner	Work	Dinner	Dinner	
7 PM	TV	Work	Study	Work	Study	Movie?	
8 PM	Study	Work	Study	Work	Study		Dance
9 PM	Study	Study	Prep. Chem Ex.	Prep. Chem Ex.	Study		Dance
10 PM	TV	Prep. Chem.	TV	Prep. Chem. Exam.			Dance
11 PM	Bed	Bed	Bed	Bed	Bed		
12 AM						Bed	

Figure 3.3 Sample Weekly Schedule

	SUN	MON	TUE	WED	THU	FRI	SAT
7 AM							
8 AM							
9 AM							
10 AM							
11 AM							
12 PM							
1 PM							
2 PM							
3 PM							
4 PM							
5 PM							
6 PM							
7 PM							
8 PM							
9 PM							
10 PM							
11 PM							
12 AM							

Figure 3.4 Weekly Schedule

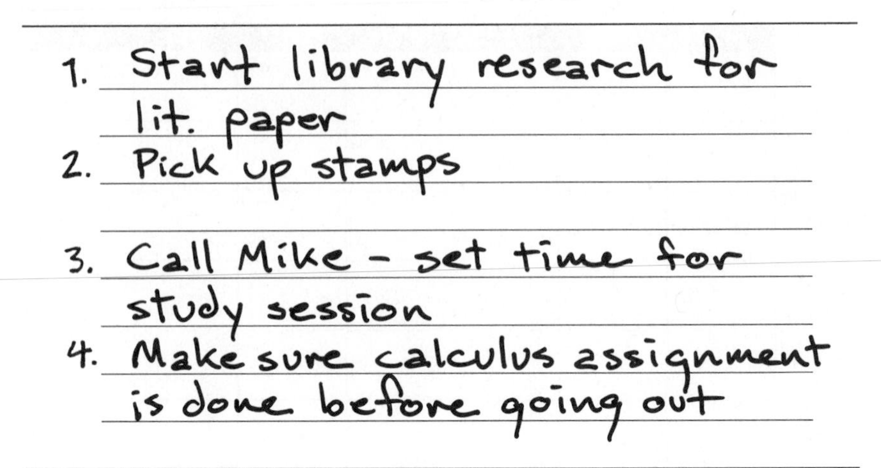

Figure 3.5 Things to Do (Sample)

you wish to accomplish each day. Don't write down *everything* you intend to do; regular activities such as classes or your job can be excluded. (These activities are already written on your weekly schedule.) Just consider your goals for the day and use the card as a daily plan to remind you of what must be done. See Figure 3.5 for an example of a "things to do" list.

Notice how this list provides guidance and helps you to monitor your progress. Once you've finished a particular activity, cross out that assignment and go on to something else. More important, don't forget to glance through the list from time to time during the day. The plan will work only if you follow it. Also consider what's reasonable. Too long a list guarantees frustration. Consider which activities you can accomplish quickly, perhaps a trip to the laundry, and which involve more commitment, such as library research. Then set some priorities. It may be worthwhile to list items by time of day: 10:30 library, 12:00 meet Joanne for lunch, and so forth. Remember, this "things to do" list should help you plan more effectively; so consider what must be done and the order of such activities, and manage your day accordingly.

Now try setting up a list for yourself, for tomorrow's activities. Use Figure 3.6.

Setting goals and planning schedules for term or semester, week and day, have been discussed thus far in this chapter. They create the framework for effective time management. But all this goal-setting and planning fail if you don't use an appropriate method for monitoring your progress and for solving problems that may arise.

1. ______________________________

____

2. ______________________________

____

3. ______________________________

____

4. ______________________________

____

Figure 3.6 Things to Do

Summary and Prediction Questions

1. To summarize the previous discussion, answer this question: How can I establish a plan of activities that will help me accomplish my goals?
2. To focus your attention on the next portion of the chapter, consider this question: How can I monitor my activities to make sure I'm on the right track?

MONITORING YOUR ACTIVITIES

Self-monitoring is critical to the success of any planning efforts. Thorough and constant examination of specific activities determines the effectiveness of your time management system. Furthermore, self-monitoring is fairly straightforward if you use a method of self-interrogation, a series of questions to judge your performance.

Questions for Self-monitoring

- *Do I have clearly established goals?*
  Goals are basic to any planning. If your goals are unclear, planning is virtually impossible.
- *Is my planning comprehensive?*
  The more thorough your planning, the more likely you are to attain your

goals. Many times students have the intent to complete an activity, but their plans fail to reflect that desire. If you want to accomplish a particular task, you must plan for it in both the short term and the long term.

- *Does my plan or schedule of activities represent each of the goals I've established?*
  It is important to remember that there are a number of goals toward which you strive at any one time. Sometimes you may mistakenly assume you only have one goal—say obtaining an education—and, therefore, fail to include time for other activities—family, work, and so forth. Make sure you devote some time to each of your goals even though they have different priorities. Keep in mind that goals are not mutually exclusive. Numerous goals are achievable with an effective management system.
- *Does my planning or scheduling reflect the priorities established by my goals?*
  Consider this example. If succeeding as a chemistry major is your goal, then classes and study time must receive first attention. When your schedule indicates that you are devoting a good deal of time to your part-time job or simply spending a lot of time with various campus activities, then your priorities are not receiving proper attention.
- *Does my schedule of nonacademic activities interfere with my attending classes and completing course assignments?*
  If the answer to this question is yes, it's time to rethink your priorities and plan accordingly.
- *Does my schedule allow a reasonable amount of time for each activity, especially enough time for study?*
  Your answer to this question will come with experience. The key is to monitor your work to see how your plans work out. Don't organize a schedule by blocking out four hours for study each evening. Organize more realistic, shorter, spaced study periods. One hour in the morning, one hour in the afternoon, and two hours at night is a much more reasonable study schedule.
- *Does my weekly schedule allow for flexibility; can it be modified in the event of a change?*
  You live in a complex world. Many events are unexpected. A bout of the flu takes time from your schedule. Building some flexibility into your schedule can mean the difference between its success and failure.
- *Does my schedule reveal any wasted time that I can use more efficiently?*
  If you think you almost never waste time, think again. Most students find themselves with time between classes. Ask what they do with the time, and they'll undoubtedly answer, "Wait for class." Waiting time is frequently wasted time. If you enjoy spending time with friends between classes, that's fine. But also consider some alternatives such as reviewing the assignment for your next class. A close review of your weekly schedule may help you locate some of that scarce time you seek. Also examine how you use scheduled activities. Perhaps you allot considerable time for study but don't use the

time as planned. Talking with friends, listening to the radio, or simply daydreaming is not study time. Make sure that your schedule reflects your true use of time.

- *Do I reward myself for following through with plans that lead to success in my activities?*
  Rewards (and punishments) are useful tools in managing your time. If you follow a specific plan that leads to a successful grade on an exam, that's a reward in itself. But rewards (and punishments) are best applied more immediately. Imagine a dilemma. You want to see a movie, but you have an extra long music history assignment. Why not schedule your preparation for the afternoon and early evening; then upon completing the assignment, reward yourself with the movie (no assignment, no movie). Rewards work well in planning activities because they offer that additional motivation sometimes needed when you find yourself faced with competing interests. With careful planning, maybe you can do both.
- *If I wanted to change my schedule to use my time differently, perhaps more efficiently, what three changes could I make?*
  Periodically reexamine your schedule for options that might be available. Consider your priorities. Look for flexibility. Consider possibilities for rescheduling certain activities. Quite simply, take control of your schedule.

As you can see, monitoring your plans and comparing those plans with goals, priorities, and actual conditions is essential for effective time management. A plan not subject to continuous monitoring easily falls into disarray. But once an organized approach to planning and monitoring becomes habitual, a natural part of your thinking, the time-management practices you are learning become virtually automatic reactions in school, on the job, with family responsibilities, and in other aspects of your life. Figure 3.7 lists each of the self-monitoring questions discussed above for quick reference. Use it as a checklist for monitoring your schedule.

A Brief Exercise

Now that you've had an opportunity to read about self-monitoring, use the self-monitoring checklist to examine your previous week's activities. How do your activities compare with the suggested approach? What improvements can you make?

Summary and Prediction Questions

1. To summarize: What questions can I use to monitor my schedule?
2. Thinking ahead: If I encounter a problem, is there a simple approach to solving problems?

_____ Do I have clearly established goals?

_____ Is my planning comprehensive?

_____ Does my plan or schedule of activities represent each of the goals I've established?

_____ Does my planning or scheduling reflect the priorities established by my goals?

_____ Does my schedule of nonacademic activities interfere with my class attendance and course assignments?

_____ Does my schedule allow a reasonable amount of time for each activity, particularly enough time for study?

_____ Does my weekly schedule allow for flexibility; can it be modified in event of change?

_____ Does my schedule reflect any wasted time that could be used more efficiently?

_____ Do I reward myself for following through with plans that lead to success in my activities?

_____ If I wanted to change my schedule to use my time differently, perhaps more efficiently, what three changes could I make?

____

____

____

____

Figure 3.7 Checklist for Monitoring Your Activities

PROBLEM SOLVING

Thus far, this chapter has presented a systematic approach to effective time management. Each step is a response to some problem. Even with careful planning, unforeseen problems arise, however. Therefore, you need one more step for effective time management, a problem-solving technique.

A helpful approach to solving problems has five steps: (1) Identify the problem, (2) decide on an appropriate response, (3) apply the strategy, (4) evaluate the results, and (5) make any necessary revision.[1] This strategy can be applied to any problem of time management.

The Situation

Imagine, for instance, that during the course of the semester you find yourself frequently late turning in papers. That's the problem. But it is not that simple. You must identify exactly what is causing the problem. Since "time" appears the issue here, you look to your schedule to identify the source of the problem.

Reviewing your schedule, you realize you have set aside very little time for library research, usually Sunday afternoons, and that you frequently use that time for much needed rest and recreation. The problem then is that "not enough time" is allotted for library research.

The Response

Next you must decide on a strategy to deal with this problem, a problem regarding both the amount of time necessary for research and when such research will be done. Imagine further that there are a couple of possible ways to deal with this problem. One, of course, is to stop changing your Sunday afternoon plans and fulfill the library commitment. That's a possibility, but since Sunday hasn't worked well in the past, another time (or times) during the week might be a better choice. You decide to try another time—Tuesday evenings and Wednesday afternoons. Tuesday evenings are study times anyway, so you simply decide to use the time differently. Wednesday afternoon was free time, but you decide to switch the free time to Sunday.

Your next step is to apply the strategy. Since your next paper is due in two weeks, you begin the Tuesday-Wednesday strategy. You must actually put the strategy to work, gathering the experience to judge the results.

The Result

The effect of the strategy can be judged in a number of ways. First, do you actually make the change in schedule it requires? Second, is the time allotted sufficient to complete the library research needed? Third, the most important issue, do you complete the new research paper by the due date, or are you late again?

Any revision that might be necessary is based on the strategy's results. If you follow the new schedule, have enough time to complete the paper, and turn it in on time, you have solved your problem. No revision of strategy is necessary. If any problems develop from this new strategy, then you must further revise until the problem is solved.

Remember, any problem can be solved if you approach it with a clearly designed procedure. Then when you encounter problems, don't throw up your hands in frustration. Use step-by-step problem solving to seek a solution.

A Brief Exercise

For an opportunity to apply the problem-solving strategy, select some problem that you regularly encounter when trying to manage your time. Carefully identify the problem. Consider how you might solve it; think of more than one approach. Then select an approach to solving the problem and give it a try. Once you've tried your new approach, evaluate the results. How did things work out? Finally, make any necessary revisions, or changes, and continue working to solve your problems. How did the problem-solving approach work for you?

Summary and Prediction Questions

1. To summarize: What approach can I take to solving problems I encounter when trying to manage my time?
2. Thinking ahead: How can I evaluate my use of a time management strategy?

EVALUATION

Evaluation is the logical conclusion to any endeavor, academic or otherwise. Evaluating a time management strategy is really quite simple. On the one hand, the results of an activity provide a basis for evaluation. On the other hand, the actual application of the strategy also provides a basis for evaluation, aside from the final results. Looking at results, the question is, "Did I accomplish my goals?" The answer should be fairly straightforward. The course was passed or not, the desired grade received or not, the plan for the term or semester fulfilled or not. Such results are obvious. And a less than satisfactory response requires that you reexamine the process in order to identify possible sources of the problem.

Yet, you must also evaluate the application of any time management strategy. This is a question of efficiency: how quickly and easily schedules are planned and tasks accomplished. Ask yourself the questions, "How efficient is my use of time management?" "Does my schedule allow me to accomplish current goals and also create additional time for new opportunities?" "How can I accomplish more within the constraints of time?" Consequently, as your awareness of the time management process increases, so does your opportunity to refine each effort and enhance your success.

Summary Question

Ask yourself: How can I evaluate my time management strategy?

A STRATEGY FOR TIME MANAGEMENT

This chapter has offered an overall strategy for dealing with the problem of time management. First, establish your goals. Consider your long-term goals as the framework for more specific goals for the short term and for the immediate situation. Clearly articulated goals provide direction and serve as the foundation for good planning.

Second, systematically plan your activities in order to reach those desired goals. Such planning by means of term/semester, weekly, and daily schedules will provide specific guidance for accomplishing each goal. In addition, be flexible enough to respond to changing conditions and unexpected situations.

Third, monitor your activities continuously. Asking questions that link your goals, plans, and efforts will help to identify problems that may impede your progress.

Fourth, be ready to attack any problems with a specific strategy. Problems are likely to arise, and any system of time management must offer a systematic strategy for resolving such unforeseen problems.

Finally, evaluate the results of your efforts. Remember, there is always enough time if you know how to use it.

Review Questions

Review your understanding of the chapter by answering each of the following questions:

1. Have I established clear goals for attending college?
2. How can I best plan in order to achieve my goals?
3. What procedures can I use to monitor my activities?
4. How can I solve problems that arise in my schedule?
5. How can I evaluate the effectiveness of my time management strategy?

CHAPTER REVIEW

To complete this chapter, answer the following questions. When you finish, review the chapter to check your answers.

1. True or False: A systematic procedure for time management helps students to take control of their schedules through organization.
2. True or False: A specific problem-solving technique allows one to attack problems by first defining the problem clearly.
3. True or False: A term/semester plan is much more important than a set of long-term goals.
4. True or False: A daily "things to do" list should be limited to special tasks for that day.
5. Which of the following monitoring questions would be most useful in determining whether you are overloading your schedule?
   a. Do I have clearly established goals?
   b. Do I reward myself for following through with plans that lead to success in my activities?
   c. Does my schedule allow a reasonable amount of time for each activity, particularly enough time for study?
   d. Does my schedule of nonacademic activities conflict with my attendance of classes and course assignments?
6. Which of the following monitoring questions would be most useful in determining whether you can respond to the unexpected?
   a. Does my weekly schedule allow for flexibility; can it be modified in event of a change?
   b. If I wanted to change my schedule to use my time differently, perhaps more efficiently, what three changes could I make?
   c. Is my planning comprehensive?
   d. Does my schedule reflect any wasted time that I can use more efficiently?

7. List each of the steps of problem solving in the appropriate order.

8. What two issues are the focus for evaluation of a time management strategy?

9. Which stage in the time management strategy seems to be most useful to your current activities? Why?

10. Discuss the similarities between the process of active learning in Chapter 2 and the process of time management in Chapter 3.

NOTE

1. Henry Clay Lindgren, *The Psychology of College Success: A Dynamic Approach* (New York: John Wiley & Sons, 1969; reprinted by Robert E. Krieger Publishing Company, Malabar, FL, 1980).

4

Purposeful Study

Preview Exercise

Take a few moments to look over the chapter, including subheadings, exercises, and figures. Compare the topics presented with your current study practices. Which topics appear similar to your current study habits? Which topics are of particular interest to you?

PURPOSE FOR READING: ______________________________

____

____

Purposeful study employs a variety of specific strategies, many of which are discussed in this chapter. Yet, the success or failure of these strategies is also linked directly to self-concept and motivation. Therefore, it is vital to approach learning, like any potentially difficult situation, with a positive attitude.

Imagine a difficult assignment. Perhaps your history instructor requires a research paper on a topic about which you have little knowledge. Initially you may experience some confusion about where to begin or some anxiety triggered by a fear of failure. A little voice in your head whispers, "I've never done this sort of thing before. Maybe I can't do it." The more difficult the situation, the more likely a fear of failure.

A POSITIVE SELF-CONCEPT

Imagine now an altogether different response to that same initial confusion and anxiety—in this case, the new assignment is viewed as a challenge. Your reaction is, "This problem looks tough, but I bet I can figure it out. I'll start by going to the library for some background reading. Then I'll . . . ." This response is motivated by a belief in yourself and your ability to succeed.

Think back over your past experiences. Can you think of a situation when your first feeling was confusion or fear? Think about how you solved the problem—going through an interview for college admission or a job, speaking before a class, passing a difficult test—and why you were able to succeed. A positive approach to any problem begins with the belief that any problem can be solved. And underlying this belief is the desire to succeed.

Persistence, the ability to keep working at a task, is also key to a positive self-concept. Tough jobs usually take a little extra time and effort. Combine persistence with a desire to succeed and you have a good start for purposeful study.

Positive Self-talk

Unfortunately the world is not a perfect place, and there are always some very trying times. For some students, it's a matter of a busy schedule—a 40-hour work week, three night classes, and children demanding attention. For others, the problem is specific—for example, discovering that the notes for a term paper are lost, or reworking a math problem three times and still not finding the answer. These can be trying times indeed.

Yet, rather than falter in the face of difficulty, renew your faith in your own possibilities for success. Your ability to succeed has brought you to this point in life. Your desire to achieve further success has placed you in this uncertain situation, so talk with yourself about how to take the next step, to solve the problem that threatens to overwhelm you.

Imagine you must solve a difficult math problem. Begin with some positive self-talk.

"Okay, this math problem is really getting to me. I'm going to take a break, relax for a few minutes, then try it again.

"I've had difficult problems like this in the past and I've managed to solve most of them. I remember when I first took geometry. It didn't make any sense at all. But I gave it a try. After a while those theorems began to make sense. Then I had to laugh about how easy it seemed.

"If I give myself some time and approach the problem step by step, I know I can get the job done.

"Let me give it another try."

Positive self-talk reminds *you* that you are the source of your success. Accept the fact that encountering difficulty and making mistakes is a natural part of learning. But persist in the desire to achieve your goals by continually reaffirming your belief in yourself.

Purposeful study also requires a well-organized strategy for achieving success. The rest of this chapter will focus on planning, monitoring, and evaluating your study program. Special attention will be given to such issues as creating an environment for study, establishing goals, and developing plans. Also discussed are techniques for relaxation, self-monitoring, and evaluating success.

Guiding Questions

Use the following questions to guide your reading. Actively search for answers and pay special attention to the specific methods presented to improve the study process.

1. What planning practices are used for purposeful study?
2. How is monitoring of the study process accomplished?
3. Why is evaluation an important part of the study process?

PLANNING PURPOSEFUL STUDY

Specific strategies for study are frequently matters of common sense. Effective study takes place in an organized fashion. Planning is accomplished by preparing psychologically, creating an appropriate environment, establishing clear goals, organizing a specific schedule to meet those goals, and applying useful methods of learning.

Preparing Psychologically

Purposeful study requires that you prepare yourself psychologically. Anxiety and learning are frequently associated and, to some extent, that is quite natural. Learning is a process of moving from the unknown to the known, from confusion to understanding. Therefore, some periodic anxiety associated with feeling out of place or not understanding what to do is quite common. Some sources of anxiety are easy to resolve, others more difficult.

Students may, for example, find themselves trying to accomplish some task—study a reading assignment, think through a science problem, or write an English paper—while worrying about something else. The answer to this dilemma is a practical one. Keep a reminder pad, or a "things to do" list. When some worry comes to mind, jot it down so you can deal with it later. That's an easy solution.

A more serious problem arises when anxiety and worry become so pervasive as to interfere with learning. Family illness, financial problems, unfinished assignments, fear of exams, all such problems interfere with study. Some alternative strategy is necessary to overcome the intrusive aspects of stress.

Positive self-talk, of course, is an important strategy for overcoming worry and anxiety. In addition, techniques that promote relaxation offer a powerful response to immediate difficulties and establish a preventive approach for the future.

Physical Exercise

Physical exercise is one popular approach to eliminating stress and tension while promoting physical health. People who maintain some sort of fitness program report feeling better physically and being able to perform more actively at work or school. Recently attention in fitness has shifted to the benefits of walking. A brisk 20-minute walk offers both physical exercise and time off from the daily responsibilities of family, work, and school. A nice walk before you settle down to study may be just what you need to clear your mind.

Visualizing a Relaxed State

Busy schedules and demanding course work contribute to stress. Special circumstances such as a particularly critical exam or a schedule that seems to become more and more overwhelming may heighten stress. Such circumstances suggest a need for special techniques that help to reestablish mental calm and clear thinking. Visualizing a relaxed state is one such technique.

Visualization exercises involve creating soothing mental pictures, or visual images, to rethink the reality of an experience. If, for instance, your stomach begins to tighten up every time you think about going to the computer lab, it may help to rethink the experience, substituting soothing images to eliminate the stressful feeling.

Virtually all visualization exercises start with attention to breathing. Relaxation is established by consciously breathing in a steady inhale . . . exhale . . . inhale . . . exhale fashion. Attention to this normally unconscious action, plus slowed breathing itself, produces a more relaxed feeling. Within that relaxed state, a visual image is created of a calm, safe, and comfortable setting. Frequently people like to visualize their favorite spot under a shade tree, on the beach, by a quiet stream, perhaps in a favorite park. The good feelings of this special place, its atmosphere, are then transferred to the stressful situation in order to reestablish a sense of calm. This is especially important to the study process since a relaxed sense of self contributes to clear thinking and active learning.

An Exercise in Visualization

If you find yourself feeling tense and anxious—muscles tight or stomach queasy—and unable to concentrate fully, try the following exercise. It may take you some time, but with practice it's an effective tool.

Step 1 Find a quiet place to lie down and relax.

Step 2 Close your eyes and begin by breathing consciously—slowly and steadily. Repeat to yourself, "Inhale . . . Exhale . . . Relax . . . Inhale . . . Exhale . . . Relax . . . ." Steadily increase your attention to breathing and forget the source of your tension and anxiety. Feel yourself relax.

Step 3 As you continue your breathing exercise, begin to count the breaths mentally from 1 to 10. "Inhale . . . 1 . . . Exhale . . . Relax . . . Inhale . . . 2 . . . Exhale . . . Relax . . . ." As you count, try to see each number in your mind's eye. Focus your attention on your breathing and visualize each number.

Step 4 When you reach the count of 10, continue slow breathing while letting your mind drift. Allow yourself to visualize your favorite peaceful place. Friendly, pleasant places warm your body and your mind with good feelings. Visualize your scene in look, sound, smell, sense. Feel yourself become totally relaxed and at peace with the moment. Enjoy the experience.

Step 5 With this fully comfortable and totally relaxed feeling, refocus your attention back to the circumstances of your stress, back to your place in the study process. Visualize yourself once again at study—now fully relaxed. In this fully relaxed state, you are now confident that you can resolve your problems, fulfill your goals, and achieve success. The sense of relaxation and self-confidence will allow you a true opportunity for success.

Step 6 Now open your eyes, feel your relaxed state, realize your sense of awareness, and begin to go about your business relaxed and with renewed self-confidence.

This visualization exercise takes about 10 to 15 minutes and should be practiced until it becomes easy to use. Take time to create vivid images of peaceful places to transfer the relaxed state of that environment to situations that create stress. Remember that this exercise is useful not only as a response to stress but also as a preventive measure, offering the benefits of a relaxed, self-confident self.

A Brief Exercise

In preparation for your visualization exercises, find a quiet place to sit and reread the exercise. Then practice the exercise, working through each step in turn. Once you feel comfortable with the activity, find a place to lie down and guide yourself through the exercise mentally. Don't worry if the exercise puts you to sleep once in a while; it's supposed to relax you.

The key to the success of visualization and relaxation exercises is practice. The effectiveness of the techniques comes with regular and continued use.

Creating a Study Environment

Learning progresses most smoothly when the activities become natural, a matter of habit. For example, when you lie down in bed your purpose is usually to sleep. You go to bed to sleep. It's habit. That's why it's not a good idea to study in bed. You're likely to fall asleep. In other words, there are places where certain activities are a matter of habit. If you want to study effectively, you need a quiet place dedicated to study.

A place for study is a place with no distractions. It's a place where you can read without interruption, write with plenty of room, and think without daydreaming. It's also a place with good lighting, plenty of paper and pencils, and lots of space. Furthermore, it's a place only for study, where your mind doesn't signal "sleep," or "dinner," or "favorite TV show." It's a place where your mind signals only, "study." For some people that may be a desk in a dorm room or in a bedroom at home. For others, it may be the dining room table, but only at a time when it serves no other purpose. For still others, particularly those with especially busy lives, the library becomes a refuge of choice.

Take the case of one student whose teenage children and full-time job left her little time to study at home. When she looked at her schedule, she realized there was time between classes that could be used for study. That time could be spent in the library, so it was worth a try. Eventually this approach proved a success. Doing her homework between classes, working quietly in the library, became a habit. She had found a place for study.

It is also crucial to avoid daydreaming wherever you study. If your attention drifts, work on breaking the habit. Observe yourself in study. When your mind begins to wander, leave the books. Take a break. Then return to your desk with the intent to study. Associate time for study with study alone, eliminating any distractions. Work toward increasing the amount of time devoted fully to study each time you sit down with an assignment, but allow yourself to take a brief break if daydreaming occurs. Try this approach whenever you catch yourself daydreaming.

Time for study also requires some regulation. Schedules help create habits. Notice how people know, without looking at a clock, when it's time to eat, or time for their favorite TV program, or time to feed the dog. Scheduling study as a regular activity prepares you to study at that time. Going to a special place at a special time with the intent to study will go a long way toward setting the stage for accomplishing your goals.

A Brief Exercise

Describe your place of study and what you might do to improve its use.

Establishing Goals

Much time is wasted if you merely read the next assignment even though the professor said, "Read Chapter 4 for Tuesday" or "Read the next story" or "On Thursday we will discuss the origins of the federal court system." At first glance, the assignment seems simple: Read the material. But a moment's thought suggests caution. Simply reading an assignment is likely to be a passive reading, with the material quickly forgotten. Such passive reading means a rereading at some later date to accomplish a different task—to prepare for an exam, for example—and perhaps even more rereading to help the memory. So why not begin with a different approach?

In Chapter 2, "Active Learning," the importance of planning study activities was discussed. These same issues apply here. The first consideration is the learner. What are your strengths and weaknesses? If, for instance, your major is biology and you have considerable interest and background in the subject, then you would probably approach an assignment in an introductory biology course in a different fashion than an assignment in art history, where perhaps you have little or no background. Knowing your strengths and weaknesses in the study process is also important because such knowledge should determine how you approach a task.

A Brief Exercise

Imagine that you are taking two different courses. For one, perhaps a course in psychology, you have considerable background knowledge and interest. That is, you are familiar with the specialized vocabulary and you have read about many of the topics. For the other, perhaps a course in anatomy, you have neither the background nor the experience. Unfamiliar terms cause confusion, and the examples used don't help to clarify ideas. How would you approach each course differently? For instance, how might your attitude be different? How would you plan your reading? Where would you go for help? Write your response on a separate sheet of paper.

A second consideration is the material. What type of material are you to read? A work of short fiction, for instance, requires a somewhat different approach than a chapter of history written in a narrative, or storylike, style. More different still is the typical informational chapter in a science text or the problem-oriented presentation of a math text. The question for readers to ask themselves is, "How is the material organized and how is it best understood?"

A third consideration, especially important to establishing goals, is the task: "What am I to learn?" While an instructor may simply ask you to read the next chapter, your purpose must be more specific if you intend to develop a working knowledge of the material. For example, a chapter in your public speaking text may be titled "An Effective Delivery," with the discussion focusing on the characteristics of effective speaking. Here your purpose might be "to understand the characteristics of good delivery, the oral presentation of a speech." Such a purpose is more focused than the goal of reading the chapter.

The fourth consideration involves learning strategies: "What methods of study are most useful?" The selection of learning strategies is determined primarily by your characteristics as a learner, the nature of the material, and your purpose.

Imagine the public speaking text again. Assume that you're familiar with some principles of public speaking, that the text is organized in a straightforward, informative style, and that your purpose is the one stated above. A good beginning question is, "What are the characteristics of good delivery?" As you read, you may decide to underline important information so you can avoid a lot of rereading. Having completed the reading, you can review the underlined material. Finally, to test your familiarity with the material, you might quiz yourself on the characteristics of good delivery.

Establishing clear goals for study is a logical consequence of these four planning issues—the learner, the material, the task, and the strategies. The goals are the foundation for a schedule.

Organizing a Schedule

Goals and schedules work together and are closely linked to the learning strategies used. Consider the public speaking assignment again. Imagine that your goal is to understand the characteristics of good delivery. Four strategies are useful: questioning, underlining, reviewing, and self-testing. Assume also that the chapter is about 25 pages long, but the material is not complex. Your schedule allows 2½ hours for the assignment. You need a plan for study.

A Brief Exercise

Before looking ahead to the sample schedule of events, describe, on a separate paper, how you think you might approach the problem of planning a schedule for studying "the characteristics of good delivery."

Sample Schedule

One approach to the scheduling process for this assignment might look something like this:

Step 1
- a. Preview the chapter to determine content and to formulate a purpose for reading (10 minutes).
- b. Establish your purpose in written form (2 minutes). Example: "To determine the specific characteristics of a good delivery."

c. Prepare a plan of action (5 minutes). Example: "Divide the chapter into five parts of five pages each. Read one section at a time, underlining important information, and briefly review before continuing to the next section. Review and self-test until the material is mastered."

At this point the preparation is complete, so take a 5-minute break before putting the plan into action.

Step 2 a. Read the first section, underlining important information, and briefly review before continuing on to the next section (10 minutes).

b. Repeat the above for the second and third sections (20 minutes).

It is again worthwhile to break for 5 minutes. This short breather is enough to ease the tension that develops during intense study and can interfere with concentration.

c. Repeat the directions in (a) for the fourth and fifth sections (20 minutes).

Take a brief break before beginning step 3, perhaps 2 to 3 minutes.

Step 3 a. With your initial purpose in mind, review the underlined material of the chapter as if preparing for a quiz (20 minutes). Example: "While reviewing the underlined material, recite the important information aloud as an aid to remembering the material."

b. For your quiz, your question might be "List the characteristics of good delivery" (5 minutes).

c. Compare your response to the quiz with the information in the text and review as necessary (10 minutes).

Allow some time to pass between steps 3 and 4, so that your next effort reinforces your memory of the information.

Step 4 After some period of time has passed, retest and review (15 minutes). This process continues until mastery is complete.

Now reward yourself for a job well done.

This schedule is only one example of how a study session might be planned and organized. A simple way to plan your activities and later to monitor them is to create a schedule of study. See Figure 4.1 for a guide to planning a study schedule.

Choosing Organizational Strategies

The preparation discussed thus far suggests a number of organizational strategies. In addition to previewing materials, establishing a purpose for

Preparation Notes	Pages	Time
(Consider preview, purpose, and plan of action.)		

Action Strategies	Pages	Time
(Requirements will vary greatly by assignment and selection of strategy; strategies are reading, underlining, note-taking, and so forth, with material subdivided into workable amounts.)		

Preview and Self-test	Pages	Time
(Major issues here include how material is reviewed and stored for memory, the type of self-test used, and when mastery of material is complete.)		

Figure 4.1 Study Schedule

study, and creating a plan of action, reexamining the sample schedule suggests that spacing study periods, using specific learning techniques, and emphasizing practice and review are critical to comprehension and memory.

Spacing study periods by dividing material into parts and taking rest breaks between them is crucial to concentration. The classic error made by students is to sit down and try to study for hours straight. Long, intense periods of study—cramming—merely lead to physical exhaustion and lack of concentration. Short, carefully planned efforts interspersed with rest sustain concentration and lead to greater learning. The sample schedule above is a good model for spacing study periods.

Selecting the best study methods for the subject and your own study style is another obvious key to success in learning. Much of this text is devoted to the discussion of specific techniques and strategies, from how to read a textbook, to how to take notes, to how to prepare for exams. Clearly a number of different strategies might be employed in any situation. The appropriateness of a study technique depends on goals to be achieved and the difficulty of the material. A simple reading would be appropriate for absorbing the facts of an article in *Newsweek* magazine in preparation for a class discussion. A much more involved effort would be required to understand and memorize formulas for solving problems from a trigonometry text. Careful planning for study involves the selection of appropriate strategies.

Finally, there is the issue of practice and review. While many students spend the bulk of their time reading assignments, their study time would produce better results if they shifted emphasis to practice and review. Have you ever spent time carefully reading assignments only to find in the exam that you can't remember the information you read? That's a problem of practice. If you want to remember information, practice it by using strategies like verbal recitation or creating imaginative stories or writing practice essay exams. The more you practice something, the better you know it. Organize your schedule so there is plenty of time for practice and review. (Additional information on this subject is found in Chapter 9, "Memory," and Chapter 10, "Taking Tests.")

Summary and Prediction Questions

1. To summarize the information presented thus far, answer this question: What planning practices are used for purposeful study?
2. To focus your attention on the next section of this chapter, think about and read for answers to this question: How is monitoring of the study process best accomplished?

MONITORING YOUR PROGRESS IN STUDY

Self-monitoring is especially important to the study process simply because it offers an easy way to keep track of what you are doing and to decide if any changes are needed. Most academic learning involves goals for which the formal results are not known for weeks or perhaps even months. Preparation for a midterm exam continues over many weeks, and the results may not be known for some time after the exam. Waiting for test results to gauge the success of your study efforts can very well spell failure. More immediate feedback serves as a check on progress and a guide to corrective action. Self-monitoring is an alternative to waiting.

Monitoring with a Checklist

One of the best ways to keep track of learning is with a checklist of activities. A monitoring checklist in the form of questions is especially effective because questions direct thinking toward specific issues and require answers. The specific questions of a monitoring checklist are based on the particular learning activity, in this case the study process. An important and appropriate first question to begin monitoring that process is the question, "Do I have a clearly stated purpose for study?"

In general any checklist should follow the basic steps used to accomplish the activity being monitored. Your purposes are to determine if your place of study is well established and clear of distractions, to decide if your plans are organized in a detailed manner with specific goals and a firm schedule, to judge how well things are going as the assignment progresses, and to identify any problems that might arise. If you ask periodically, "Am I meeting the goals of my plan?" and the answer is only "sometimes," then you will need to reexamine both the plan of action and the strategies. Why are these goals not being met? It may be that in one activity—say, completing a reading assignment—you did not allow enough time. Another activity—studying a user's manual for a computer program—may require a more elaborate learning strategy such as note-taking.

The following checklist is a good place to start when monitoring the study process. You may wish to add questions addressing other needs or problems you frequently encounter.

A Self-monitoring Checklist

_____ Is my place of study clearly established, free of distractions, and regularly used?

_____ Do I have a clearly stated purpose for study?

_____ Are my plans organized in a detailed manner with specific goals and a firm schedule?

_____ Am I able to concentrate on my studies and avoid daydreaming?

_____ Does my schedule of activities allow me to complete assignments on time with positive results?

_____ Am I meeting the specific goals of my plan?

_____ Are my specific learning strategies—reading, note-taking, self-testing, and so forth—effective?

_____ Am I working to reduce distractions—from people, radio, stereo, thinking about future events?

_____ Is my understanding and retention of the material satisfactory for my purpose—preparing for class discussion, organizing information for a paper, practicing a speech?

_____ Am I experiencing any problems that require immediate attention? If so, what corrective action should I take?

Problem Solving and Strategy Revision

Chapter 3 presented a problem-solving method for time management. The same approach is useful for resolving problems revealed by your self-monitoring of the study process: Identify the problem, decide on an appropriate strategy, employ the new strategy, evaluate the results, and make appropriate revisions. This approach is one effective way to approach any problems identified by a monitoring checklist.

Imagine, for example, that you are taking a course in child development. You have always enjoyed working with children and have some experience working in a day care center. You believe that a thorough understanding of child development is important to your future career plans. The text for the course seems extremely difficult, unfortunately, even though you've planned your study activities carefully. Not only is the text difficult to understand, but strategies like underlining and rereading don't seem to help either in grasping concepts like "sensorimotor development," "egocentrism," and "object permanence." There seems to be a serious comprehension problem.

A Brief Exercise

The discussion above presents a comprehension problem. You are using some useful strategies for study, but they appear ineffective. On a separate piece of paper, consider the following questions: Why might these problems occur? How would I try to solve this problem?

There are many reasons why such problems arise. Distractions in the study environment may be interfering with concentration. It could be the plan of study is unrealistically ambitious; perhaps too much material is being covered at one time. New ideas take time to absorb. Perhaps other strategies for study would be more effective. Perhaps another approach is necessary. If, in fact, the problem does involve ineffective strategies, then the direction is set to look for alternatives.

A Think-aloud Strategy

One common reason for comprehension difficulty is too little use of prior knowledge and experience to decipher new ideas. One way to solve this problem is to use a think-aloud strategy to help you make use of what you already know to grasp new ideas.

Thinking aloud brings your thoughts into the open for a clearer understanding of how you are thinking about a subject. The strategy works as follows: First read a portion of text, perhaps a paragraph. Next, translate the information into your own words, talking aloud to yourself. Third, think aloud about any prior experience that seems to parallel the author's discussion or for examples that might help clarify an idea. Comparing your past experience with new information is one key to understanding, because similarities help you become more familiar with the material. Fourth, draw some conclusions about the meaning of the text. The think-aloud strategy offers a step-by-step approach to developing that understanding. Look at how it works with an example.

Take the concept of egocentrism in child development. Perhaps the definition in the text is technical, and your initial reaction is, "I don't understand." Take a second look at the word itself. People talk about "ego" all the time. If a student is talking about what a great job he did on that last test, really boasting about it, a classmate might say, "What an ego you have!" You think about that and reason, "The student was really saying, 'Hey, I'm great,' so ego must have something to do with how you feel about yourself." Next, look again at examples in the text. Do they suggest a similar idea? Think some more about what you have learned. "Egocentrism must have something to do with paying attention to yourself." That's your conclusion. In fact, the concept of egocentrism in child development relates to how children experience themselves as the center of their world. (See Chapter 6, "Reading Textbooks," for a more detailed discussion of the think-aloud strategy.)

Cooperative Learning

While a think-aloud strategy may be useful in resolving certain problems, there may very well be times when more resources are necessary. This is where cooperative learning may help. It is not uncommon to have some experience working with others in school. Most students, at one time or another, have worked in study groups—revising lecture notes, organizing a group presentation, or studying for a major exam. Small groups can work together in many ways, but the secret of success in cooperative learning is clear organization.

Two heads are better than one, the saying goes, and cooperative learning is best accomplished in pairs. For example, first both students read a passage from the text. Then one student summarizes the passage and the other asks questions to help the first student clarify the summary. Next the two work together to relate their prior experience to the new information by offering examples, comparing similar experiences, and explaining how this new information offers insight into some prior knowledge or situation. As understanding builds, the pair continue working together with techniques to aid memory. One student may, for instance, identify a concept for which the other provides an example. Or one student may ask a question for which the other provides an answer, and so forth. Continually reversing roles, each has an opportunity to use a different learning strategy.

Cooperative learning enables you and others to resolve specific problems. And you can develop a better understanding of the learning process as you look for better ways to interpret, translate, and communicate new information.

A Brief Exercise

To practice this technique of cooperative learning, pair up with a student in one of your classes, and work together on a textbook assignment. Try to follow the procedure in the steps presented, so that there is order and consistency in your study activities.

1. Both read a portion of the text.
2. Student A summarizes, student B asks questions, and A then clarifies.
3. Both students discuss how the new information fits in with their prior experience—offering examples, telling of similar experiences, explaining how this new information offers insight into some prior situation.
4. For retention, student A identifies concepts for which student B offers examples, and so forth.

5. Roles regularly reverse as the process continues. The goal of the process is understanding and retention.

It may seem to you that some of these ideas for planning and monitoring are somewhat time consuming. At times they surely demand extra effort. But it's important to recognize that you are in the process of learning how to organize and carry out a systematic program of study. Once you understand the process and begin to practice it, you will find that most of the planning, monitoring, and study activities recommended in this book proceed rather quickly. After a time much of the study-thinking-reading process becomes virtually automatic. In addition, you don't have to use all these strategies all the time. Once familiar with them, you can choose the most appropriate to your purpose and the difficulty of the task. The emphasis in purposeful study is on flexibility, choosing from a variety of techniques to accomplish your task in the most effective and efficient manner.

Summary and Prediction Questions

1. To review the monitoring process, answer the following question: What strategies can I use to monitor my study activities?
2. To consider the next topic of discussion, think about and read to answer this question: Why is evaluation an important part of the study process?

EVALUATING THE STUDY PROCESS

The evaluation stage is one of the easiest, yet one of the most essential, steps in the study process. It is a logical extension of the self-monitoring process because it reviews success in the study process. It also assesses not only ongoing efforts but also the long-term results of those efforts.

If the purpose of study is to pass a particular exam or to complete a research paper, evaluation looks at the results of the effort. To pass the exam means that you were successful in meeting your goal. To complete the research paper brings the same result. One important question in evaluation is, thus, "Am I accomplishing my goals?" That question also applies more broadly when evaluating success in a given academic course or progress toward a career. Success in your efforts also suggests the next important issue.

Flexibility

Goals are met in many ways, some more efficient than others.. Therefore, it is important to evaluate your learning strategies with an eye toward becoming more flexible and efficient.

Occasionally, for instance, students ask instructors for permission to use a tape recorder in class to copy lectures. When asked why, they usually comment that they don't take good notes, or they're afraid of missing something, or they need to hear things twice to grasp them. Many instructors do let students tape lectures. But is this the most efficient and effective way to improve note-taking? Is tape recording a positive way to instill self-confidence in a learner? What are the limitations? The problem with taping lectures is obvious. It wastes a lot of time. Each lecture is heard at least twice, and quite frequently notes are a time-consuming verbatim transcript of the lecture. Improving note-taking skills, revising notes with other students, and asking questions in class are all more efficient ways to obtain lecture information and lead to a more flexible system of study.

With the results of your efforts in mind—the amount of time involved, the degree of success achieved, the commitments planned for the future—evaluate your learning strategies. How are you using them, and what alternatives are available? Remember, you must decide which strategies are most appropriate to your particular purpose and the ease or difficulty with which it is accomplished. Difficult, lengthy assignments require more planning, more time, and use of more complicated strategies. Less difficult assignments require less planning, less time, and use of fewer strategies. Emphasize flexibility—choosing the best strategy for the task. Ask yourself, "Am I using my study strategies in a flexible fashion?"

Seeking Additional Help

Perhaps one of the most important questions in the evaluation stage is, "Should I seek help?" Too often students let problems grow because they are afraid to ask anyone for help. It's a bit like being in class and having an instructor ask if anyone has any questions. Most often no one says a word. Does that mean everyone fully understands the instructor's presentation? You know better. The truth is that students are reluctant to raise their hands because they're afraid they'll look stupid. What's the result? It's a question left unanswered or a problem left unsolved.

If you are having difficulty with a course, or with a learning strategy, or with remembering what you've learned, or anything else in school, seek the additional help you need. Everyone needs help at some time, and to imagine this is not the case is to undermine your self-awareness. In some cases asking for help may be the key to survival.

A Final Point

Identifying success in the study process, whether during the activities themselves or in the final outcome, offers another opportunity to influence the study process—this time through rewards. Students are very busy people with commitments to school, to work, to family, to themselves. There are times when creating time for purposeful study is extremely difficult. The solution is to set priorities and decide what to do first.

There are no simple answers to the question of what to do first. But one approach is to save the things you enjoy doing, the things you *want* to do, as rewards for accomplishing the more difficult tasks in life—like studying.

Imagine, for example, that on Thursday night at 9 o'clock there is a movie you want to see. Maybe you even asked a friend along. But you have a composition due Friday morning. Planning, scheduling, and a reward system will let you do both.

At a minimum, you'll need time to outline your paper, compose a rough draft, and write the final paper, so you carefully budget time for each step. Then you make a deal with yourself and your friend: "If I complete my paper early Thursday evening, we'll go to the movie. If not, I'll have to cancel."

If you meet your goal, you have the satisfaction of completing an assignment and the reward of relaxing with a friend. If you are unable to finish, cancel the reward. Rewards must be tied to success. A treat such as "going to the movie" is an excellent incentive for getting down to business and not wasting time. Moreover, with a plan like this, canceling is not necessarily a punishment. The extra time needed to complete the paper is now available because of the planning. The punishment comes only if you go to the movie, don't finish the paper, and receive a failing grade.

Success should be rewarded, and those rewards are, at least, one way to reinforce your self-image as a successful student and to motivate further effort. A final question for evaluation is thus, "Am I using rewards effectively to reinforce my success and motivate further efforts?"

A Brief Exercise

On a separate sheet of paper, make a list of activities you could use as rewards for your efforts, and describe how you would use one or two with a particular assignment.

Summary Question

To review the evaluation process, answer this question: Why is evaluation an important part of study?

SUMMARY

The study process requires a good deal of attention because it is so crucial to success in education. Planning carefully for study, monitoring specific activities closely, and evaluating final results effectively are the building blocks of purposeful study. Knowledge of this process is one step toward active learning. Application of this process is the road that leads to success.

Review Questions

Review your understanding of the chapter by answering each of the following questions:

1. What planning activities aid purposeful study?
2. How is self-monitoring of the study process best accomplished?
3. Why is evaluation an important part of the study process?

CHAPTER REVIEW

To complete this chapter, answer the following questions. When you are finished, review the chapter to check your answers.

1. True or False: Creating a quiet study environment is crucial to establishing good study habits.
2. True or False: Self-questioning is not a useful approach for monitoring the study process.
3. True or False: Establishing clear goals is a logical beginning for careful planning.

4. True or False: Think-aloud strategies and cooperative learning may be effective responses to difficulty in learning.

5. Which of the following is not an important consideration in organizing a schedule?
   a. clearly established goals
   b. regular practice and review
   c. an interesting assignment
   d. periodic self-testing

6. Why is visualization an effective technique for relaxation?
   a. It is an opportunity for students to forget about their assignments.
   b. It offers students time to reestablish a sense of calm and clear thinking.
   c. It relies primarily on physical exercise and sports activities.
   d. It is a technique most students already use to avoid tension and stress.

7. Which of the strategies discussed in this chapter seem most useful for improving your study habits? Which less so? Discuss why certain strategies appeal to you and others don't.

____

____

____

____

____

____

8. Using the sample checklist for self-monitoring, analyze two or three study sessions. What appear to be your strengths and weaknesses? What steps can you take to improve your approach to learning?

____

____

____

____

9. Imagine that you are limited to selecting only one strategy from this chapter to help improve your study habits. Which would you choose and why?

____

____

____

____

10. Spend the next 15 minutes practicing the visualization exercise for relaxation. Then describe your reaction.

____

____

____

____

5

Taking Lecture Notes

Preview Exercise

Take a few moments to preview the chapter. Determine what topics are discussed. Think about your current approach to listening and note-taking. Identify your strengths and weaknesses. Then study the chapter for specific strategies for improvement.

PURPOSE FOR READING: ______________________________

____

____

Listening plays a significant role in everyone's life, whether in school, on the job, at home, or during leisure time. Careful listening is critical to success in daily affairs. Interestingly, studies of listening suggest that people tend to listen less attentively than many situations require and that much listening is fairly lax. Some studies go so far as to suggest that while growing up people may actually learn *not* to listen, at least not very carefully.

Poor listening may be partially a consequence of having no clear purpose. Without good reason for listening, one's attention is likely to stray.

Poor listening may also be a consequence of the many distractions that intrude upon listening situations. Loud conversations, noisy machinery, nearby activity, all have the potential to interfere with good listening.

Poor listening and the troublesome problem of misunderstanding are also closely linked. An inattentive listener may simply misinterpret a speaker. And this may occur more often than imagined because meaning and understanding are influenced by the listener's experiences, point of view, and reactions to the consequences of an idea, all of which may differ from the speaker's. Even further, poor listening contributes to forgetting. Perhaps the information is so obvious or heard so briefly that it is not processed to the point of storing it in memory. If there is really nothing to remember, what is heard is forgotten.

Since listening is one of the fundamental issues in the learning process, this chapter examines some practical aspects of active listening, some useful techniques for taking lecture notes (including revising and reviewing), a self-monitoring procedure, and some sample lecture exercises.

Guiding Questions

Use the following questions to guide your reading. Look for specific answers as the ideas are discussed.

1. How can I become a more active listener?
2. What techniques promote effective note-taking?
3. When and how should I revise and review my lecture notes?
4. Why should a checklist for self-monitoring lecture notes include the elements of active listening, note-taking, and revising and reviewing?

ACTIVE LISTENING

Active listening is one key to success in an academic setting. Students spend a good deal of time listening to classroom lectures, discussions, laboratory demonstrations, and small group presentations. They can learn more by listening actively.

A positive attitude once again provides the framework. Approaching a lecture with a "Who needs this?" attitude obviously will interfere with listening. The contrasting attitude, "Let me see if I can find out why . . ." reflects a conscious desire to learn from a lecture or class discussion and motivates careful listening.

Purpose in Listening

Of course, the desire to listen is only a first step. A purpose for listening offers direction. The more specific the purpose, the better the focus. If the lecture, for instance, is about "management styles," then your purpose is "to define the different management styles and determine what the benefits and disadvantages of each might be and how effective each is in the marketplace." You begin the listening process by deciding what you hope to learn, and your purpose directs your attention toward the subject of the presentation and its subsequent development.

A BRIEF EXERCISE

Assume that each of the following statements is a lecture topic. Establish a purpose for listening to each.

1. Regulations Governing Day Care Centers
2. Three Approaches to the Prewriting Process
3. Reasons Why Businesses Leave Urban Areas
4. Benefits and Losses Associated with Using Computer Technology in the Office

Preparation for lectures is also an important foundation for good listening. Completing reading assignments listed in the course syllabus or the instructor's "suggested readings" list provides the foundation for listening. The background you acquire not only increases your awareness of the subject under discussion, but gives you some sense of where the instructor is heading. It also gives your purpose for listening a sharper focus: You will be listening for clarification of ideas that confused you in the reading and answers to questions the reading brought to mind.

Listening to Lectures

Getting to a lecture on time is another responsibility you owe yourself. Because lecturers frequently begin with a preview of the presentation, missing the first few minutes places you at a serious disadvantage. Previews help establish purpose in listening and suggest the organization of the presentation. Your American history instructor may begin, "Today I want to talk about three facets of government policy after World War II: the containment of the Soviet Union, the Marshall Plan to rebuild Europe, and the industrial conversion to a peace time economy." This brief preview identifies the subjects to be covered, the probable order of presentation, and the information necessary to establish specific purposes for listening.

Be sure to come prepared. Pens, pencils, notebooks, and textbooks are the student's tools for transferring the insights of classroom listening into long-term learning. Make sure to carry them with you.

As the lecture begins, take the role of an active listener. Anticipate the lecturer, ask yourself questions to focus your thinking, listen for the organization of ideas, and listen for cue words to identify key points in the presentation.

Anticipate a lecturer by making informed guesses about the direction of a lecture. If the history instructor begins, "After World War II the objective of U.S. foreign policy was containment," the active listener anticipates that the instructor will next define *containment* and explain its importance to the postwar foreign policy. It's a good bet that an explanation will follow. Remember also that even the act of anticipation, whether the guess is right or wrong, stimulates more active listening.

Asking Questions

Asking yourself questions is similar to anticipation. In this case, the information is used to ask questions that help focus your attention and stimulate thinking about the content of the lecture. As you listen to the history preview above, you might ask yourself, "What was the containment policy and how was it carried out?" or "What was containment and why was it necessary?" Your listening is now directed toward answers for those questions. If you feel the lecture does not provide the answers, you might ask the instructor to clarify the point or further elaborate.

Asking questions also contributes to active listening by linking information in the text together with information in the lecture. More general questions like, "How did the text present that idea?" or "What example was used to explain that concept?" help promote more critical thinking about the information under consideration. Comparative questions such as, "How is the lecturer's view similar to or different from the text presentation?" stimulate you to analyze ideas. Moreover, at an appropriate moment in the lecture, you may want to ask the instructor to explain points of disagreement or to clarify areas of confusion. Such questions clearly aid both listening and understanding.

Asking questions can help you identify the organization of a lecture. If a lecturer says, for example, "There are three major stages in demographic transition," the logical question to ask is, "What are the three stages?"

With that question in mind you not only are listening for a description of those stages but also are alert to the fact that there are three stages under discussion.

Following the Organization

Following the organization of a lecture is crucial not only to understanding information but also to recording that information in your notes. Preparation provides background to the content of a lecture, and the lecturer's preview establishes a focus to the presentation. In addition, specific language cues help you identify the lecturer's organization. Listen for sentences that begin with phrases like these: "There are three major stages of. . .," "Important here . . .," "There are several reasons why . . .," or "The key to understanding this is . . . ." Such cues direct listeners to the main ideas and should trigger note-taking.

Similarly, other language cues alert you to supporting points that illustrate and clarify concepts. One of the most common cues is the phrase "for example." When a lecturer says, "For example, . . .", you're alert for specific information that will clarify major ideas. Listen carefully for phrases like "For instance . . .," "To illustrate that point . . .," "Imagine that . . .," and "Put into specific terms . . . ," and use the examples to clarify the information in your own mind.

Patterns of Organization

Lecturers also use language cues to organize lectures according to specific patterns. These patterns of organization are actually patterns of thinking—such as explaining a problem from a cause-and-effect perspective, or analyzing the similarities and differences between two events through comparison and contrast.

Common patterns of organization include: (1) enumeration, a listing pattern that might be used with a presentation like "Five Quick Ways to Accomplish Your Task"; (2) sequence, a pattern of ordered steps such as a lab experiment; (3) cause and effect, a pattern that shows a certain relationship between two conditions such as, "I was late for class this morning [the effect] because my alarm didn't go off [the cause]"; and (4) comparison and contrast, a pattern that examines similarities and differences between two or more things such as "The two planes are similar in their engineering design [the comparison]; however, they perform in radically different ways [the contrast]."

Figure 5.1 offers a list of some common words, sometimes called transitional or signal words, used to identify patterns of thought. These words will help you identify the development of an idea and are useful for organizing information as you take notes.

A Brief Exercise

Take a few minutes to study Figure 5.1 to make sure you're familiar with the patterns of organization. Then, without looking back to the figure, identify the patterns suggested by the language cues that follow.

1. "Safety precautions had been taken; however, . . ."
2. "To complete the exercise, we must first. . . . Second. . . . Finally. . . ."
3. "The author had skillfully manipulated the plot of the story, so . . ."
4. "There are many ways to analyze the situation. First. . . . Another. . . . Finally. . . ."

Active listening is much more than simply hearing what someone has to say. The more important the listening situation, the more actively you must listen. Remember, listening ability can improve with the use of effective strategies, frequent practice, and a conscious desire to learn.

Still, academic activities require something more. Lectures, class discussion, special presentations, and so forth frequently require that you retain information for some period of time, and that's where good note-taking strategies become very important.

Summary and Prediction Questions

1. To summarize the points of discussion for active listening, answer this question: How can I become a more active listener?
2. To focus your attention on the next stage in the discussion, read to answer this question: What techniques promote effective note-taking?

TECHNIQUES FOR TAKING LECTURE NOTES

As previously noted, preparation is one of the foremost requirements for good listening and note-taking. Preparation means coming to class on time with reading assignments complete and questions ready. It also means coming to class on time with a notebook, a couple of pens (one could run out of ink) or pencils, and the textbook, ready to begin.

Major points

The major point here . . .
There are several reason why . . .
Most significant is . . .
More importantly . . .
Of special note . . .
The primary purpose is . . .

Examples and illustrations

for example	imagine
for instance	more specifically
to illustrate	a case in point

Enumeration

first	another
also	next
in addition	finally

Sequence

first	next
second	after
then	the fifth step
following that	finally

Cause and effect

because	so
reasons for	therefore
source of	consequently
led to	as a result of

Comparison and contrast

like	in contrast
similarly	but
in the same	however
analogously	on the other hand

Figure 5.1 Word Clues to Patterns of Organization

Now the question is *how* to take notes, and to be quite frank, there are many points of view. Some instructors believe that most of your time in class should be spent listening and thinking, with note-taking only to highlight ideas for later consideration. Others believe that you might just as well write down everything you can. The more detailed the notes the better; you can organize them later. Still others suggest a middle ground between these two extremes and discuss a format for note-taking that is useful for most students.

A Format for Note-taking

Spacing is what makes a good note-taking format useful. Leave yourself room to use your notes in a variety of ways. For instance, when you are actually taking notes of important ideas, definitions, and explanations, supporting points, and examples or illustrations during the lecture, do not fill the page from margin to margin. Leave space for making revisions within the notes themselves such as clarifying terms or adding examples. Also leave space for making connections to the text and for answering questions you may have. Finally, be sure to organize your notes so that they are useful for later study.

To begin, always use an 8½″ × 11″ notebook with lined pages. Use only one side of each page for notes, so the back side is available for additional information. Title and date each page for quick reference. To set up the page, create a left-hand margin of approximately one-third of the page for review activities. The other two-thirds is for taking notes, with plenty of space between points. See Figure 5.2 for an idea of what this layout looks like. Keep a separate notebook, or a separate section within a large notebook, for each course.

Organizing Notes

The discussion of active listening gave considerable attention to organization, not only because it's one sure approach to good listening but also because it's crucial to organized note-taking. Notes need some organization that makes sense long after the lecture is over. You can follow the organization of the lecture or create some pattern that makes sense to you.

One option is to follow an outline that identifies major ideas, supporting points, and specific examples. In outline form, such an approach looks like this:

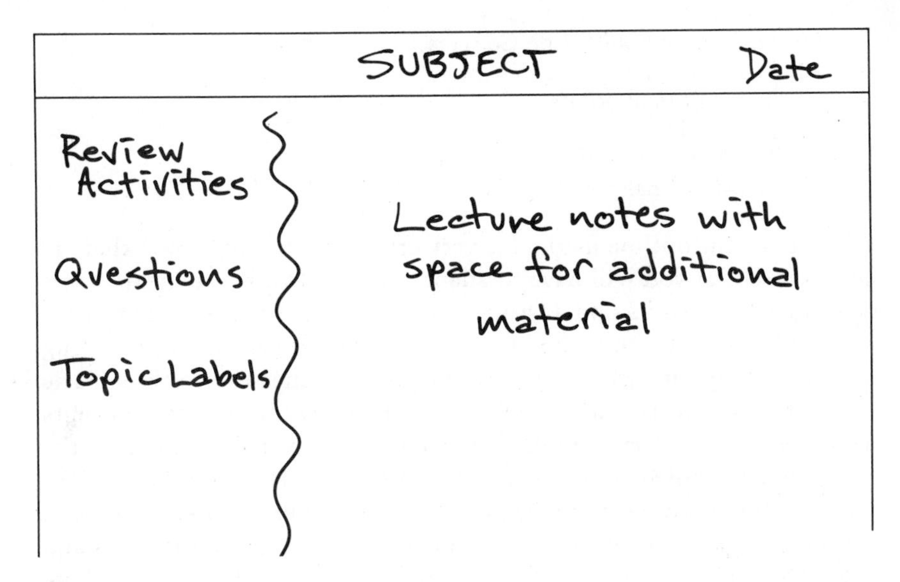

Figure 5.2 Format for Note-taking

Topic

I. Major idea
    A. Supporting point
        1. Specific example
        2. Specific example
    B. Supporting point
        1. Specific example

II. Major idea

And so the pattern would continue. But what if the lecturer is not following this organization in the lecture? To avoid confusion, remember this principle in outlining: Create some pattern of organization when you take notes.

An outline works well for describing a hierarchy, as shown below for an introduction to government.

Branches of Government

I. Federal govt. divided into 3 major parts with certain responsibilities.
    A. Executive branch (the president)
        1. Commander-in-chief
        2. (additional points)

B. Legislative branch (the Congress)
   1. Makes laws
   2. (additional points)
C. Judicial branch (the courts)
   1. Arbitrates conflicts over laws
   2. (additional points)

In this case, the outline method is very effective. Still, for topics that are not hierarchical you will have to adapt your note-taking to create some other form of organization. Listing points may be appropriate when an instructor begins, "There are eight ways . . . ." Some other form of grouping may be appropriate when a lecture begins, "Businesses use three basic types of . . . ." Creating a "time line" may be useful for recording events discussed in a history lecture that begins, "Today I want to trace the changing economic conditions between 1865 and 1890, ..."

The important point is that you listen carefully in the first minutes of the lecture for a preview of its contents. Be alert to pattern words and cues. Then organize your notes accordingly.

Sample Notes

Figure 5.3 presents an example of effective note-taking in a sociology class. This sociological look at childhood shows how to use idea phrases rather than complete sentences, a good time saver. It suggests how information in lectures might be grouped. It uses abbreviations when possible, such as "sys" for *system*, "sch" for *school* and "beh" for *behavior.* It uses symbols where possible to show relationships such as "=," "+," and lines suggesting the direction of an argument. Each of these techniques is useful for note-taking, but it's best to find your own shortcuts for note-taking.

A BRIEF EXERCISE

Take a few moments and on a separate sheet of paper make a list of abbreviations and symbols that you could use to make your note-taking more efficient. Consider for example, "=" for *means,* "ex." for *example,* and so forth. Remember that abbreviations and symbols should be used consistently.

A PRACTICE EXERCISE

Once you've taken a careful look at Figure 5.3, try your hand at this process of listening and note-taking. To complete this exercise, have a friend read aloud the

SOCIOLOGY 9/25

TOPIC: Children learn roles

Childhood = a status, a place in a sys. of social relations

Status is

achieved OR ascribed

↓ individuals achieve something

EX doctor (+)
alcoholic (-)

↓ individuals assigned something by birth or situation

EX sex, race

Status has a "role" → a set of expectations, required beh.

↓

Childhood = obey parents, attend sch. . . .

↓

Expected beh. associated with a status is learned thru experience — social interaction

Figure 5.3 Sample Notes

following selection on marketing research as if it were a classroom lecture. On a separate sheet of paper, take notes during the "lecture," applying the suggestions presented in this chapter. Listen for organization and create your notes accordingly. Try to use idea phrases, abbreviations, and symbols where possible.

Sample Lecture: Marketing Research[1]

For any business, the marketing research associated with identifying consumer needs begins with a clearly established purpose, the origin of which is the recognition of a problem or an opportunity. Clearly defining one's purpose, or defining the problem under research, is crucial to the success of the effort.

Assume for a moment that a product your company markets shows a decline in sales. The purpose of the research is to identify the causes for the decline, and the research activity is sometimes referred to as "exploratory research."

Exploratory research follows two basic tracks. On the one hand, it consists of examining internal sources of information such as sales information, marketing costs, and other financial records. On the other hand, it also requires an examination of external sources of information such as customer surveys, retail market evaluations, and government marketing data like the U.S. Census.

Once information from these sources is obtained, the data is analyzed and interpreted with the initial problem or purpose in mind.

Now that you have completed the note-taking exercise, compare your notes with the sample notes in the appendix (See Figure 5.6 in the appendix). Remember that identification of major ideas is your most important concern. The sample notes are one approach for you to compare with your notes. Having reviewed the sample notes, continue with the next exercise.

A Practice Exercise

Once again you will need a friend to read the following lecture titled "Understanding plot structure." Use a separate sheet of paper and try taking notes that clearly reflect the content of the lecture. This lecture contains a sample illustration the instructor would sketch on the blackboard. Be sure to incorporate it in your notes.

Sample Lecture: Understanding Plot Structure

Plot is one fundamental aspect of the short story. We typically consider it the structure of events in a story from beginning to end. And the question that frequently guides our investigation of a story's plot is, "What happens?"

If we think about plot as the structure of events, then we can create a general framework for examining plot. A plot may be divided into six basic parts: the in-

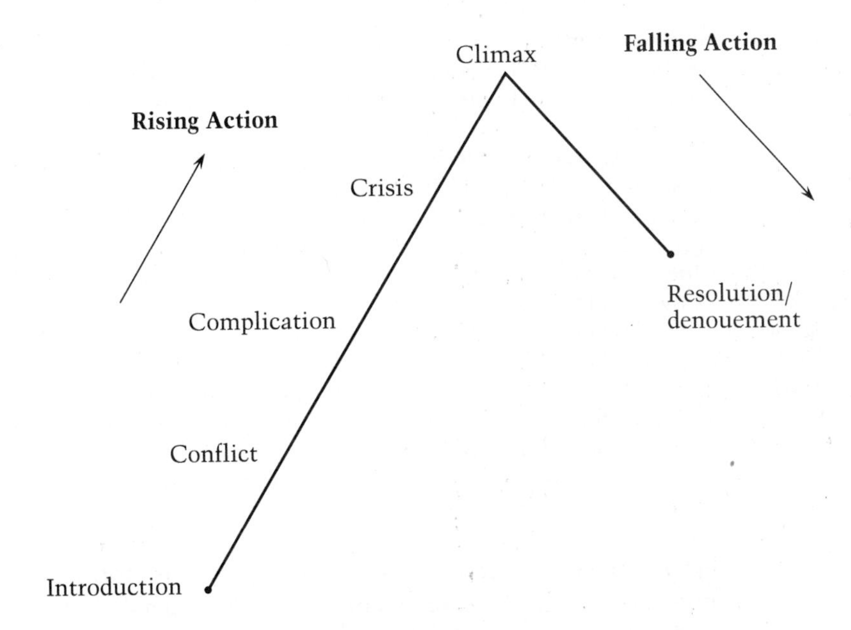

Figure 5.4 Blackboard Figure of Plot Structure

troduction, the conflict, complication, the crisis of events, the climax, and the resolution, (also called denouement, pronounced: "day'-noo-mon"). From the introduction of the story to its high point—the climax—is the *rising* action; and from the climax to the conclusion—or resolution—is the *falling* action. The sketch on the board shows a helpful way to think about plot structure (see Figure 5.4). Understanding the workings of plot structure is a way to better understand short stories, and what's happening.

Richard Wright's short story "The Man Who Was Almost a Man"[2] is a useful example for examining plot structure. The story presents a young black man's struggle for his manhood in the old South. As the story begins, we are immediately introduced to Dave, the central character, and his discontent with people around him. We also become aware of Dave's desire to own a gun so he can show others that he is not a child but a "man" and that he deserves their respect. The beginning of a story is the *introduction*, and our knowledge of Dave's desire to prove his "manhood" with a gun establishes the *conflict* of the story.

As the story progresses so does the *complication* of events. Dave manages to manipulate his mother into letting him buy a gun, which is supposed to be for his father. But Dave keeps the gun, and takes it to his job on a nearby plantation. The reader can foresee problems.

The *crisis* of events comes when Dave attempts to shoot the gun. Closing his eyes and waving his arm, Dave fires. Aside from nearly blowing off his hand, he accidentally shoots a mule. He is at a loss as to what to do, so he hides the gun and tries to lie about the death of the mule.

Yet once the truth is known, he is ridiculed by his co-orkers, threatened with a beating by his father, and placed in debt for two years by the plantation owner to pay for the mule. Dave's desire to prove his manhood with a gun has brought his life to a point of crisis.

Desperate and angry, Dave vows to himself that he will be a victim no longer. This decision leads to the high point of the story.

The *climax* comes when Dave returns to the site of the earlier shooting; finds the gun and fires it a second time; this time with his eyes open and his hand held steady. This is the turning point in the story, a point that sees Dave firmly attempt to take control over his life.

At this moment of change, Dave hears the whistle of a train heading north. His decision is made, and the *resolution* of events comes as Dave climbs aboard the passing train in search of a future. The reader has only to interpret events.

Plot structure is the series of events that make up a short story. Thinking about a story while keeping in mind the elements of plot structure (introduction, conflict, complication, crisis of events, climax, and resolution) will help you, the reader, better understand what's happening.

Now that you have completed this exercise, compare your notes with the sample notes in the appendix (see Figure 5.7 in the appendix). What similarities and differences are there? Can you think of any specific problems that you might need to correct? Remember, becoming a good listener and a good note-taker requires attention and practice.

Summary and Prediction Questions

1. To summarize the discussion for note-taking: Describe the techniques for effective note-taking.
2. To focus your attention on the next section, read to answer the question: When and how should I revise and review my lecture notes?

REVISING AND REVIEWING

Active listening and effective note-taking are two critical stages in the note-taking process; but if you were to stop at this stage and assume that you had finally mastered the process, you'd be in trouble. Like most learning activities, this process requires further revision and review. Once the classroom exercise in note-taking is complete, the revision process begins. Regardless of how well you take notes, there is always the possibility of missing points, writing phrases that mean little to you later, or recording information that requires further elaboration. Quite simply, once class is over, it is time to begin filling in the gaps.

Revision

Begin revision as soon as possible after a lecture while it is still fresh in your mind. You will frequently remember information from the lecture that you neglected to note during class. Moreover, you may be able to clarify points of confusion once you are quietly away from the classroom and have time to think about the lecture's content. This revision period also serves as an opportunity to highlight important concepts for special attention, and to link the information to the text.

That left-hand margin you saved for later can now be used in a couple of helpful ways. You can jot questions there as you study your notes. For example, if your notes on marketing research indicate that there are three sources of internal information, then you might write a question in the margin like, "What are the three sources of internal information?" Creating the question helps you focus on important points, and practice-testing during the review will help you remember the information.

The left-hand margin is also a good place for topic labels for important information contained in the notes. These labels then serve as guides for reviewing and for practice testing. Covering the notes with a sheet of paper, you can use the topic label as a stimulus for recalling information. Read the topic label, explain its meaning, provide appropriate examples, and then check your response with your notes. Figure 5.5 presents a set of sample notes on "demographic transition"[3] with questions or topic labels included.

Periodic Review

For lecture notes to be of value in the learning process, periodic review of them is an absolute necessity. Notes are reviewed during the revision stage, but the purpose then is to clarify information, to identify key ideas, and to create questions. Once that task is accomplished, it is time to schedule the study-type, periodic review activities discussed in Chapter 4. Each review period provides additional practice and experience with the revised lecture notes. By posing questions and answering them, by creating topic labels and providing explanations, by coming to understand the material, you will achieve the success you desire.

ECOLOGY 10/27

	TOPIC: Demographic Transition
When did the pop. begin to rise?	Historically pop. grows slowly, but 15TH cent. begins to rise rapidly because people are living longer
What held pop. low?	Hist. poor nutrition, unclean water, infectious disease = a high birth rate and a high death rate (child).
Health care causes...	Health care ⟶ decline in death rates
Developed countries...	Past 100 yrs. improved health care & improved agriculture & food dist. = high birth & low death rates (developed countries) ↓
How is pop. stab. after rapid rise?	People begin to recognize change = decline in birth rates ↓ Decline in birth & death rates = pop. stability

Figure 5.5 Sample Notes for Demographic Transition

ECOLOGY 10/27

Poor coutries . . .	Demo. trans. cont. Poor countries not exp. gradual change ↓ Dramatic improve in health care = decline in death rates & cont. high birth rates = rapid pop. growth
Summarize demographic transition.	Demographers summarize change: 1. poor health care = high birth/high death → pop. stability ↓ 2. modern medicine = high birth/low death → rapid pop. growth ↓ 3. people recogn. new cond. = low birth/low death → pop. stability called "demographic transition"

Cooperative learning is beneficial in both the revision and the review stages. Classmates can share notes and discuss class lectures in order to refine and clarify their lecture notes. Additionally, cooperation among classmates can assist in the review process, especially if the students help each other clarify the information and practice testing by exchanging roles in the question-and-answer sessions. Revision and review can proceed both individually and collectively.

AN EXERCISE

Once again you will need a friend to read a lecture to you. The title of this lecture is "The value of children's picture books." Your purpose in this exercise is twofold. First you want to listen carefully and take well-organized notes. Second, when you've completed the notes, you want to revise them and use the left-hand margin to write sample study questions. Complete this exercise in your notebook.

Sample Lecture: The Value of Children's Picture Books

Children's books have been a phenomenal success among book buyers in recent years and much of this success can be attributed to the high-quality production of "picture books."

Children's picture books are basically stories told through a fine blend of text—the written story—and illustration. The text and illustration complement each other and share in telling the story through their integral relationship.

Both parents and children are attracted to these books for their vividly told stories and excellent illustrations.

The values picture books have for children are many. Today we will consider four of the more important ones: that the books "entertain," that they create "engagement," that they promote "language development," and that they stimulate "visual imagination."

Entertainment

All good literature should, first of all, entertain, and children's literature is no different. Picture books have a particular advantage in this because while the story is read to children, they can immerse themselves in the illustration. Even the cover of Peter Spier's book, *A Fox Went Out on a Chilly Night,*[4] with its red fox running across an old corn field filled with the colors of autumn and early evening, is a moment to remember.

Entertainment comes from good storytelling, and in picture books through both story and illustration. So when Ezra Jack Keats tells the story of a little boy named Peter in *The Snowy Day,*[5] children are taken on an adventure of winter when the city fills with snow. Little things are remembered as when Peter makes angels in the snow, or when he puts a snowball in his pocket for tomorrow . . . and goes inside.

Engagement

While children are being entertained by books, those especially fine works of literature also create a true engagement, where the children are literally drawn into the story, asking to hear it again and again. A book such as Maurice Sendak's *Where the Wild Things Are*[6] has such appeal. Children are attracted to Max, who has been sent to bed without his supper for acting like a wild thing. What really draws their attention is Max's imaginary trip to "where the wild things are" and the "wild rumpus" of Max and all other wild things. The engagement comes full circle when Max returns home to where someone loves him most of all and finds his supper waiting for him. Rare is the child who forgets Max and the wild things.

Engagement of a similar kind is presented in Paul O. Zelinsky's illustrated version of *Hansel and Gretel*,[7] retold by Rika Lesser, where the bold use of oils and large-image illustrations create an atmosphere of excitement and suspense, where characters seem to come alive. Children become a part of this story through its illustration. Text is merely an aid to their engagement.

Children are especially attracted to books that explore the problems of childhood. Consequently, many works engage the young by providing a warmth of understanding for what may seem to a child an insurmountable problem. Ann Grifalconi's *Darkness and the Butterfly*[8] accomplishes the task of understanding and assurance in this dramatically illustrated story of a young girl's efforts to overcome her fear of the night. Realism and fantasy blend together in a flow of watercolor illustrations to show how Osa "found the way to carry her own Sight through the darkness."

Language Development

Picture books also promote language development. As children grow, they tend to repeat the language of their experience, or their environment. Children's books contribute to that experience. Books like Sendak's are read again and again, while children become familiar with the rhythmic language of sailing "off through night and day and in and out of weeks and almost over a year to where the wild things are." Books like Robert McCloskey's *One Morning in Maine*[9] not only offer children a splendid story about a young girl named Sal losing a "baby tooth" but also a tightly knit story line where dialogue and narrative intermix. " 'Why it's gone!' she said sadly, feeling once more to make sure. . . . The salty mud from her fingers tasted bitter, and she made a bitter-tasting face that was almost a face like crying." Picture books offer children the language they need to understand and interpret their world. Language grows as experience grows and children's literature adds much to that experience.

Visual Imagination

Finally, picture books stimulate visual imagination. Images of the mind are parallel to the power of language in that they too grow with experience. The essential value of artistic quality in children's picture books is the incredible range of art work—an immense scope of artistic impressions—from conventional realism to abstract impressionism. All forms of art can be shared with children through illustration in picture books. The vivid images cut in wood to illustrate Gail E. Haley's *A Story a Story*[10] leave us with unforgettable impressions of Ananse, the spider man, and his attempt to obtain stories for the children. The abstract water color and textured collage images of Leo Lionni's *Swimmy*[11] give us an altogether different view of a young fish's ingenious approach to survival. And even the most basic technique may contain a wealth of character, as does Judith Viorst's pen and ink presentation of *Alexander and the Terrible, Horrible, No Good, Very Bad Day.*[12] Picture book illustrations offer children a continuously replenished reservoir of visual images that their imaginations may tap for all time.

So we have the values of entertainment, engagement, language growth, and visual imagination in children's picture books. To explore the wealth of opportunities in children's literature, spend some time at the library before our next class and see what you can find.

Now that you have completed the exercise, compare your notes and revisions with the sample in the appendix (see Figure 5.8 there). How well did your work compare? What steps might you take to eliminate any problems?

Summary and Prediction Questions

1. To summarize the discussion above, answer this question: When and how should I revise and review my lecture notes?
2. Now, read to answer this question: Why should a self-monitoring checklist for taking lecture notes include the elements of active listening, note-taking, and revising and reviewing?

SELF-MONITORING CHECKLIST

Active listening, organized note-taking, thorough revision, and periodic review are the major stages in taking effective lecture notes. Understanding this process is one step toward improving the value of your notes. Regular practice is another. And monitoring your efforts is a third. To accomplish this third step, you can use the following self-questioning checklist. It works much like the monitoring checklists in many of the other chapters, but it has been specifically designed for taking lecture notes. Notice that the questions concern active listening, note-taking, and revising and reviewing.

A Sample Checklist

_____ Am I prepared for the lecture—notebook, pens, reading assignment complete?

_____ Do I listen for a preview of the lecture?

_____ Am I listening for organizational language such as "the important point here" or "for example" or "the result was" as a guide for organizing my notes?

_____ Do I ask questions—of myself and the instructor—as the lecture progresses in order to keep actively involved in the lecture?

_____ Am I using an appropriate format to organize my lecture notes, including a left-hand margin and plenty of space for necessary revisions?

_____ Am I using abbreviations and symbols to make note-taking faster and more efficient?

_____ Do I record information not only from lectures but also from class discussions and small group activities?

_____ Is there space in my note-taking format to relate ideas to the text?

_____ Am I revising, adding information, and checking for errors after class, before I forget things?

_____ Am I reviewing my notes on a regular basis in preparation for exams, discussions, and so forth?

_____ Is my left-hand margin used effectively for sample questions and topic labels?

_____ Have I established contact with other students in the class to compare notes and discuss ideas?

_____ Am I experiencing any problems that require special attention?

Each of these self-monitoring questions helps you to judge your progress taking notes. Accomplishing each task indicates progress toward learning. Identifying potential difficulty suggests the need for corrective action. In either case, you can judge the success of your efforts.

Summary Question

To summarize: Why should a self-monitoring checklist for taking lecture notes include the elements of active listening, note-taking, and revising and reviewing?

SUMMARY

Listening, note-taking, revising and reviewing, and self-monitoring are all crucial stages in the note-taking process. Once you have a firm grasp of how to listen, take efficient notes, and use periodic reviews for learning, the monitoring checklist allows you to keep track of your activities and take action to resolve any problems that arise. The final evaluation of your efforts is similar to the evaluation of any purposeful study activities: Are you able to accomplish your goals? The greater your awareness and control over the learning process, the greater is your opportunity for success.

Review Questions

Review your understanding of this chapter by answering each of the following questions:

1. How can I become a more active listener?
2. What techniques promote effective note-taking?
3. When and how should I revise and review my notes?
4. Why should a self-monitoring checklist for taking lecture notes include the elements of active listening, note-taking, and revising and reviewing?

CHAPTER REVIEW

To complete this chapter, answer the following questions. When you are finished, review the chapter to check your answers.

1. True or False: Most listening is highly efficient.

2. True or False: Effective note-taking is accomplished by writing down everything in a lecture.

3. True or False: An effective note-taking format leaves plenty of space for review activities.

4. True or False: Active listening is a consequence of preparation and purpose.

5. The purpose of revision is
   a. to clarify points of confusion.
   b. to highlight important concepts.
   c. to link information to the text.
   d. all of the above.

6. Questions are most useful in the review process because
   a. they are a principal means of study.
   b. they identify points of misunderstanding.
   c. they are easy to work with.
   d. they are the only way to identify key points.

7. Describe the suggested format for taking notes.

____

____

____

____

8. How does the self-monitoring checklist guide your note-taking and review and help to eliminate problems?

____

____

____

____

9. Use active listening, organized note-taking, and self-monitoring for two or three classroom lectures. Then assess your efforts. What are your strengths or weaknesses? What is your next step?

____

____

____

____

____

____

10. Discuss how active listening can be of benefit to understanding not only classroom lectures but also everyday experiences on the job, in the family, and with friends.

____

____

____

____

____

____

NOTES

1. Adapted from Louis E. Broone and David L. Kurtz, *Contemporary Marketing,* 2nd ed. (Hinsdales, IL: Dryden Press, 1977).
2. Richard Wright, "The Man Who Was Almost a Man," in *The Story and Its Writer,* 2nd ed., edited by Ann Charters (New York: St. Martin's Press, 1987).
3. Adapted from J. Turk, *Introduction to Environmental Studies* (Philadelphia: W. B. Saunders, 1980), pp. 92–93.

4. Peter Spier, *The Fox Went Out on a Chilly Night* (New York: Doubleday, 1961).

5. Ezra Jack Keats, *The Snowy Day* (New York: Viking Press, 1962).

6. Maurice Sendak, *Where the Wild Things Are* (New York: Harper & Row, 1963).

7. Paul Zelinsky, *Hansel and Gretel,* retold by Rika Lesser (New York: Dodd, Mead, 1984).

8. Ann Grifalconi, *Darkness and the Butterfly* (Boston: Little, Brown, 1987).

9. Robert McCloskey, *One Morning in Maine* (New York: Viking Press, 1952).

10. Gail E. Haley, *A Story a Story* (New York: Atheneum, 1970).

11. Leo Lionnie, *Swimmy* (New York: Pantheon, 1968).

12. Judith Viorst, *Alexander and the Terrible, Horrible, No Good, Very Bad Day,* Illustrated by Ray Gruz (New York: Atheneum, 1972).

6

Reading Textbooks

Preview Exercise

Preview the chapter. Predict some good ways to read and study textbook chapters. Think about these questions: What is your attitude toward reading textbooks? How would you judge your earlier experience with textbooks? Successful? Frustrating? Depends on course? Why is mastery of textbook information so important to academic success?

PURPOSE FOR READING: ______________________________

____

____

"I can't read this book." "This material is really boring." "Do I have to memorize all of this?" "These words are like a foreign language." "I keep rereading, but nothing makes any sense." Do these statements sound familiar? They are just a sampling of students' complaints about their textbooks. Textbooks are a frequent source of difficulty for many students. Yet, textbooks are the basic tool for learning, and the information they present is critical for student success.

Textbooks may be confusing initially for quite logical reasons. The main reason, quite simply, is that their purpose is to present complex information that is typically new to the reader in a very precise and detailed manner. So textbooks are experienced by many readers as confusing because so much information is new, and as overwhelming because of the wealth of detail. Moreover, subject areas—academic disciplines such as sociology, biology, computer science, art history, and physics—all use their own specialized vocabulary to present their ideas. This situation complicates matters for some students, although such specialized vocabulary is necessary for a precise understanding of a subject. (Chapter 8 examines vocabulary and concept learning in detail.)

The purpose of this chapter is to discuss the organization of textbooks and to present a systematic approach to reading. Specific methods for processing and monitoring information such as underlining and note-taking, think-aloud strategies for clarifying information, fix-up strategies to overcome confusion, and visual imagery techniques are also considered.

Guiding Questions

Use the following questions to guide your reading; look for specific answers as the ideas are discussed.

1. What is the typical format of a textbook chapter?
2. How can an understanding of patterns of organization be helpful for reading and studying textbooks?
3. Why is a systematic approach to reading textbooks so important?
4. What are fix-up strategies?
5. How do think-aloud and visual imagery strategies help to clarify information?
6. What questions can you ask to monitor your textbook reading?

INFORMATIONAL TEXT

As a child, you undoubtedly learned many things from books read to you by parents and teachers. For one thing, you learned that books can introduce you to unusual characters, interesting places, exciting adventures, and a wealth of information about the world. For another thing, you probably learned that books influence people's lives. Perhaps you imagined yourself as one of the many characters in stories, played out imaginary adventures first experienced through books, or dreamed about those far-off places that books so aptly described.

Interestingly, those early years also provide a framework for understanding textbooks. You probably learned quite quickly that books provide a wealth of information. Books can inform readers about explorations in space or about the early history of human society, about computer technology or tribal customs. Moreover, you learned, consciously or otherwise, about the organization of a book, from a simple understanding of "beginning, middle, and end" to a more complex sense of "reading for an explanation." Understanding textbook organization and how to use it systematically is merely an extension of that early learning experience.

A Typical Chapter

The typical textbook chapter has a fairly standard form of organization. In fact, your experience with *this* text already suggests some likely elements of a chapter. A textbook chapter commonly has a title, introduction, subheadings, illustrations, and a summary, all of which help to organize the information presented. There may also be additional elements such as chapter objectives, or discussion questions, or suggested readings. Each of these elements has a particular purpose.

Each chapter in a textbook begins with a title that identifies the general topic, or focus, of the chapter. The title is important because it can stimulate you to draw upon your prior knowledge about a subject as preparation for reading.

A list of objectives or a topic outline often begins a chapter. The purpose is to help the reader discover the purposes for reading and to provide an overview of important topics. In either case, readers can use these elements to prepare themselves for reading or, later, to assess the results of their efforts. For instance, if a chapter objective is "to describe the functions of a political party," a good purpose for reading is "to understand the functions of a political party." Then, after reading, you can assess your understanding by describing the functions. Objectives and topic outlines can be used as a guide to reading and a method of assessing comprehension.

The Content of a Chapter

The content of a chapter follows a common pattern. The chapter begins with an introduction and is followed by the body of the chapter, which is usually subdivided by topical subheadings and clarified with illustrations of various types. It concludes with a summary of important points. Each of these elements is discussed later in the strategies section of this chapter, but a couple of points are important to remember. First of all, most textbook chapters are fairly long, so previewing the introduction, the subheadings, and the summary is a useful way to identify the focus of the chapter and important points of emphasis. The preview will help keep the author's focus in mind.

Second, since much information is presented in the course of a lengthy chapter, the various subdivisions identified by subheadings are manageable units for working through a presentation. Instead of trying to read straight through a chapter before checking your understanding, proceed on a unit-by-unit basis, monitoring your understanding as you go along. Subheadings, for instance, can be turned into questions; subdivisions can be read for answers; and understanding can be monitored by your ability to identify, understand, and retain important information. A subheading like "The Role of Political Parties in Local Politics" becomes the question, "What is the role of political parties in local politics?" Your answer to each question indicates how well you understand the material.

Textbook illustrations help the reader understand the written material. History texts, for instance, make frequent use of photographic illustrations of artifacts, characters, and events in history. Science texts offer a wealth of graphic illustrations to help translate the language of science into clear visual examples. Social science texts make extensive use of charts and tables to help readers visualize statistical presentations (for example, "65% of those surveyed indicated that . . ."). Whatever the type, illustrations typically create a better understanding of the written presentation.

Discussion Questions and Suggested Reading

Frequently, chapters conclude with discussion questions that may be used to reconsider the information presented or to explore the implications of various ideas. These questions stimulate further thought about the information and help increase the reader's familiarity with new ideas. Some texts go one step further, providing a chapter quiz as an opportunity to test your knowledge. Both of these organizational elements are useful for monitoring your learning and preparing for exams.

Finally, there may be a list of suggested readings at the chapter's end that offers direction for further reading about information discussed in the chapter. There may also be a list of references, that is, a list of books and periodicals the author used as resources when writing the chapter. These references can be an additional guide for further investigation.

Each element of chapter organization has its purpose in the presentation of information and each can guide you toward understanding and remembering what you read.

A Brief Exercise

In the discussion of textbook organization, a number of elements are presented, including: the chapter title, the chapter objectives or topic outline, the introduction, the subdivisions identified by subheadings, the illustrations, the summary, the discussion questions, and the suggested readings or references. With these elements in mind, first compare a chapter in this book with these elements. Which elements are present? Which are not? Why do you think there are some differences? Second, examine a chapter in a text from another course. Which elements are present? Which are not? Are there any differences? Why? Write your response on a separate sheet of paper.

Summary and Prediction Questions

1. To summarize: What is the typical format of a textbook chapter?
2. To prepare for the next section: How can an understanding of patterns of organization be helpful for reading and studying textbooks?

Patterns of Organization

Chapter 3, "Taking Lecture Notes," discussed patterns of organization. Special attention was given to language cues that identify important patterns of thinking. Such patterns are readily apparent in textbook writing, as well. Statements like "The most important point here . . .," or "There are several reasons why . . .," or "Most significantly . . .," are clues that a major point is to be presented. Statements such as "for example," or "in this instance," or "to illustrate this point," identify the supporting examples or clarification of ideas.

In addition, four basic patterns of organization are frequently used to present information in textbooks, just as they are in lectures and in everyday conversation. These patterns are enumeration, or listing; sequence; cause and effect; and comparison and contrast.

Words like "first," "in addition," and "another" indicate a list of information follows. Numbers or words like "first," "second," "next," and

Major points

The major point here . . .
There are several reasons why . . .
Most significant is . . .
More importantly . . .
Of special note . . .
The primary purpose is . . .

Examples and illustrations

for example	imagine
for instance	more specifically
to illustrate	a case in point is

Enumeration

first	another
also	next
in addition	finally

Sequence

first	next
second	after
then	the fifth step
following that	finally

Cause and effect

because	so
reasons for	therefore
source of	consequently
led to	as a result of

Comparison and contrast

like	in contrast
similarly	but
in the same	however
analogously	on the other hand

Figure 6.1 Word Clues to Patterns of Organization

"finally" establish a specific sequence of events. The words "because," "therefore," and "consequently" indicate the pattern of cause and effect. And words such as "similarly," "but," and "however" identify points of comparison and contrast. Such words clearly identify a pattern of organization and show how to think about the subject presented. (See Figure 6.1 for a list of common words or cues that identify points of information and patterns of organization.)

AN EXERCISE IN PATTERNS

Below is a list of phrases excerpted from a text on American government.[1] Each phrase includes a word or words that suggest a specific pattern of organization. Using the categories of "major point," "examples and illustration," "enumeration," "sequence," "cause and effect," and "comparison and contrast," your task is to identify the pattern of organization for each phrase. The answers are in the appendix.

1. "Democracy is best reflected in the principle of political accountability . . ." (p. 139)

   ____

2. "Third, even when election campaigns seem to offer clear choices . . ." (p. 82)

   ____

3. "One result of this growth . . ." (p. 240)

   ____

4. "However, the cities are not . . ." (p. 188)

   ____

5. "On the other hand, the humanities program . . ." (p. 181)

   ____

6. "Still other factors are public opinion . . ." (p. 66)

   ____

7. "For example, it is not clear . . ." (p. 152)

____

8. "There are several ways of assessing the service performances of the national government. One is . . ." (p. 151)

____

9. "Thus, if a lobbyist desires . . ." (p. 105)

____

10. "Two striking illustrations of creative federalism were . . ." (p. 118)

____

11. "The most prominent units in the national administration are . . ." (p. 268)

____

12. "The second phase of the budget cycle . . ." (p. 280)

____

13. "The primary disadvantage is . . ." (p. 181)

____

14. "After considerable debate . . ." (p. 154)

____

15. "On the other side of the coin, a weak governor . . ." (p. 256)

____

16. "Also, participation is highest . . ." (p. 76)

____

17. "Finally, we should remember . . ." (p. 170)

____

18. "Citing only one example . . ." (p. 123)

____

The Reading Process

A good question to consider here is, what is reading? A simple enough question perhaps; but before you attempt an answer, think about some typical reading activities.

Many people read the newspaper to see what's happening around town or around the world. But they don't usually stay up late memorizing what they've read. Many people read for pleasure, human interest stories in magazines or a good novel late at night. But when they read for pleasure, no one is requiring that they take an examination on what they've read. And many people also read to solve problems like how to fix a carburetor, or how to remove a stain, or how to refinish a piece of furniture. They select their reading material according to their particular interests. Examples of reading are many, but still no one checks most readers' comprehension to see how well they do.

So what is reading? Think of reading as an active process in which the reader has some purpose and is consciously engaged in constructing some meaning, some understanding of the material being read. Because the process is an active one, reading involves not only examining the information of the text—language, ideas, insights, and applications—but also the reader's use of prior knowledge and experience and the purpose of the activity.

Reading textbooks has a particular purpose. It involves learning—coming to understand something previously unknown—and it involves studying—storing and retrieving knowledge from memory. Reading textbooks is a special form of learning with a special purpose. Getting the most out of studying textbooks requires a general strategy for reading that aids both understanding and memory. The strategy presented here involves four basic steps: preview, read, self-test, and review.

Summary and Prediction Questions

1. To summarize: What is the value of understanding patterns of organization? How do you define reading?

2. To prepare for the next section: Why is a systematic approach to reading important? What are fix-up strategies? How can think-aloud and visual imagery strategies help to clarify information?

A SYSTEMATIC APPROACH TO READING

Ask another student how he reads a textbook assignment and he will probably tell you, "That's easy. I start at the beginning and continue until I finish the assignment." His approach seems reasonable, but it has limitations. Ask the student what the purpose of his reading is and he'll probably look at you strangely and then say, "To read the assignment, what else?" His purpose is to read some pages. Your next question is, "Is that a good approach to reading for understanding? Does an instructor just want you to 'read through' some pages?" Undoubtedly the purpose is more involved: to understand important information, to reflect on its significance, to analyze it critically, and to retain it for later use.

A systematic approach to reading is important because it involves a much more serious effort than just "reading the assignment." (See Figure 6.2 for an overview of this reading strategy.)

Preview

You are already familiar with preview strategies because each chapter in this book begins with a preview exercise. The purpose is fairly obvious: to prepare you for reading.

The preview prepares you in a number of ways. It increases your awareness of a chapter's content and focus. It provides information you need to assess the chapter's difficulty, such as how many unknown concepts it contains or how much specific detail. It is also an opportunity to compare your prior knowledge and experience with the content of the chapter. Furthermore, it provides information necessary for establishing purpose. And, perhaps most important, the preview provides the background you need to plan an approach to studying the chapter.

Step by Step

An effective preview proceeds step by step, beginning with the title. Read the title of the chapter and the introduction—the first two or three

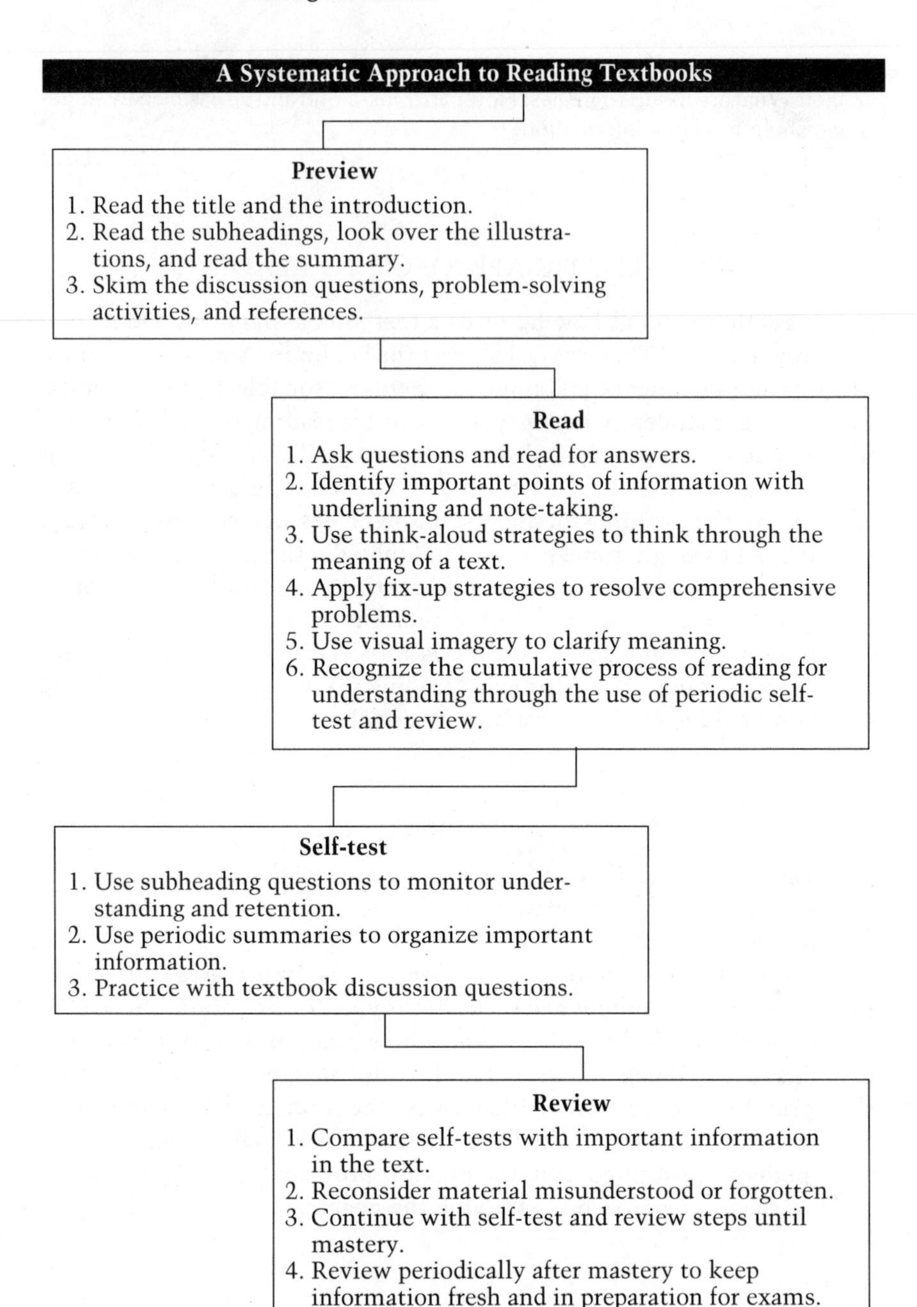

Figure 6.2 A Systematic Approach to Reading Textbooks

paragraphs—and use that information to think about what you already know about a subject. If the title is "Conditions of Colonial Settlement," ask yourself what you know about the subject. Try to create a mental image of colonial settlement. Then predict what the chapter might discuss.

Next, read over the subheadings of the chapter. Subheadings may identify subjects like "The English Colonization of Virginia" or "The Tobacco Plantations of the Chesapeake." Look over the illustrations—a good illustration is sometimes more helpful than the most carefully written text. For instance, a map of the colonial settlements would create a good visual frame of reference for detailed reading. Then read the chapter summary carefully. Summaries frequently restate the major points of a chapter, reviewing important information. Again, draw to mind your prior knowledge about the subject, predict the important aspects of the chapter's content, and establish a clear purpose for reading. Imagine, for example, that the chapter presents a detailed examination of the conditions of colonial settlement. What do you already know about the subject? The focus is "conditions" and the information is presented in considerable detail. Your purpose is "to identify those conditions as they occurred throughout the colonies." Reading is much more productive if you know where you're going and what your purpose is for reading.

Finally, complete the preview by skimming—quickly looking over—the discussion questions, problem-solving activities, references, or anything else at the end of the chapter and decide how they might be useful for reading and especially studying the chapter.

AN EXERCISE IN PREVIEWING

Read over the following material including a chapter title, chapter subheadings, a brief excerpt of the introduction, and a summary. Then in three or four sentences predict what the chapter will discuss and establish a purpose for reading. Use a separate sheet of paper to complete the exercise. A sample response is included in the appendix.

Chapter 2

Title:	The Environment of the Political System[2]
Introduction:	We cannot analyze the American political system without first looking at the culture within which it works—and fails to work.
Subheadings:	Politics as a Cultural Heritage
	Democracy as Ideas and Activities

The Natural Environment: A Setting for Politics
The People: The Base of American Politics
Economic Influences on American Politics
New Demands: The Continuing Struggle for Democracy

Summary: Our political system is a part of our culture—the way our society thinks, feels, and behaves .... One value on which most Americans agree is the desirability of democracy.... Political parties and a free election system are the basic institutions of democratic government necessary for majority control on a continuing basis.... America's geography has influenced its political development.... The U.S. population has increased steadily since 1900 and Americans have become more mobile.... As America changed from a nation of farmers and small business enterprises to an industrialized economy, the government became more actively involved in the economy.... Over the past decade, Americans have become more insistent that laws and the government work as they should.

Reading Textbooks

Reading textbooks is a fairly complex task, much more involved than reading the newspaper and generally more purposeful than reading a novel. So the task of reading textbooks centers around (1) asking and answering questions, (2) identifying important points of information, (3) thinking about the meaning of the information, and (4) recognizing that reading for understanding is a cumulative process.

As you read a chapter, make up questions to guide your reading and keep it more active. Converting subheadings into questions is an effective way to use the author's organization as a guide for questions. For instance, a subheading such as "The Organization of Political Parties" can become a question like this: "What is the organization of political parties?" or "How are political parties organized?" With such questions in mind you are ready to read for answers and to read more purposefully.

Ask Who? What? When? Where? Why? and How? questions to guide your reading and focus your attention when reading textbooks.

A Brief Exercise

Refer back to the previous exercise, on previewing. For practice in converting subheadings into questions, use each of the subheadings in the exercise to create as many questions as you can think of asking who, what, when, where, why, and how. Note how such questions offer specific purposes for reading. Use a separate sheet of paper to complete this exercise.

Identify Important Information

Subheadings are an important clue to what's important in a particular section, but subheadings tend to be somewhat general. Therefore while reading a text, you need to decide which information is most important. That's one reason for the special attention given to patterns of organization. Look for the author's language cues to major points such as "the point here" or "the major reason." Phrases like "for example" alert you to details supporting important points that precede or follow the examples. And since some points of information are complex, additional pattern words such as "because" and "therefore" help identify specific types of important information.

Once you have located key information, it needs to be identified in some way. Consequently, you may wish to use underlining and note-taking as useful techniques for identifying information for future attention. Besides identification, underlining and note-taking serve another purpose. As you read, these techniques help to keep track of important information; and when you review a text, they help to avoid simply rereading everything. The review is directed toward underlined points, or special notes made while reading. However, underlining and note-taking work best when used selectively and organized carefully. (See Chapter 7, "Marking Texts and Taking Notes" for a detailed discussion.)

For the purposes of this chapter, look at how another approach to identifying important information and thinking about the meaning of the material can be combined with underlining and note-taking.

A Think-aloud Strategy

A think-aloud strategy is just what it sounds like, bringing your thinking out into the open so that you have a clearer sense of how you're thinking about the information you're reading. Although the thought process can easily occur mentally, thinking aloud offers you greater control of reading and thinking and a clearer understanding of whether or not you are accomplishing the task.

To make this point clearer, take a close look at the following application of a think-aloud strategy to a textbook section titled, "Limitations of the National Government."[3] On the left-hand side of the page is the actual text and on the right-hand side are the thoughts of the reader. Remember, the purpose of a think-aloud strategy is to think about the meaning of a text and to help identify important information.

Text	*Think-aloud*
One political scientist has identified three kinds of restrictions on the national government.	Okay, this seems like an important point. I'll probably underline this. I want to find out what the three restrictions are. I'll bet one has to do with government control over people because that's what the Bill of Rights is all about.
First, there are limits on its authority over the political rights of an individual.	Good guess. There are limits to government control of individuals. This is the first point, so I should make note of that. I wonder what the limits are.
It cannot abridge a citizen's voting rights because of race, creed, color, or sex;	I didn't think of that. Okay, voting rights are an example of individual rights.
nor can it violate an individual's right to speak, publish, or assemble in an attempt to express his political views.	Now that's what I was thinking about, things like free speech. This is the sort of thing that's in the news a lot. So voting rights and free speech are two good examples of restrictions on government, when it comes to individuals.
While these limits may seem straightforward, they have caused controversy.	The controversy—this is why these things are in the news. This is probably why my dad and I argue about what somebody has a right to do or not to do. Now that I have examples of the limitations, I probably should have some examples of the controversy.
In defining the limits of free speech, for example, courts have held that the burning of draft cards does not constitute a form of "speech" deserving constitutional protection.	Here's an example. Burning a draft card is not considered free speech. Some people may disagree, so that's part of the controversy. What else?
But they have ruled that arresting persons with the American flag sewn to the seat of their pants constitutes a violation of political freedom.	Different example. The flag on seat of pants is okay. Now I know that makes people angry.

Okay, now let me summarize. One restriction on government involves people's political rights like voting and free speech. But there's controversy about these rights. Burning draft cards is not free speech, but sewing a flag on the seat of your pants may be. People disagree. Now, what's the second restriction?

Note that the think-aloud strategy is simply a natural way of thinking through information by identifying important points, asking questions, looking for examples, and summarizing ideas. Notice also that the think-aloud strategy makes extensive use of prior knowledge and experience. The strategy need not be used all the time and in fact is most effective when used selectively. But it has many benefits. It helps you become actively involved in your reading, it helps you organize your thoughts, it helps you concentrate more fully, and it helps you consciously think through material that is complex or confusing. Quite simply, think-aloud strategies help increase reading with understanding.

A Brief Exercise

Take a selection from any of your reading assignments and practice the think-aloud strategy. Talk your way through the material by identifying important points, asking questions, looking for specific examples, summarizing information in your own words, and thinking about how the information in the text is related to your own prior knowledge and experience. The more you practice a strategy like this, the more useful it will be when problems arise.

Fix-up Strategies

To encounter problems when reading is not uncommon. The purpose of reading is understanding, and reading is a process of constructing meaning. That process may go smoothly; that is, the material makes sense and is read with ease. Or it may be filled with obstacles; that is, the material is confusing, does not make sense, and is difficult to understand and remember.

What causes this breakdown in reading comprehension? There are many sources. Sometimes the problem lies with the reader, sometimes with the complexity of the material, or the textbook author's writing style. The purpose of this section is to present strategies for overcoming such difficulties. Monitoring strategies are an important step, especially so that problems can be identified and some action taken to correct those problems. Monitoring your reading comprehension helps alert you to problems that require some specific corrective action.

Comprehension fails for one of four major reasons: (1) failure to understand a word, (2) failure to understand a sentence, (3) failure to understand how sentences relate to one another, and (4) failure to understand how the information fits together in a meaningful way. Six "fix-up" strategies may help you to correct these problems,[4] beginning with some simple procedures and continuing to some that are more disruptive to the flow of reading.

The first strategy is to ignore the problem and read on. If, for instance, you encounter a problem, such as an unknown word or a difficult passage, you might decide that it's not especially important to your purpose or for understanding the chapter. It may be practical to ignore the problem and read on, but be selective in making the decision. Ask yourself, "How important is this word, or this example, or this discussion to my understanding of the text?" A major point cannot simply be ignored, but some less important details can be.

A second strategy is to "suspend judgment"—to wait. In other words, problems that arise at one point in a text may be resolved at another point, if you read ahead looking for clarification. Frequently you must await an author's further explanation of an important concept before you understand the point. That's the purpose of explanation and illustration in a text. If you don't understand a concept, read the explanation. If the explanation is not totally clear, study its examples. And so forth. Even the discussion of additional concepts may clarify an earlier point.

Another strategy is to "form a tentative hypothesis" to make an educated guess. This strategy is like saying, "I think the point here is . . . ," then reading on to find out if your prediction is correct. Forming a tentative hypothesis, or making a prediction, helps focus your attention, directing your search for answers. Such a search for meaning is an active approach to learning.

A fourth strategy is to "reread the current sentence" or sentences. Two things probably trigger this response. One is the feeling that a sentence or an idea does not make sense in terms of what was read previously. Another is the thought that you are having difficulty with the current sentence because you misread it. Therefore, the corrective action is to reread the current sentence. Used selectively, this rereading may clear up any

1. Ignore and read on
2. Suspend judgment
3. Form a tentative hypothesis
4. Reread the current sentence
5. Reread the previous context
6. Go to an expert source

Figure 6.3 Fix-up Strategies

momentary confusion and allow you to move forward. Such rereading is in response to a specific problem, not a regular activity.

A fifth strategy is to "reread the previous context." At this point, there's a serious breakdown in comprehension. Perhaps earlier strategies have not worked, or there's an extensive amount of information to be considered. Whatever the case, your sense of the situation is that you may be able to resolve the confusion by rereading an earlier portion of the text. Again, rereading to resolve a specific point of confusion may be a useful strategy, but it must be a selective strategy, not a general one. Remember, though, the rereading strategy tends to be overused, so be selective with its use. In addition, other strategies discussed in this chapter may be more useful for resolving comprehension problems.

A final strategy in response to a comprehension difficulty is to "go to an expert source." Applying this approach may be as simple as using a dictionary to define a word or asking a friend to explain an idea. Or it may be as involved as arranging a conference with an instructor or reading additional background material. Whatever the case, this can be a good way to clear up a difficult problem. But it is also an approach that is very disruptive to reading. Since you must literally stop reading to accomplish the task, it is usually a response of last resort. Look for other ways to solve a comprehension problem before going to an outside source, but realize that it is an option, especially with complex subjects.

Use these fix-up strategies when you read; they may be one solution to your problems. (See Figure 6.3 for a checklist of fix-up strategies.)

A Brief Exercise

Find a magazine article that interests you, perhaps a major feature in *Newsweek* or *Time*. Read it with the purpose of fully understanding the subject in order to discuss it with a classmate. As you read, be very alert to any comprehension problems that arise and use one or more of the fix-up strategies in response to each problem. Keep track of which strategies you use and try to determine how effectively you're using them. Which strategies seem most useful? Why should these strategies be used selectively?

Visual Imagery

Visual imagery is another strategy for improving comprehension. Visual images are a natural form of thinking. People frequently—and quite automatically—create pictures in their minds when making plans for some future event or trying to remember something from the past. When solving problems, it is also quite common for people to visualize a solution to the problem before actually trying the solution. This imagery exercise allows them to "see" if the solution is likely to work before they try it.

Here's an example. It's not unusual for people to leave their car keys lying around the house. Then, when it comes time to use the car, they can't remember where they left the keys. The problem is, "Where are those keys?" So how do they go about solving the problem? Typically, they start by pondering, "Now let's see, when did I use them last?" Recalling the day's events they remember, "I used the car this morning." Then, visualizing the events, "I came into the house, put down the groceries, and ran for the phone." The events suggest a solution, "The keys are by the phone!"

So the keys are found not so much by the "facts" remembered as by the images created. Once a point in time is identified, a sequence of events is established and each additional fact is an image—"the house," "the groceries," and "the phone"—which leads to the solution: "the keys." The importance of visual imagery is probably the reason behind the maxim "a picture is worth a thousand words."

Visualizing the images conveyed by information in textbooks can be extremely useful for both understanding and remembering information. Fluent readers report creating visual images of text quite readily. In fact, most textbooks include illustrations of one sort or another to help clarify ideas. Science texts, in particular, make extensive use of illustrations to make their point. But you can go beyond what a text might offer and create your own visual images, or representations, of ideas in a text. Most often descriptions are easy to visualize whether they are characters in novels, or historical events, or a carefully planned sequence for a scientific experiment. Yet, the mind can create images of many things and visualization is one more strategy for understanding textbooks.

For a closer look at how someone might create visual images in response to a text, read the following think-aloud activity. Notice how the reader makes extensive use of prior knowledge and attempts to "see" the information of the text. The selection is about early 1600s farming settlements around the Chesapeake Bay region of the Eastern United States, surrounded by Virginia and Maryland.[5]

Text	*Think-aloud*
The marshy coastal plain that became known as the Chesapeake settlements was threaded by countless navigable streams along which the first planters extended their estates.	Now let's see. I've been down to the Chesapeake, so I remember what a huge bay it is, like having an ocean separate Maryland into two parts with a bit of Virginia at each end. And it's true that the lower Chesapeake has rivers and streams everywhere and it's really a marshy wetland. Even today there are still a lot of big farms. I guess the farms were called estates because they looked more like southern plantations than New England farms. A lot of the homes were like mansions. I wonder who worked on those plantations, indentured servants or slaves?
Oceangoing vessels could sail right up to plantation wharves, making it unnecessary for the planters to send their tobacco to export centers.	This reminds me of Mark Twain's *Life on the Mississippi*. In the movies they have the big paddlewheel steamboats pull up to a riverside landing and unload supplies or pick up farm produce. It was probably like that around the Chesapeake, except they used sailing ships. I guess they were tobacco farmers. I wonder if tobacco grows best around watery regions because I think they used to grow tobacco, which looked like huge corn fields, along the Connecticut River Valley.
This geographic circumstance helps account for the development of a society of independent plantations and smaller farms more or less sufficient to themselves, often uncooperative and difficult to administer.	If you look at how large an area the Chesapeake is and then imagine everyone separated by bay and river and stream, it's no wonder the plantations became self-sufficient. People were probably limited in travel, so they made a life on their plantation. It's like the stories and movies about southern plantation life.

What people needed to live was made, or raised, or grown right on the plantation. And if they could ship their goods right from their own wharf, they didn't really need to work with others. They didn't even need a town full of stores to provide the plantations with goods and services because the plantation provided it all. In fact, they probably argued over who raised the best tobacco for the best price. Plantations look like little communities.

For more than a century this society did not 'have any one place of Cohabitation . . . that may reasonably bear the Name of a town.'

Even today if you drive down to the Chesapeake, after driving through the highly urbanized and industrialized east coast, it's like entering a different world of small towns, open farmland, and the great bay and its waterways.

Using visual imagery helps you to see what you are reading in a text. But to make visualization a conscious strategy, you must draw upon your prior knowledge and experience in multiple ways. You must think about where you've been and what you've seen, about what you've read and what you've imagined, and how your understanding may grow as a consequence of your "vision" of a text and the information presented.

An Exercise in Visual Imagery

Read the following paragraph about "the almanac" in colonial America.[6] As you read, create an image of the almanac in you mind—what it looked like and how people used it. How might you translate the language of the text into a visual image of the mind? See the appendix for a sample response.

A more popular medium than newspapers for spreading scientific and political information, especially to rural Americans, was the almanac, an old English institution. The first colonial almanac appeared in New England in 1639; by 1731, almanacs were being read in all the colonies. Pocket-sized and paper-bound, they served as calendars, astrological guides, recipe books, and children's primers. Sandwiched in between bits of practical information were jokes, poems, and maxims. The better almanacs (published by Nathaniel Ames and Benjamin Franklin) punctured superstition, provided simplified summaries of the new science, and presented tasteful selections from the best British authors. Franklin's *Poor Richard's Almanac*, published in 1732, soon sold 10,000 copies a year.

Reading as a Cumulative Process

Another point to be considered is that reading is a cumulative process. Understanding and insight increase as you absorb new information as you progress through the text. Therefore, the understanding of each subdivision within a chapter steadily builds toward a cumulative understanding of the complete chapter. Recognizing that comprehension builds through this steady accumulation of information focuses attention on the manageable subdivisions of a chapter and suggests that the pace of reading be geared to the successful comprehension of each subdivision.

Within each subdivision, you read for understanding. You combine important new information with your prior knowledge and think about how this new information fits into or adds to your understanding of a subject. Such a process is exciting because you come to realize, "I never thought about that before!" Moreover, by recognizing the cumulative process of reading for understanding, you avoid reading to memorize. Confusing the goal of understanding with the goal of retention creates an overly detailed reading that merely slows you down and overwhelms you with specifics. Memorizing important information or specific details is best handled during the self-test and review stages, after you have gained a basic understanding of the information. The value of working with chapter subdivisions is simply that they are manageable units of information that can be mastered a step at a time and that allow knowledge to become cumulative as progress with the text continues. Cumulative experience is the goal of the reading process.

Self-testing

Self-testing is a principal method for monitoring reading comprehension in study situations. This strategy is especially critical to success simply because it provides the feedback necessary for determining the success of comprehension and retention efforts. In addition, self-testing focuses review activities more efficiently on areas that require additional attention. Without some self-testing strategy to determine what is known or unknown, any review activities become merely a continuous rereading of the text.

Using the Subheading Questions

Probably the easiest approach to self-testing is to use subheading questions as test questions once a section is complete. Following this approach, first you create a question to guide your reading, next you read the section for important information to answer the question, and then you test your understanding and retention of the text by answering the question.

Imagine that you are reading a selection with the subheading "Functions of Bureaucracy."[7] The logical question is, "What are the functions of bureaucracy?" The selection indicates that the primary function is "to administer the policies of government." Another function is "to introduce specialized knowledge and expertise into the policy making process." A third is "to lend continuity to work of government." And a fourth is "to make decisions on the basis of rules and objective standards."

Since there are four functions of bureaucracy presented in the text, a good self-test question might slightly modify the initial question to, "What are the four functions of bureaucracy?" Your ability to answer such a question will determine both your understanding and retention, and determine what you may need to review.

A Brief Exercise

Using reading assignments for your other classes, practice self-testing by turning subheadings into questions, reading for answers, and testing yourself by answering the questions. Avoid unnecessary rereading by continuously testing your comprehension and reviewing material that was misunderstood or forgotten.

Periodic Summaries

Periodic summaries are also useful for testing understanding as you progress through a chapter. If you think back to the example of a think-aloud strategy, you will recall that a brief summary was the logical conclusion to reading for understanding. In the think-aloud sample, important information and key supporting examples were identified. Eventually that information was combined to summarize the material. The summary then actually served two purposes. It helped the reader organize the information into a brief statement and it helped the reader judge the success of the effort. Consider using summaries to monitor your progress as you read. (Further discussion of summaries, along with appropriate exercises, can be found in Chapter 7, "Marking Texts and Taking Notes.")

Chapter Quizzes

Many textbooks include discussion questions or chapter quizzes with each chapter. Such aids, while frequently overlooked, can be most useful for a conscientious reader. Since these questions are created to reinforce the information presented and to measure a student's comprehension, they are an excellent method for self-testing. If you can judge your strengths and weaknesses with such a test, then you can take corrective action with the necessary review. You'll know you're ready for an examination on the chapter when you're successful with chapter quizzes.

Self-tests using subheading questions, periodic summaries, and chapter quizzes also prepare you for more effective reviews.

The Review Process

The review process is a familiar one, which in its simplest form means to go back over material. Unfortunately, there's a common fault to most reviewing efforts—it is that students think of reviewing as merely another term for rereading. Students assume, all too often, that reading material over and over will create the comprehension and retention desired. That view is probably false, and even if it weren't, continuous rereading is clearly too inefficient and time consuming for purposeful study.

Efficient and effective reviews require purpose. To rework material already read for understanding, you need specific direction. What's the purpose of the review? What do I need to accomplish? What information requires more attention? Is total mastery necessary? Do I need to focus on specific problems? How will my understanding be evaluated? A clear focus will create a specific purpose for each step in the review process.

Comparing Self-tests

One reason for reviewing is to check your comprehension from the initial reading. Here's where the self-testing helps. When you review material to check the accuracy of your self-tests, a specific purpose for review is established. "Did I understand the information?" "Have I included important points and specific illustrations?" "What information requires restudy?" With a purpose in mind, a review is not an unguided reading but a directed effort to monitor comprehension and to resolve specific problems.

In addition, if you're using subheading questions and periodic summaries for your self-tests, review efforts focus on subdivisions within the chapter. Therefore, you're not likely to be overwhelmed by the amount of material studied. Instead, you're working with more manageable amounts of material, which are more readily mastered. In addition, effective underlining and note-taking strategies provide an immediate source of information for comparison with self-testing, linking together important reading, study, and memory techniques.

Reconsidering Material

Aside from comparing information with the results of your self-tests, reviews also have the purpose of reconsidering material initially misunderstood or forgotten. In the case of misunderstanding, a selective rereading is appropriate. For whatever reason, some material will not make sense the first time (an example of such material is a difficult chemistry experiment or a technical discussion on economic conditions). It will be necessary for you to carefully reread the material, perhaps employing a think-aloud strategy or visual imagery to reinforce your comprehension.

Selective rereading to overcome confusion or to clarify ideas is a very purposeful activity, and quite distinct from a general, unguided rereading. Moreover, when this rereading is complete, the self-test comes into play again. And you check the results of the self-testing against the text with a new review, so the cycle continues until the material is mastered.

In the case of forgotten material, the review should proceed a bit differently. Many times information is quickly forgotten simply because you are processing a lot of new information and really haven't had time to store it in memory. Therefore, the approach to the review in this circumstance is different. Your purpose is not simply to reread but rather to relocate important information and use appropriate memory techniques to help you store the information. Reciting or rehearsing the material is a typical corrective measure for overcoming forgetfulness, as are mnemonic techniques (memorizing acronyms and rhymes as reminders of important information) and visual imagery.

Imagine, for example, that you were reading a chapter in national government about political parties. The section you read noted that there are five major factors affecting the success of political parties, but your self-test shows that you only remember three. Your review purpose is to identify the five points, repeat the factors aloud to yourself two or three times, and then test yourself again, continuing until you remember all five points. This approach is vastly different from rereading because it focuses activities on developing memory.

The important point here is that there is a distinction between misunderstanding and forgetting, and your method of review is influenced by that distinction. (See Chapter 9, "Memory," for a discussion of techniques for remembering information.)

A Brief Exercise

Take four or five sections of a chapter you are reading for another class. Using subheading questions or periodic summaries, test yourself after each section. Then review the results with the test. Next examine the differences between your response and the text. Are your differences problems of misunderstanding or problems of forgetting? The distinction is important because the review process is different for each case.

A Continuous Process

Self-testing and review are continuous processes ultimately judged by your mastery of the material. Once again self-tests become critically important because they provide accurate information for making judgments about progress. Also keep in mind the goals of your efforts and your specific purposes for reading. In some instances, virtually total mastery of the information is necessary. That is typically the case, for instance, with the anatomy course for the nursing student or the calculus course for the engineering student. In other instances, such as an American history course, it may only be necessary to determine the underlying reasons for some event, such as the Civil War, rather than a detailed recollection of the event itself. Both your personal goals (you may simply want to pass a particular course) and your specific purpose for study (total mastery versus basic understanding) will influence when the continuous cycle of self-test and review is complete.

Then all that is required are regularly planned periodic reviews to keep fresh in your mind material mastered and to keep fully prepared for exams. Regular practice with appropriate memory techniques, combined with adequate test preparation, is a sound formula for success.

An Exercise in Reading Textbooks

The following excerpt on "public opinion" is taken from a textbook on politics in the United States.[8] The exercise is designed to guide you through the four steps of preview, read, self-test, and review; and a sample quiz follows the selection. Simply follow the directions for each step. Sample responses can be found in the appendix.

Step 1 Preview the selection by reading the title, the selection subheading, the first and last sentence of the selection and the sample quiz. Then answer the following questions:

What did you learn from the preview?

____

____

What is your purpose for reading?

____

____

Step 2 Read the selection, first turning the subheading into a question. As you read, underline important information or make any notes you wish. Think about how your prior knowledge and experience help you understand the text. Write your question and your notes below.

Question:____________________________________

____

Notes:______________________________________

____

____

____

____

Public Opinion

Professional opinion makers. Television has become preeminent among the mass media as a source of political news. More than four out of five Americans say they get most of their news from television, especially during great crises. The assassination of John F. Kennedy and the attempted assassination of Ronald Reagan were experienced largely through television. Through its coverage of the resistance to the civil rights movement in the South, television gave that movement much of its popular support. Televising the eruptions of violence in cities such as Watts and Detroit in the 1960s had a great impact on the public consciousness.

The bloody battlefields of Vietnam, coming into American homes at the dinner hour night after night, helped turn public opinion against the war. And the televised Senate and House investigations and debates over the Watergate scandal were a principal means of establishing the climate of opinion that led to Richard Nixon's resignation from the presidency.

Presidential elections are fought increasingly in the arena of television. Even the traditional personal tours of the candidates are scheduled to get the best coverage on the local television stations. Vast amounts of money are poured into television commercials. And in 1960, 1976, and 1980, the televised debates between the major candidates probably had a critical effect on the election results. Radio, a potent instrument of mass persuasion for political leaders in the 1930s and 1940s, has now taken a secondary role. However, the increasing number of all-news radio stations is an important source of information for people driving to and from work and for homemakers.

Thus newspapers are no longer the public's primary source of political information and opinions, although one-half of the population still cites them as such (often in conjunction with television). However, they can explore issues in depth, give the full background to a news story, and present problems that, though of crucial importance, are difficult for television to convey visually. Not all newspapers do this. But those that do—*The New York Times, The Washington Post,* the *Los Angeles Times,* the *Chicago Tribune* and others—almost certainly contribute significantly to the shaping of public opinion. Nor is the impact of such newspapers limited to the general public. *The New York Times* and *The Washington Post* are read regularly in the White House and in Congress. Many political and organizational leaders, like the public at large, frequently do not form an opinion about a subject until they have read columnists such as Mary McCrory (generally regarded as a liberal) or George Will (usually perceived to be conservative).

As we noted, television news and newspapers are not unrelated sources of information. The most likely watchers of the network news programs are newspaper readers, and the day after a major story has appeared on television newspaper circulation will generally rise, because many people want to know more than they can glean from the usually superficial television coverage.

Is there a particular bias in the presentation of news and opinion in the mass media? We shall have more to say on this question later in this chapter. For the moment we can indicate that some process of selection is inevitable in the presentation of news, because it is impossible to cover everything that happens, and the values and preconceptions of the individuals who decide what is important and what is not cannot be completely excluded from the selection process. In general, the majority of journalists are centrist to left-of-center, and the majority of publishers, whose editorial views are printed by their publications, are centrist to right-of-center.

In addition to the mass media, an array of general and specialized journals speak to particular publics. Magazines with a primarily political emphasis offer analyses that cover the complete spectrum of opinion. In the center, *Time* and *Newsweek* have the largest circulations in this category (*Newsweek,* which is owned by *The Washington Post,* is somewhat more liberal than *Time*); *U.S. News and World Re-*

port is more conservative. Opinion weeklies such as *The New Republic, Nation,* and *The National Review* have much smaller circulations, and many organs of opinion on the far left and far right speak to still smaller constituencies. Among the vast number of weekly and monthly publications that appeal to various tastes, hobbies, professional activities, and leisure-time pursuits, some give at least occasional attention to politics, particularly if legislation is being proposed or considered that would affect a significant number of its readers. Finally, a number of scholarly journals, especially those in political science and economics, bring the findings of recent research to bear on governmental affairs.

Another source of opinion in any society is its intellectuals—people whose primary interest is in philosophical, social, aesthetic, scientific, and political ideas. They work in a diversity of professions, but the bulk of them are found in colleges and universities, where they undertake the most characteristic functions of intellectuals: research, writing, and teaching. They influence opinion in the first place through their impact on their students and their peers. They reach the public at large through lectures, articles in the press and popular journals, and radio and television appearances. They also act as consultants to government and, as in the case of Henry Kissinger or Zbigniew Brzezinski, are even appointed to high official posts.

In general, college and university faculty members are considerably to the left of the public at large. However, there is no one pervasive ideology common to all academics. According to one study, 64 percent of social scientists and 57 percent of humanities professors call themselves "liberal" or "very liberal." The more distinguished universities with the largest number of research awards have more politically liberal faculties than do the less prestigious schools. However, in business and engineering 60 percent of the professors describe themselves as "conservative" or "very conservative." The governing boards of universities and colleges are generally more conservative than their faculties, which has occasionally caused acute conflicts.

Three other kinds of agencies are concerned with the development of ideas. First there are social science research centers, such as the Rand Corporation, the Brookings Institution, the Hoover Institution, the American Enterprise Institute, the Institute for Policy Studies, and others. Then there are organizations such as the Council on Foreign Relations and the Committee for Economic Development that help top-level business and professional people explore political and economic issues, and other organizations, such as the Foreign Policy Association, that are concerned with the education of the broader citizenry. Finally, several of the private philanthropic organizations, including the Ford and Rockefeller foundations, have provided large amounts of money over the years to facilitate research in many areas of public policy. However, philanthropic foundations may jeopardize their tax-free standing if their grants are used for partisan political purposes.

Step 3 Once you've finished reading the selection, test yourself by answering your initial question and by summarizing the important points of the selection. Use a separate sheet of paper if necessary.

Answer:____

Summary:______________________________________

Step 4 Now review the selection by comparing the results of your self-test with the information. How does your work compare? Continue the self-test and review until you are ready to take the quiz. Then check your results in the appendix.

Quiz:

1. Why is television preeminent among the mass media as a source of political news?

____

____

2. Give two examples of television influencing public opinion.

____

____

3. Explain how newspapers may go beyond television in influencing public opinion.

____

____

4. Is there a particular bias in the presentation of news and opinion in the mass media?

____

____

5. How are intellectuals a source of public opinion?

____

____

6. What do the surveys tell you about the political attitudes of college and university faculty?

____

____

7. How do agencies like the Rand Corporation or the Council on Foreign Relations influence public opinion?

____

____

Summary and Prediction Questions

1. To summarize: Why is a systematic approach to reading important? What are fix-up strategies? How can think-aloud and visual imagery strategies help to clarify information?
2. To prepare for the next section: What questions can be used to monitor textbook reading?

MONITORING TEXTBOOK READING

Reading textbooks requires a step-by-step approach. Each step has a purpose and each accomplishes a specific task. To keep track of your progress requires not only attention to your comprehension of the text, usually accomplished through self-testing and review, but also attention to your application of this step-by-step approach.

A checklist of questions can alert you to important steps in this process and to any problems that might hinder your success. Whatever questions are used, they should help you determine how well you are accomplishing your goals.

A SELF-MONITORING CHECKLIST

_____ Do I carefully preview the chapter by reading the introduction, subheadings, and conclusion; and by looking over illustrations, sample problems, and chapter questions?

_____ Do I establish a purpose for reading before I begin and do I turn subheadings into questions to guide my reading?

_____ Am I identifying important points of information by underlining or note-taking?

_____ Am I using think-aloud, fix-up, and visual imagery strategies to overcome comprehension problems?

_____ Am I monitoring my comprehension through regular self-testing, including the use of subheading questions, periodic summaries, and chapter quizzes?

_____ Do I plan and carry out a systematic review of my reading-study activities and use these reviews to improve my understanding and retention of the text?

_____ Are regularly planned periodic reviews a part of my long-term study schedule?

_____ Am I experiencing any particular difficulties that suggest I need to change my strategies or seek further assistance?

Use these self-monitoring questions until you master the process of comprehending textbooks.

Summary Question

What questions can be used to monitor textbook reading?

SUMMARY

The purpose of the chapter has been to explore the subject of reading textbooks. Both chapter organization and a systematic approach to reading were emphasized as an alternative to less purposeful activities. Specific strategies to improve comprehension such as questioning, underlinry ? fix-up, think-aloud, and visual imagery were also discussed.

The point of all this is quite simple. Once you are aware of how a text is organized, and once you have a clear method for reading and studying that text, you are in an excellent position to become a fluent reader. Your knowledge of the text and the process for reading and study prepares you to use particular strategies when appropriate, whether previewing a chapter to determine its content or reviewing a section to check your comprehension. Moreover, as your experience with these strategies increases, the efficiency with which you apply them increases, and your success grows correspondingly.

Review Questions

Review your understanding of this chapter by answering each of the following questions:

1. What is the typical format of a textbook chapter?
2. How does an understanding of patterns benefit a reader?
3. Why is a systematic approach to reading textbooks so important?
4. What are fix-up strategies?
5. How can think-aloud and visual imagery strategies help to clarify information?
6. What questions can be used to monitor textbook reading?

CHAPTER REVIEW

To complete this chapter, answer the following questions. When you are finished, review the chapter to check your answers.

1. True or False: A frequent error in reading textbooks is reading without purpose.

2. True or False: The reading process is directed toward constructing a meaningful understanding of a written text.

3. True or False: Think-aloud strategies are of limited use for students experiencing reading difficulty.

4. True or False: Visual imagery is a natural way of thinking that can be consciously used to understand a reading assignment.

5. Which of the following is not a useful self-test strategy?
   a. using subheading questions
   b. using a think-aloud strategy
   c. using periodic summaries
   d. using the chapter's discussion questions

6. Self-testing guides the review process by
   a. providing feedback about a reader's understanding.
   b. suggesting strengths and weaknesses in comprehending the text.
   c. directing the reader to pay special attention to areas of confusion.
   d. helping the student to do all of the above.

7. Describe each of the four basic steps in the systematic approach to reading a textbook.

____

____

____

____

8. Discuss how you think strategies such as "fix-up," "think-aloud," and "visual imagery" may (or may not) benefit you as a reader.

____

____

____

____

____

____

9. Apply the four-step strategy of preview, read, self-test, and review to one of your reading assignments. Then discuss the results of your efforts. What benefits did you experience? What problems did you encounter?

____

____

____

____

____

____

10. Discuss how the chapters "Active Learning," "Purposeful Study," and "Reading Textbooks" work together to create a systematic approach to learning.

____

____

____

____

____

____

NOTES

1. I. Sharkansky and D. Van Meter, *Policy and Politics in American Government* (New York: McGraw-Hill, 1975).
2. M. D. Irish, J. W. Prothro, and R. J. Richardson, *The Politics of American Democracy*, 6th ed. (Englewood Cliffs, N.J.: Prentice-Hall, 1977), pp. 26–65.
3. Sharkansky and Van Meter, *Policy and Politics in American Government*, pp. 138–139.
4. A. Collins and E. E. Smith, "Teaching the Process of Reading Comprehension," Technical Report 182 (Urbana: The University of Illinois, Center for Study of Reading, Sept. 1980).
5. R. Hofstadter, W. Miller, and D. Aaron, *The United States: The History of a Republic*, 2nd ed. (Englewood Cliffs, N.J.: Prentice-Hall, 1967), p. 48.
6. Ibid., pp. 119–120.
7. Irish, Prothro, and Richardson, *Politics of American Democracy*, pp. 354–355.
8. L. Freedman and R. A. Riske, *Power and Politics in America*, 5th ed. (Monterey, Calif.: Brooks/Cole, 1987), pp. 59–61.

7

Marking Texts and Taking Notes

Preview Exercise

Preview the chapter by identifying the various marking and note-taking techniques. Compare with your current approach. Think about how different techniques might be appropriate to different circumstances. Do you have a specific strategy for using the different techniques?

PURPOSE FOR READING ____________________

Marking texts and taking notes are rather common study practices. They are strategies that help identify important information and create a sense of control over the study process. Furthermore, they promote an active engagement with the text and constant attention to comprehension and retention. As a consequence, such practices are essential to the learning process.

ACTIVE INVOLVEMENT

Many times students are lulled into a false sense of security by a passive intake of information. They find themselves thinking, "I understand this material," "This makes a lot of sense," or "This subject isn't as difficult as I thought." Yet, some time later, they find to their dismay that they can't remember what was read. So they begin rereading. Continuous rereading becomes a routine part of study.

Marking texts and taking notes can decrease the time spent rereading while increasing active involvement in learning. In fact, an effective system for marking a text helps to focus attention and concentration, while an effective method of note-taking promotes understanding and memory. Furthermore, much educational research suggests that memory of text reflects the level of meaningful interaction with the text during learning.[1]

Marking texts and taking notes serve a number of useful purposes: Such procedures help you identify important information as you read and monitor your understanding of the text; they also help organize (reorganize actually) the material into manageable units that are more easily remembered; and they offer a workable format for study in preparation for exams.

Guiding Questions

As you read this chapter, think about the following questions and read to find answers:

1. What benefits are derived from marking texts and what techniques can be used to distinguish different types of information?
2. What four techniques are used for taking notes and how does each help clarify important information?
3. How does memory benefit from the use of graphic note-taking techniques and why is flowcharting considered useful with complex material?
4. What questions can be used to monitor the text-marking and note-taking processes?

MARKING TEXT

Ask a group of fellow students what study techniques they use with textbook assignments, and the majority will probably report using underlining and some note-taking. Some sort of highlighting approach is used by most students. Such an approach alerts readers to important information. In addition, identifying important information while reading helps you relocate it later, during review.

Unfortunately, underlining has many pitfalls. New college students tend to feel overwhelmed by the amount of new information in a text and begin underlining much too much. The result is lack of focus on important information. For others underlining is almost random—a word here or a thought there grabs the reader's attention. The purpose for underlining becomes unclear. Marking seems to range from "much too much" to "little or nothing" and therefore is often ineffective. The critical issue then in marking texts is to have a clear understanding of purpose combined with a systematic approach.

A Marking Technique

Although the specific purposes for reading an assignment vary, most assignments have as general purpose reading for understanding and remembering. Hence, a text is approached with the purpose of identifying and understanding important information, points of information frequently referred to as the "main idea" or "the author's point."

Identify Important Information

The first emphasis of any system of marking should be to identify important information, and the simplest way is with an underline. Imagine, for example, that you finished reading a paragraph or a series of paragraphs. The logical question is, "What is the author's central point?" Find the sentence (or sentences) that establish the point most clearly, and underline it with a solid line. Asking questions about the material helps you think through ideas, and the underlining helps you identify important information for later study.

Note Specialized Vocabulary

Identifying important points of information, though, is only part of a more comprehensive marking system. Learning is frequently guided by the introduction of the specialized vocabulary a specific discipline uses to discuss its subject matter. Sociology, for instance, might emphasize terms like socialization, kinship patterns, social stratification, and so forth. So a part of your purpose in marking is to identify new concepts phrased in the specialized vocabulary. Since most textbooks present a wide range of new concepts, it is especially crucial to recognize their importance and mark them for later study, perhaps by underlining with a wavy line. Using a wavy line for new concepts helps to distinguish types of information, although the categories "important information" and "new concepts" may overlap.

Note Supporting Points

Your marking system needs to include a technique for noting supporting points, such as key examples, useful illustrations, and clarifying explanations. A simple numbering system may do; simply mark these items #1, #2, #3, and so forth. If, for instance, the sociology text presents the family, the neighborhood, and the community as examples of where socialization takes place, you might number them as three examples.

It is also worthwhile to use some notation that alerts you to specific patterns of organization since understanding and remembering are greatly influenced by these patterns. Circling key words such as "because" and "therefore" helps you monitor the organization of a presentation and study the material with that pattern in mind. If, for example, an author explores an unfamiliar period in medieval history by comparing it with a more contemporary period, attention to the comparison and contrast pattern of organization may prove critical to understanding the subject. (Refer to Chapters 5 and 6 for more on organizational patterns.)

The basic method for marking text demonstrated here includes a solid underline of important information, a wavy underline of new concepts, the numbering of principle supporting points, and the circling of key terms that identify patterns of organization.

A Closer Look

To give this presentation some practical value, let's look at the following examples. Read the paragraph on "small groups"[2] and think about how you might mark the text using the methods presented above. Then examine the sample paragraph that is marked for you.

The term *small group* is relative. It refers to the many kinds of social groups such as families, peer groups, and work groups, that actually meet together and contain few enough members so that all members know each other. The smallest possible group contains only two members, and its technical label is *dyad*. An engaged couple is a dyad, as are the pilot and copilot of an aircraft. Dyads resist change in their group size: On the one hand loss of one member destroys the group, leaving the other member alone; on the other hand the addition of a third member, creating a *triad*, adds uncertainty because it introduces the possibility of two-against-one alliances and group pressure directed at one member.

Now examine the sample.

The term *small group* is relative. It refers to the many kinds of social groups such as families, peer groups, and work groups, that actually meet together and contain few enough members so that all members know each other. The smallest possible group contains only two members, and its technical label is *dyad*. An engaged couple is a dyad, as are the pilot and copilot of an aircraft. Dyads resist change in their group size: on the one hand loss of one member destroys the group, leaving the other member alone; on the other hand the addition of a third member, creating a *triad*, adds uncertainty because it introduces the possibility of two-against-one alliances and group pressure directed at one member.

Notice, first of all, that the critical information on "small group" is presented in the first two sentences; thus both sentences are underlined. It is also apparent that two new concepts related to small groups are introduced, "dyad" and "triad." Both are identified with a wavy underline. Noting the examples of a dyad seems unnecessary. What do seem important are the pattern words, "on the one hand" and "on the other hand," since these words indicate an important shift from dyad to triad. A good marking system helps you distinguish important points of information.

A Brief Exercise

Now you try reading through and then marking the next two paragraphs on "small groups."[3] Keep in mind the importance of being selective when marking the text. Decide what's most important and underline, identify key concepts with a wavy line, number supporting points, and circle any key terms identifying patterns. Samples of marked text for this exercise are found in the appendix.

> Triads at times can be more adaptable than dyads. However, on occasions they can be more unstable. "Two's company, three's a crowd" derived from this view. Triads are more stable in those situations when one member can help resolve quarrels between the other two. When three diplomats are negotiating offshore fishing rights, for example, one member of the triad may offer a concession that will break the deadlock between the other two. If that does not work, the third person may try to analyze the arguments of the other two in an effort to bring about a compromise. The formation of shifting pair-offs within triads can help stabilize the group. When it appears that one

group member is weakening, one of the two paired members often will break the alliance and form a new one with the individual who had been isolated (Hare, 1976). This is often seen among groups of children engaged in games. In triads where there is no shifting of alliances and the configuration constantly breaks down into two against one, the group will become unstable and may eventually break up. In Aldous Huxley's novel *Brave New World* the political organization of the earth was organized into three eternally warring political powers. As one power seemed to be losing, one of the others would come to its aid in a temporary alliance, thereby assuring worldwide political stability while also making possible endless warfare. No power could risk the total defeat of another because the other surviving power might then become the stronger of the surviving dyad.

As a group gets larger, the number of relationships within it increases, which often leads to the formation of *subgroups*—splinter groups within the larger group. Once a group has more than five to seven members, spontaneous conversation becomes difficult for the group as a whole. Then there are two solutions available: The group can split into subgroups (as happens informally at parties), or it can adopt a formal means of controlling communication (use of *Robert's Rules of Order,* for instance). For these reasons small groups tend to resist the addition of new members because increasing size threatens the nature of the group. In addition there may be a fear that new members will resist socialization to group norms and thereby undermine group traditions and values. On the whole, small groups are much more vulnerable than large groups to disruption by new members, and the introduction of new members often leads to shifts in patterns of interaction and group norms.

Now compare your work with the sample in the appendix.

PRACTICE PARAGRAPHS IN MARKING

To provide you with some additional experience with marking a text, read the following selection on problems in race and ethnic relations.[4] Read each paragraph through before marking anything; then use the suggested method to mark the text. A sample of the marked text is found in the appendix.

Problems in Race and Ethnic Relations

As different kinds of people have come together, there have been difficulties between and among the various groups. People's suspicions and fears are often aroused by those whom they feel to be "different."

Prejudice

People, particularly those who have a strong sense of identity, often have feelings of prejudice toward others who are not like themselves. Literally, *prejudice* means "a prejudgment." According to Louis Wirth (1944) prejudice is "an attitude with an emotional bias." But there is a problem with this definition. All of us, through the process of socialization, acquire attitudes, which may not be in response only to racial and ethnic groups but toward many things in our environment. We come to have attitudes about cats, roses, blue eyes, chocolate cheesecake, television programs, and even ourselves. These attitudes run the gamut from love to hate, from esteem to contempt, from loyalty to indifference. How have we developed these attitudes? Has it been through the scientific evaluation of information, or by other, less logical means? For our purposes at this point we will need to define prejudice more precisely: *prejudice* is an attitude that predisposes a person to think, perceive, feel, and act in favorable or unfavorable ways toward a group or its individual members (Secord and Backman, 1974). In most cases prejudice takes a negative form.

What is the cause of prejudice? Although pursuing that question is beyond the scope of this book, we can list some of the uses to which prejudice is put and the social functions it serves. First, a prejudice, simply because it is shared, helps draw together those who hold it. It promotes a feeling of "weness," of being part of an in-group—and it helps define such group boundaries. Especially in a complex world, belonging to an in-group and consequently feeling "special" or "superior" can be an important social identity for many people.

Second, when two or more groups are competing against each other for access to scarce resources (jobs, for example), it makes it easier if one can write off its competitors as somehow "less than human" or inherently unworthy. Nations at war consistently characterize each other negatively, using terms that seem to deprive the enemy of any humanity whatsoever.

Third, psychologists suggest that prejudice allows us to "project" onto others those parts of ourselves that we do not like and therefore try to avoid facing. For example, most of us feel stupid at one time or another. How comforting it is to know that we belong to a group that is inherently more intelligent than another group! Who does not feel lazy sometimes? But how good it is that we do not belong to that group—the one everybody knows is lazy!

Of course, prejudice also has many negative consequences, or dysfunctions, to use the sociological term. For one thing it limits our vision of the world around us, reducing social complexities and richness to a sterile and empty caricature. But aside from this effect on us as individuals, prejudice also has negative consequences for the whole of society. Most notably it is the necessary basic ingredient of discrimination, a problem found in many societies—including our own.

Now compare your work with the sample in the appendix.

Summary and Prediction Questions

1. Summary: What techniques are used for marking texts?
2. Prediction: What techniques are used for taking notes and how is each used to clarify material?

TAKING NOTES

While marking a text is particularly useful for identifying important information and monitoring your progress in learning it, taking notes is the crucial step in organizing information into manageable units for remembering. Useful note-taking practices include sentence summaries, paraphrases, periodic summaries, and graphic techniques.

Sentence Summaries

Single-sentence summaries of important information are especially useful for furthering your understanding and memory of text. Since paragraphs are a primary unit of organization, they are the central focus for taking notes. The first step is to read the paragraph. Then ask yourself the critical question, "What important point, or points, has the author made?" Your response forms the basis for the sentence summary, essentially restating the meaning of the paragraph in your own words. This reorganization and restatement of important information helps to clarify the author's meaning in your own mind and to create more distinct units of information—a familiar sentence—for storing the information in memory.

To Clarify a Point

To clarify this point, read the following paragraph about vegetables as a food group from a popular health text.[5] Identify the important information and think about how you could summarize the material in a single sentence.

Vegetables are important sources of minerals and vitamins when they are prepared correctly. Overcooking, cooking at high temperatures, or cooking in large amounts of water decreases the amounts of water-soluble vitamins present in this group. Vegetables also supply needed bulk and roughage and give a variety of interesting colors and flavors to daily meals. The recommended two or more servings a day are easy to plan in the form of cooked or raw vegetables and salads. A dark-green leafy vegetable or a deep-yellow fruit or vegetable should be eaten daily for vitamin A. Because water will absorb the nutrients, vitamins, and flavors of vegetables, it is nutritionally sound to use the water in which vegetables have been cooked to make soups, gravies, and sauces.

The paragraph emphasizes the value of vegetables both for nutrition and for dietary variety. Key points include their value as sources of vitamins and minerals, as a source of bulk and roughage, and as a source of variety in color and flavor. The caution is that their nutritional value not be lost in overcooking. A sentence summary of this information may look like this:

Vegetables are an important source of vitamins and minerals, bulk and roughage, and variety of color and flavor, but do not overcook.

The summary sentence indicates an understanding of the paragraph, reviews key points, and eliminates any need for rereading the text.

A Brief Exercise

Now try the following exercise. Read the following paragraph about fruits as a food group,[6] identify the important information, and then summarize the paragraph in a single sentence.

> Two servings of fruit each day are recommended. At least one of them should be a citrus fruit or tomato or other food high in vitamin C. Since vitamin C is believed by some to be stored somewhat in the body, the absence of the vitamin from the diet should not affect a person for several days. But, though technically not necessary, daily intake of vitamin C is considered desirable. Fruits are easily included in the diet as fresh, frozen or canned whole fruits, juices, fruit desserts, or snacks. Fruits and vegetables and their juices supply approximately the same nutrients whether they are fresh, frozen, or canned. Children should be encouraged to enjoy fruits in place of other sweets for desserts and snacks.

Summary: ______________________________

____

____

____

____

The focus of this paragraph is the importance of eating fruit. Key points include having two servings a day, making sure a source high in vitamin C is used, and noting the ease of incorporating fruit into the diet. Your summary sentence may look something like the following:

Fruits should be a part of the daily diet, especially those like citrus fruits high in vitamin C, and two servings are easily accomplished with whole fruits, juices, or fruit desserts.

The single-sentence summary is a beneficial form of note-taking because you generate the summary yourself. You do not copy it from the text, a frequent mistake on the part of many note-takers that undermines the value of note-taking by making it a copy exercise rather than a *thinking* exercise. The summary you generate yourself requires an understanding of important information and organizes your new knowledge for future use. Such notes help put you in charge of the *learning process*.

Practice Paragraphs in Sentence Summaries

Read each of the following paragraphs on "self-concept and consistency,"[7] identify the important information, and then summarize the material in a single sentence. Sample summaries are found in the appendix.

Self-concept and Consistency

Our everyday lives give us a great deal of information about ourselves. Teachers and employers may either praise or criticize us. Friends may act interested or disinterested in what we have to say. Strangers may react with warmth or coldness when we try to get to know them. We are faced with much information that can often be contradictory. The information must be processed or filtered so that it seems to fit together. In other words, we have a need for consistency.

Summary: ____

____

____

____

Self-concept, or the way in which we view ourselves, will influence the manner in which we process information about ourselves. We tend to accept feedback that is consistent with our self-images. We tend to reject feedback that does not fit our self-concepts. In other words, people tend to distort information in order to make it consistent with their existing self-concepts. For example, if someone's boss tells her that she is doing a good job, and her self-concept is in agreement with this, she will probably feel that she deserves the compliment. If, on the other hand, the same person is told that her work needs improvement, she might think that the boss is having a bad day.

Summary: ____

____

____

____

Students in one experiment were asked to take a series of personality tests. On the basis of one of the tests, students were divided into three groups. One group had a good self-concept, another had a moderately good self-concept, and the third group had a poor self-concept. In the second part of the experiment, the students were given feedback that they believed was based on the tests' results. Actually, it was made up by the experimenter, and all students got exactly the same test interpretations.

Summary: ____

____

____

____

As predicted, it was found that students with a favorable self-concept accepted positive feedback (for example, when they were told, "You are a well-adjusted individual who has several close friends"), and rejected negative feedback (for example, "You tend to have trouble getting along with other people"). Students with poor self-concepts did just the opposite. They tended to reject favorable feedback and accept unfavorable information. After a number of these interpretations were read to the students, they were asked how favorably the interpretations described them. Students with a good self-concept reported that the interpretations described them in a favorable manner. Students with a poor self-image said that the interpretations described them in an unfavorable light. This was true even though all students received exactly the same information.

Summary: ____

____

____

____

The experiment demonstrates that those with positive feelings about themselves tend to filter out negative feedback. Individuals who see themselves in a negative fashion filter out positive feedback. It also demonstrates that individuals with different self-concepts interpret information about themselves in different ways. Persons with good self-concepts who are told by friends that they are serious-minded individuals will probably view the remarks as a compliment. Persons with poor self-concepts might view the same information as criticism.

Summary: ____

____

____

____

Self-concept also influences the way people regard their own behavior—both achievements and failures. Clinical psychologists are well acquainted with people who have poor self-concepts. These individuals are likely to feel that nothing they do is quite good enough. Louis Janda saw a young woman in therapy who was a brilliant student. She got excellent grades, was respected by the faculty, and was accepted by the graduate school of a famous university. In spite of these accomplishments, she felt that she was not as intelligent or capable as other students. When asked about her accomplishments, she answered that she was "just lucky."

Summary: ______________________________

____

____

____

There are others with unrealistically favorable self-concepts. They refuse to take responsibility for their failures. Such individuals are quick to point out that hard work and ability are responsible for their accomplishments. They also believe that their failures are due to bad luck or other external causes.

Summary: ______________________________

____

Research confirms the observation that individuals high in self-esteem tend to attribute success to internal factors (for example, ability and effort) and failure to external factors (for example, bad luck). Low self-esteem individuals do just the opposite.

Summary: ______________________________

____

In one experiment students were asked to estimate the number of dots on a series of slides. Regardless of actual performance, half the students were later told they had done very well. The other half were told they did poorly. As predicted, students who were high in self-esteem were more likely to believe their successes were due to internal causes and their failures were due to external causes. Low self-esteem students tended to view success as resulting from external causes and failures as resulting from internal causes. It seems as though low self-esteem individuals have difficulty in believing anything good about themselves. High self-esteem individuals probably have difficulty in believing anything bad about themselves.

Summary: ____

____

____

____

Now compare your summaries with the sample summaries in the appendix.

USING PARAPHRASE

Quite similar to the single-sentence summaries are paraphrases of important information and major concepts. The purpose of paraphrase is to restate ideas in different words—your own—in order to monitor or check your understanding of new information. Paraphrases aid comprehension by prompting you to apply your prior knowledge to the text information.

An Example

Read the paragraph below about cognition.[8] Think of how you might paraphrase the concept of cognition as it appears in this paragraph. Then read the discussion that follows.

Cognition refers to the ways in which human beings perceive, understand, and organize their responses to the environment. Interest in the relationships among culture, perception, and cognition has a long history in anthropology. Because they relied on the reports of travelers and missionaries, early scholars were mainly concerned with the *differences* in perception and thought between Europeans and the non-Western peoples they encountered. Some of these scholars attributed the differences to innate differences in mental processes. They characterized non-Western peoples as mentally deficient, childlike, incapable of abstract thinking, lacking ideas of causality, and unable to differentiate between reality and fantasy. By the turn of the twentieth century, however, anthropologists were arguing that there was a basic similarity in both mental and perceptual processes among all human groups.

Paraphrase: ____

The central concept is cognition, and the immediate definition, "ways in which human beings perceive, understand, and organize their responses to the environment," presents the important information. Additional discussion serves to clarify the concept. A paraphrase of this material may read something like this:

Cognition is the way people think about the world, the way they become aware of it, understand it, and decide how to react to it.

While you may translate the author's ideas in a slightly different manner, this paraphrase combines the information presented with one reader's prior knowledge and experience. Moreover, once you have a better understanding of an author's meaning, you can give additional attention to learning the language of the author's definition. The paraphrase helps you understand new information with the help of prior knowledge.

A Brief Exercise

Read the following paragraph on "stress,"[9] paying attention to the major concept. Then paraphrase the information, in this case a process, in your own words.

> How does a person physically respond to stress? According to Hans Selye (1956), the response occurs in several stages. The first stage is the *alarm reaction,* which is similar to the physiological aspects of fear and anger that we discussed earlier. As the body prepares to cope with the stress, there is increased activity in the sympathetic nervous system, digestion stops, the level of blood sugar rises, heart rate and blood pressure increase, and blood flow to the muscles increases. Then comes the stage of *resistance*. Now the body's resources are mobilized to overcome the stress (fight) or escape it (flight). If these efforts are successful, the body returns to normal. If not, as is

the case with long-term stress, the stage of *exhaustion* is reached. Failure to cope with stress eventually results in physical and psychological breakdown and sometimes even death.

Paraphrase: ____

____

____

____

The subject of this paragraph is the physical response to stress that occurs in three stages. Your paraphrase may be similar to the following:

Physical responses to stress occur in stages: (1) the alarm reaction of physical changes similar to fear; (2) the resistance stage of either fighting the stress or leaving it with a return to normal, and (3) the exhaustion stage resulting in breakdown, and perhaps death.

Paraphrasing may seem difficult at first, but the effort is worthwhile. You'll learn much from the experience because of the thought required to understand the information well enough to condense and rephrase it. This activity is not used in all instances; rather, it is used as an aid in understanding and clarifying complex information. Once you have a feel for paraphrasing, you can apply it when necessary. The alternative is unacceptable—continuous rereading. For additional practice, review the paragraphs used in the marking activities earlier in this chapter and write paraphrases.

PERIODIC INFORMATION SUMMARIES

Typically textbook chapters are subdivided into sections, based on an author's organization of the material. In fact, limiting your focus to individual paragraphs may very well hinder your understanding of ideas that are developed over a series of paragraphs. Short summaries are a tremendous aid to both understanding and organizing lengthy amounts of material because they focus on important information and condense the material into more manageable chunks. Once again you yourself generate summary rather than copying sentences from the text. The summary serves as a practical method for increasing comprehension and monitoring progress. And once again concisely translating ideas into your own words increases your ability not to understand important information but to remember it.

To begin to write summaries of lengthy selections, consider the techniques you have already developed. The point is to identify important information, to translate the information into a concise restatement, and to organize the information into a manageable unit of study.

An Example

Consider the following selection on the cultural patterning of food habits.[10] First read the selection with attention to the important information. Use a marking technique to keep track of the information. Consider using sentence summaries to understand it. Then combine the information into a concise summary of three or four sentences.

Every individual must eat to survive. But what people eat, when, and in what manner are all patterned by culture. No society regards everything in its environment that is edible and might provide nourishment as food. Certain edibles are ignored, others are tabooed. Food taboos may have such a hold on a society that just the thought of eating forbidden foods causes individuals to feel sick. A Hindu vegetarian would feel this way about meat, an American about eating dogs, and a Muslim about pork. Most Americans will shudder at eating insects, though this is a common practice in many parts of the world.

Cannibalism is probably the human food practice that arouses the most horror in our culture. Although in most societies in which cannibalism is practiced it occurs only under special conditions and in ritual contexts, there have been a few societies in which human flesh was simply another available source of animal protein. In societies in which cannibalism is strongly tabooed, however, the taboo is rarely overcome. Two famous cases of cannibalism in Western societies are that of the Donner Pass party, which got caught in a snowstorm in the winter of 1846–47 crossing the Sierra Nevada mountains, and the recent case of the South American soccer team whose plane crashed in the Andes. These two exceptions and the furor they generated prove the rule. Many individuals have been in equally desperate circumstances and have not resorted to eating the flesh of their dead companions.

Anthropologists have attempted to understand some seemingly irrational food habits in terms of their long-term adaptive significance. We have already mentioned the Hindu taboo on beef as an ecological adaptation. It is also possible that there is a biological component in the avoidance of certain foods. The Chinese aversion to milk may have to do with the fact that lactase, an enzyme that acts to digest the sugar lactose in milk, ceases to be produced in many Mongoloid populations after weaning has occurred. As a result, the milk sugar cannot be digested, and the use of milk and milk products frequently causes intestinal distress. But evidence supporting biological interpretations of food taboos is scarce. Given our knowledge at this point, it seems safe to say that it is primarily culture which channels hunger so that only some edible substances and not others can satisfy it.

Summary: ____

____

____

____

Throughout this selection a single idea dominates—what and how people eat are patterned by culture. The details of the selection elaborate on that idea through an extensive discussion of the taboo against cannibalism and other influences on eating behavior. The material may be summarized as follows:

What and how people eat is patterned by culture with some foods ignored or tabooed. Most strongly tabooed is cannibalism, although it may be practiced ritually or even totally accepted in certain cultures. Anthropologists look for adaptive significance or biological reasons for eating habits, but it seems that culture channels hunger toward certain foods and away from others.

If your summary differs considerably from this example, take another look at the selection with these ideas in mind.

A Brief Exercise

Reread the earlier selection on problems in race and ethnic relations. Review the marking technique to keep track of important information. Consider using sentence summaries. Then combine the information into a concise summary of three or four sentences. A sample summary is in the appendix of this chapter.

Summary: ______________________________

____

____

____

Now compare your summary with the sample in the appendix.

There are times when summary writing seems difficult or time consuming. Initially this can be somewhat of a problem because the procedure is unfamiliar. Changing habits takes time. Your current study habits have been effective enough to bring you successfully to this point in life, and changing habits is difficult even when you have the motivation. Yet the benefits of the activity are many, from increasing understanding to aiding memory, and the time spent in writing summaries avoids the time wasted in needless rereading.

Summary and Prediction Questions

1. Summary: What is the purpose of each of the note-taking techniques: sentence summaries, paraphrase, and periodic summaries?
2. Prediction: How can graphic techniques benefit study?

GRAPHIC TECHNIQUES

Graphic techniques are useful as tools for "seeing" the organization of information. If you have some method for visualizing how ideas are organized and interrelated, you are much more likely to understand and remember them. Two such techniques that are relatively easy to employ are mapping and flowcharting.[11] The primary benefits of such graphic techniques are the visual representation of large amounts of complex material and the ease of study afforded by these techniques.

Mapping Information

A map of any reading selection is simply a visual representation of important information selected from the text. The central focus of the map is the focus of the material, such as the topic or the main idea of the piece. It is represented as the center of attention. (See Figure 7.1.)

Figure 7.1

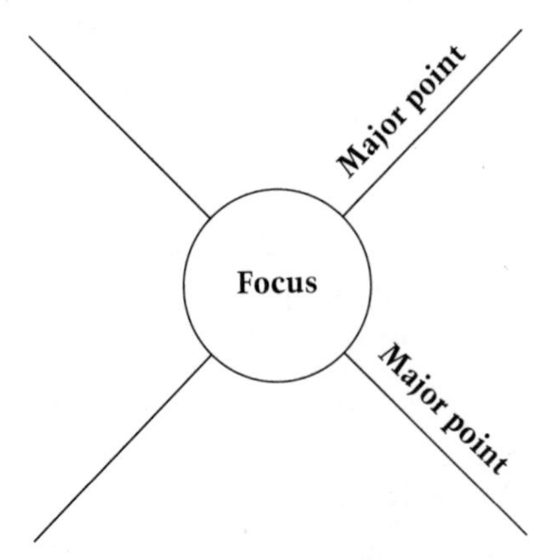

Figure 7.2

Extending from that focus are the key aspects, or important points of information, developed in the material. Identification of important information and organization is crucial to this stage. (See Figure 7.2.)

The number of extending arms is based on the number of major points in the material. Then additional details that help to clarify key points of information are connected to the major points on the map. (See Figure 7.3.)

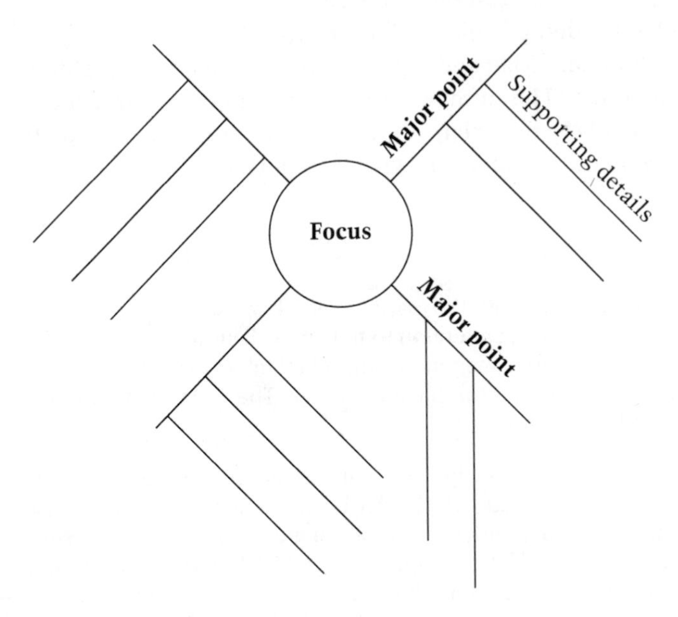

Figure 7.3

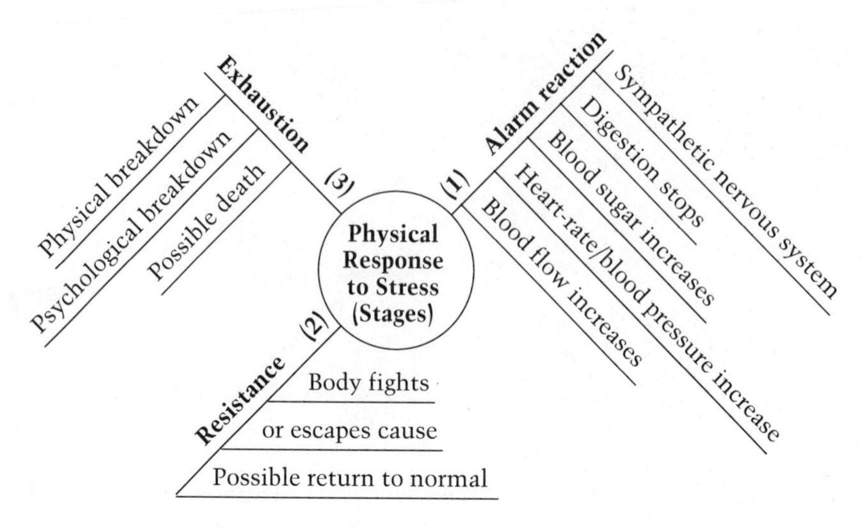

Figure 7.4

An Example

To clarify the manner in which mapping represents a graphic view of written information, compare the map in Figure 7.4 with the earlier selection on the "physical response to stress."

Considerable detail is included in the map to identify the specific organization of the material, and the numbering of major points shows the sequence of stages. The number of major points on a map depends on the organization of the material; whereas, the number of details included will depend on some judgment of what's important.

A Brief Exercise

For some experience with the mapping process, try the following exercise. First read the selection, paying attention to how it explains the relationship of stress to disease.[12] Then prepare a map of the important information following a pattern of organization similar to the sample map above. The initial stages of the map have been started for you in Figure 7.5.

> Some scientists now believe that virtually all diseases are related to emotional stress (Colligan, 1975). For example, it has been demonstrated that people who work under conditions of great urgency and pressure are especially likely to suffer from hypertension (high blood pressure) and eventually to suffer heart attacks (Friedman and Rosenman, 1974). Other diseases that frequently seem to result from stress include arthritis, asthma, and ulcers.

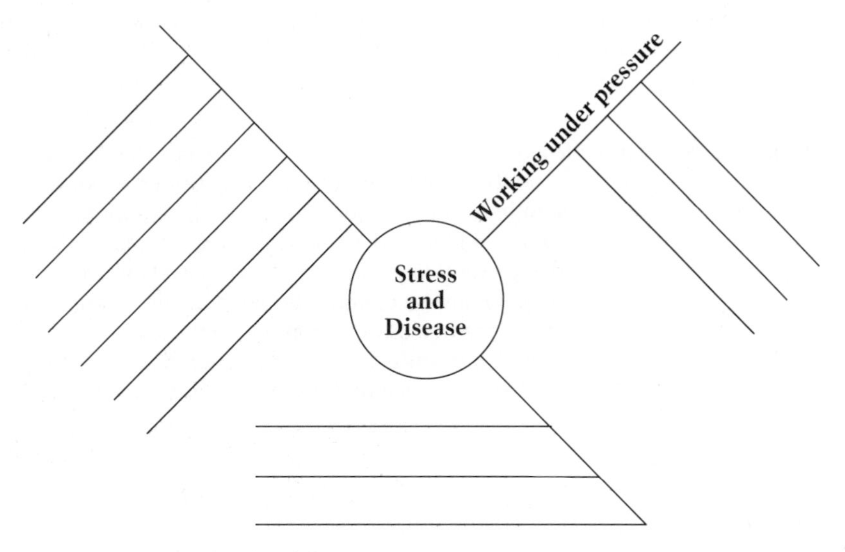

Figure 7.5 Mapping Emotional Stress

And stress may also increase a person's susceptibility to infectious diseases, by lowering the body's resistance to bacteria and viruses.

Physical diseases that are caused at least in part by stress or other psychological factors are called *psychosomatic* diseases, although the distinction between psychosomatic and nonpsychosomatic diseases is often quite arbitrary. Needless to say, the fact that diseases may often have psychological origins does not mean that they are any less real. Such diseases can incapacitate or kill just as easily as diseases that seem to have solely physical causes.

How does stress cause a disease to develop? Let's take the example of stomach ulcers (or peptic ulcers). According to the National Health Survey of the National Center of Health Statistics, peptic ulcers are one of the leading chronic conditions leading to disability. Stomach ulcers afflict 1 out of every 20 people at some point in their life, and each year stomach ulcers cause more than 10,000 deaths in the United States. Ulcers are a common affliction among people in many different occupational groups, from business executives to physicians. One group of workers with a particularly high frequency of ulcers is air traffic controllers. At least one-third of the traffic controllers in America reportedly suffer from ulcers, a much higher incidence than in any other profession or group. In March 1970, 111 air traffic controllers walked off the job and staged a "sick-out" to protest stressful job conditions. Subsequently, 66 of them were diagnosed as having some sort of gastrointestinal disorder, and 36 were found to have peptic ulcers.

Why do air traffic controllers develop ulcers so frequently? Stress appears to be the culprit. For these people, stress seems to come from the combination of constant vigilance and uncertainty. The controllers must remain alert and watchful at all times; they cannot afford to let their guard down for even a moment. In addition, there is the constant fear and uncertainty. There is always the possibility of an accident, no matter how careful the controller may be.

Your map should provide a reasonable overview of the selection. Stress and disease is the focal point. Beyond that point you must make decisions about what's important, about what categories of information to include. One approach is to have three major subdivisions: working under pressure, psychosomatic disease, and stomach ulcers. Then the decision for including detail is based on what is sufficient to clarify each category. For instance, under stomach ulcers, references to details like widespread, cause of death, many occupations, high incidence in pressure jobs, and closely associated with stress could be considered. Each is a separate supporting detail. A sample map is included in the appendix. (See Figure 7.9 in the appendix.)

A PRACTICE EXERCISE

To gain just a bit more experience with mapping, consider the following selection on "the rewards of self-disclosure."[13] First read the selection, perhaps marking important information. Then, using a separate sheet of notebook paper construct a map that provides a clear graphic overview of the material. A sample map is provided in the appendix. (See Figure 7.10 in the appendix.)

The Rewards of Self-disclosure

The obvious question when the topic of self-disclosure arises is, *Why?* Why should anyone self-disclose to anyone else? What is it about this type of communication that merits its being singled out and discussed at length? There is no clearcut answer to these very legitimate questions. There is no great body of statistical research findings that attests to the usefulness or importance of self-disclosure. Yet there is evidence in the form of testimony, observational reports, and the like that has led a number of researchers and theorists to argue that self-disclosure is perhaps the most important form of communication in which we can engage. Self-disclosure enables us to:

- Increase our knowledge of self
- Increase our ability to cope
- Increase our available energies
- Increase communication efficiency
- Increase the chances for a meaningful relationship

Self-knowledge

One argument is that we cannot know ourselves as fully as possible if we do not self-disclose to at least one other individual. It is assumed that by self-disclosing to another we gain a new perspective on ourselves, a deeper understanding of our own behavior. In therapy, for example, very often the insight does not come directly from the therapist; while the individual is self-disclosing, he or she realizes some facet of behavior or some relationship that had not been known before. Through self-disclosure, then, we may come to understand ourselves more thoroughly. Jourard, in *The Transparent Self*, notes that self-disclosure is an important factor in counseling and psychotherapy and argues that people may need such help because they have not disclosed significantly to other people.

Coping Abilities

Closely related is the argument that we will be better able to deal with our problems, especially our guilt, through self-disclosure. One of the great fears many people have is that they will not be accepted because of some deep dark secret, because of something they have done, or because of some feeling or attitude they might have. Because we feel these things are a basis for rejection, we develop guilt. If, for example, you do not love—or perhaps you hate—one of your parents, you might fear being rejected if you were to self-disclose such a feeling; thus a sense of guilt develops over this. By self-disclosing such a feeling, and by being supported rather than rejected, we are better prepared to deal with the guilt and perhaps reduce or even eliminate it. Even self-acceptance is difficult without self-disclosure. We accept ourselves largely through the eyes of others. If we feel that others would reject us, we are apt to reject ourselves as well. Through self-disclosure and subsequent support we are in a better position to see the positive responses to us and are more likely to respond by developing a positive self-concept.

Available Energies

Keeping our various secrets to ourselves and not revealing who we are to others takes a great deal of energy and leaves us with that much less energy for other things. We must be constantly on guard, for example, lest someone see in our behavior what we consider to be a deviant orientation, or attitude, or behavior pattern. We might avoid certain people for fear that they will be able to tell this awful thing about us, or avoid situations or places because if we are seen there others will know how terrible we really are. By self-disclosing we rid ourselves of the false masks that otherwise must be worn. Jourard puts this most clearly:

Every maladjusted person is a person who has not made himself known to another human being and in consequence does not know himself. Nor can he be himself. More than that, he struggles actively to avoid becoming known by another human being. He works at it ceaselessly, twenty-four hours daily, and it is work! In the effort to avoid becoming known, a person provides for himself a cancerous kind of stress which is subtle and unrecognized, but none the less effective in producing not only the assorted patterns of unhealthy personality which psychiatry talks about, but also the wide array of physical ills that have come to be recognized as the province of psychosomatic medicine.

Communication Efficiency

Self-disclosure is also helpful in improving communication efficiency. We understand the messages of others largely to the extent that we understand the other individuals—that is, we can understand what an individual says better if we know the individual well. We can tell what certain nuances mean, when the person is serious and when joking, when the person is being sarcastic out of fear and when out of resentment, and so on. Self-disclosure is an essential condition for getting to know another individual. You might study a person's behavior or even live together for years, but if that person never self-discloses, you are far from understanding that individual as a complete person.

Relational Depth

Perhaps the main reason why self-disclosure is important is that it is necessary if a meaningful relationship is to be established between two people. Without self-disclosure, relationships of any meaningful depth seem impossible. There are, it is true, relationships that have lasted for 10, 20, 30, and 40 years without self-disclosure. Many married couples would fall into this category, as would colleagues working in the same office or factory or people living in the same neighborhood or apartment house. Without self-disclosure, however, these relationships are probably not terribly meaningful, or at least they are not as meaningful as they might be. By self-disclosing we are in effect saying to other individuals that we trust them, that we respect them, that we care enough about them and about our relationship to reveal ourselves to them. This leads the other individual to self-disclosure in return. This is at least the start of a meaningful relationship, a relationship that is honest and open and goes beyond the surface trivialities.

Mapping can be used to organize information from sections of a chapter, or even a total chapter, depending upon the complexity of the material. It serves best as an aid to study, organizing information into manageable parts with observable relationships that can be easily understood and remembered.

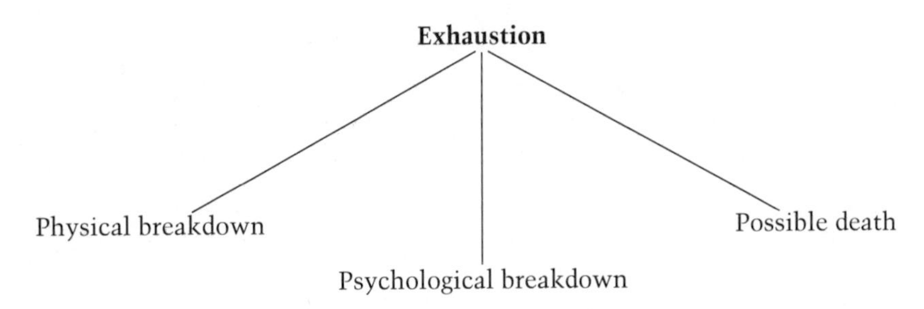

Figure 7.6

Flowcharting Information

Flowcharting is a rather specialized technique that may benefit you in a couple of areas. Initially, it's useful as a tool for understanding complex material. It gives special emphasis to the relationship among ideas. For instance, if an example is presented to clarify an idea, the two thoughts are connected with a simple code, a straight line. Consider the earlier exercise on the physical response to stress. Three examples were given for exhaustion as a physical response to stress: physical breakdown, psychological breakdown, and possible death. That relationship can easily be represented in the manner of Figure 7.6.

If, on the other hand, you want to represent a cause-and-effect relationship leading to a conclusion, one code, ——→, indicates cause and effect, and another code, ⇒, indicates a conclusion. Consider the selection of self-disclosure. According to this piece, self-disclosure causes an increase in one's knowledge of self, ability to cope, available energies, communication efficiency, and chances for a meaningful relationship. The implication, or conclusion, is that self-disclosure makes you a better person. That relationship can be represented as in Figure 7.7. The direction of the arrows designates cause to effect in the flowchart.

The following relationships can be identified through flowcharting, although you may find that some codes, such as elaboration and cause and effect, are more useful than others, such as those distinguishing between example and detail. The point is to use some graphic image to aid you in understanding and organizing information.

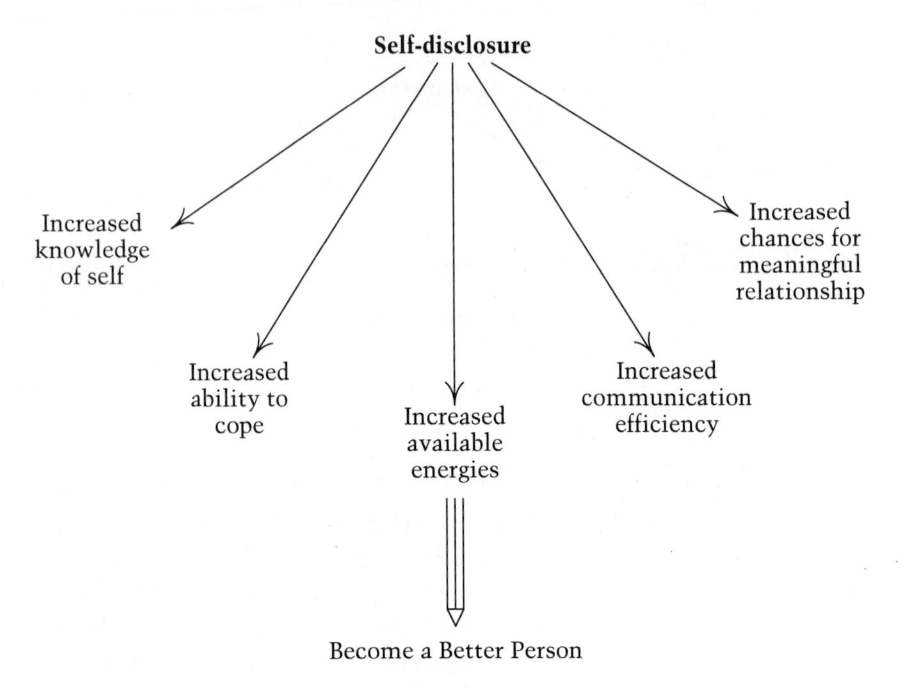

Figure 7.7

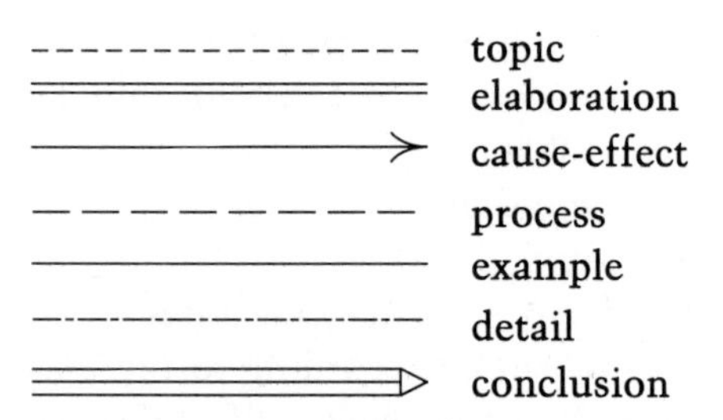

Flowcharting helps readers investigate the relationship among ideas in complex material and then chart them out.

Flowcharting is also very useful for studying. By helping you to sort out and understand relationships, it promotes long-term memory. The flowchart's visual image of relationships also provides the mental picture so helpful in retrieving information from memory.

A Practical Look

A practical look at flowcharting is presented below for the selection on

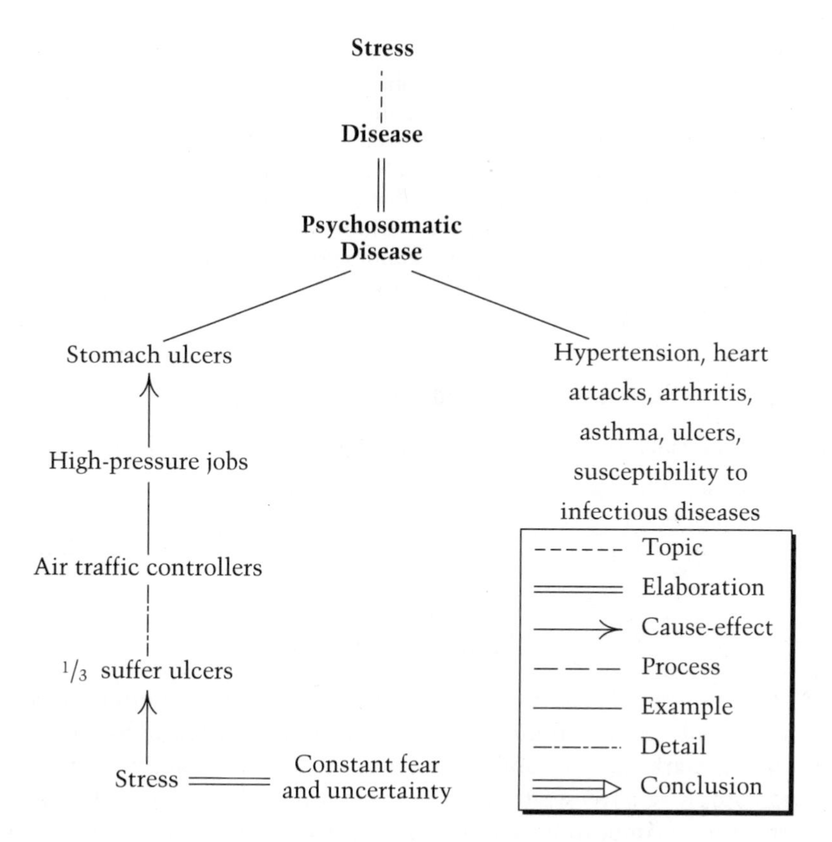

Figure 7.8

stress and disease. Notice both the similarities and differences compared with mapping. (See Figure 7.8.)

Notice how the flowchart covers the same basic information as the earlier map. At the same time, it shifts the emphasis so that the relationship between stress and disease is more thoroughly examined through the example of stomach ulcers and the air traffic controllers. Such clarity is the benefit gained from flowcharting.

A Brief Exercise

Reread the earlier selection on "self-concept and consistency." Read it with the intent to further understand the relationship between these two concepts and with the flowchart assignment in mind. Then flowchart the selection on a separate sheet of notebook paper. Use the model and code from the presentation above as a guide.

Your flowchart should center on self-concept and consistency and consider the discussion of experiments. Make sure that the codes you employ indicate the correct relationships, most of which will be example, detail, and cause-effect. Also learn to judge the success of your efforts by comparing your flowchart with the text. Then take a look at the sample flowchart in the appendix. (See Figure 7.11 in the appendix.) Remember, this procedure is most useful with complicated reading assignments, simply because your attention to creating a graphic representation not only helps you clarify information but also helps you recognize the distinctiveness of important information.

Summary and Prediction Questions

1. Summary: How can graphic techniques benefit understanding and memory?
2. Prediction: What questions can be used to monitor the marking and note-taking process?

SELF-MONITORING

A self-monitoring strategy for the note-taking process should probably be integrated with the monitoring strategy for reading textbooks. In most instances, marking texts and taking notes is a specific activity within a more comprehensive strategy for reading and studying specific assignments. But it is important to monitor yourself to determine if you are taking notes when necessary and to judge how well you are doing. A self-monitoring checklist for marking texts and taking notes also suggests that different techniques will be used in different circumstances. In addition, you may want to add questions of your own.

A Self-monitoring Checklist

_____ Do I follow a systematic approach to marking texts and taking notes?

_____ Am I using a marking technique such as underlining to identify important information as I read?

_____ Do I distinguish between important ideas and specialized vocabulary or major concepts with my marking technique?

_____ Am I using note-taking—sentence summaries, paraphrases, or periodic summaries—as necessary to organize information into manageable units for study?

_____ Do I use mapping or flowcharting to promote understanding and memory for large amounts of complex information?

_____ Am I encountering any problems that require some change in my approach to marking texts or taking notes?

Use self-monitoring to keep yourself alert to the note-taking process and to judge the effectiveness of your efforts.

Summary Question

What questions can be used to monitor the marking and note-taking process?

A FINAL NOTE

Throughout this chapter, numerous techniques for marking texts and taking notes have been presented. The techniques are many and varied, from the simple underlining of important information to the detailed flowcharting of complex presentations. Yet, the purpose of this chapter is not to suggest that you employ all of these techniques each and every time. Rather, it is to offer you a series of options for understanding information and monitoring your progress, for thinking about information and organizing it into manageable units, and for creating workable formats for study.

Active learning involves making decisions about how to read and study any given assignment, and how to plan an efficient approach to successful learning. Once familiar with available strategies, it is your responsibility to use them wisely. Among your options for learning are marking important information, creating well-organized notes, and using graphic techniques for study. Choosing the appropriate technique for a specific assignment determines how efficiently and effectively you will learn the material the assignment covers—that is, how successful you will be.

REVIEW QUESTIONS

Review your understanding of the chapter by answering each of these questions:

1. What benefits are derived from marking texts and what techniques can be used?
2. What techniques are used for taking notes and how does each help clarify important information?

3. How can graphic techniques help clarify information?
4. What questions can be used to monitor the marking and note-taking process?

CHAPTER REVIEW

To complete this chapter, answer the following questions. When you are finished, review the chapter to check your answers.

1. True or False: Marking is one good way to monitor progress with a text.
2. True or False: Paraphrasing new information helps increase understanding though the use of prior knowledge.
3. True or False: Flowcharting is most useful for understanding complex information.
4. True or False: Mapping is probably not a useful technique for most students because it is so confusing.
5. If your reading was progressing smoothly and you felt comfortable with the material, which technique would be most helpful?
   a. sentence summaries
   b. underlining important information
   c. periodic summaries
   d. flowcharting
6. If the material was rather difficult and you were having trouble with concepts, which technique should you use?
   a. flowcharting
   b. paraphrase
   c. sentence summaries
   d. periodic summaries
7. Discuss the usefulness of writing periodic summaries when studying textbooks.

____

____

____

____

8. Compare and contrast mapping and flowcharting, and describe your reaction to these graphic techniques.

____

____

____

____

9. Make a map of this chapter, emphasizing the basic techniques for marking texts and taking notes.

____

____

____

____

10. Describe your reaction to the techniques discussed in this chapter. Which might most benefit your study activities?

____

____

____

____

NOTES

1. J. A. Glover, B. S. Plake, B. Roberts, J. W. Zimmer, and M. Palmere, "Distinctiveness of Encoding: The Effects of Paraphrasing and Drawing Inferences on Memory from Prose," *Journal of Educational Psychology* 731 (1981): 736–744; M. Doctorow, M. C. Wittrock, and C. Marks, "Generative Processes in Reading Comprehension," *Journal of Educational Psychology* 70 (1978): 109–118.

2. Henry L. Tischler, Phillip Whitten, and David E. Hunter, *Introduction to Sociology* (New York: Holt, Rinehart and Winston, 1983), pp. 172 173.

3. Ibid., pp. 172–173.
4. Ibid., pp. 315–317, excluding p. 316.
5. Kenneth L. Jones, Louis W. Shainberg, and Curtis O. Byer, *Principles of Health Science*, 2nd ed. (New York: Harper & Row, 1980), p. 66.
6. Ibid., p. 66.
7. Valerian J. Derlega and Louis H. Janda, *Personal Adjustment: The Psychology of Everyday Life*, 2nd ed. (Glenview, Ill.: Scott, Foresman, 1981), pp. 74 76.
8. Serena Nanda, *Cultural Anthropology* (New York: D. Van Nostrand, 1980), pp. 66–67.
9. Elton B. McNeil and Zick Rubin, *The Psychology of Being Human*, 2nd ed. (San Francisco: Canfield Press, 1977), p. 302.
10. Nanda, *Cultural Anthropology*, pp. 66en67.
11. M. Buckley Hanf, "Mapping: A Technique for Translating Reading into Thinking," *Journal of Reading* (January 1971): 225–229; Esther Geva, "Facilitating Reading Comprehension Through Flowcharting," *Reading Research Quarterly* (Summer 1983): 384–405.
12. McNeil and Rubin, *Psychology of Being Human*, p. 303.
13. Joseph A. DeVito, *Human Communication*, 3rd ed. (New York: Harper & Row, 1985), pp. 38–40.

8

Vocabulary and Concept Development

Preview Exercise:

Carefully preview the chapter. Then create a "map" of the chapter using the note-taking technique of Chapter 7 and paying attention to the chapter subheadings. The map should give an overview of the important topics under discussion.

PURPOSE FOR READING: ______________________________

____

____

Problems of vocabulary and concept development are pervasive in the study of new and complex information. Unfamiliar words provoke confusion or make the information hard to remember. Typical approaches to word recognition may fail, and the sheer number of new words seems overwhelming. What can you do to overcome these problems?

You can begin by distinguishing between two major types of unfamiliar words: "general vocabulary," such as the word *infatuation*, and "concepts," such as the word *impressionism*. Knowing that some terms are general words and others are complex concepts determines how to approach an unfamiliar word.

It is especially important to take a very close look at a systematic approach to understanding and retaining those key concepts that serve as the foundation for most academic study. The specific aspects of this strategy for learning vocabulary and concepts are the focus of this chapter. Finally, it is necessary to consider how vocabulary and concept learning can be integrated with the process of active learning.

Guiding Questions

1. What is the difference between general vocabulary and concepts, and how does that difference affect learning unfamiliar words?
2. What steps are suggested for a systematic approach to understanding and retaining both general vocabulary and specific concepts?
3. Why does prior knowledge and experience play such an important role in development of vocabulary and concepts?
4. How can vocabulary and concept learning be readily integrated with the active learning process?

DISTINGUISHING WORDS

To begin this chapter, see how well you can define each of the following words. As you search for a definition, think about how you typically try to define unfamiliar words.

1. *garner* ______________________________

____

2. *infatuation* ______________________________

____

3. *pernicious* ______________________________

____

4. *sedentary* ______________________________

____

5. *tempestuous* ____

____

Now attempt to define these same words after reading the example sentences, which are typical contexts in which they might be found. Notice how each word is used in the example sentence provided.

1. We had great fun that autumn morning in the woods watching the squirrels garner acorns for the winter ahead.
   garner ____

   ____

2. Even though Ted and Mary had been dating for a rather long time, their relationship seemed merely an infatuation.
   infatuation ____

   ____

3. The constant arguing of their parents had such a pernicious effect on the children that they had difficulty sleeping at night.
   pernicious ____

   ____

4. Joe was a rather sedentary sort, unlike Laura, who was always on the go.
   sedentary ____

   ____

5. She was as tempestuous as the sea on a stormy day.
   tempestuous ____

   ____

Comparing your ability to define these five words either separately or within a sentence, you may have noticed a couple of things. One is that words in isolation tend to be much more difficult to define than words in context. The reason is that when you hear an isolated word you either recognize it from previous listening and reading or you don't. There is little to go on except prior knowledge. The other thing you may have noticed, on the contrary, is that for words in context even if you do not know a word like *pernicious* or *tempestuous* by itself, reading the word in a sentence helps you to guess its meaning. The surrounding words give you a clue to meaning.

Look at the sentence containing the word *pernicious*. What information does it present that helps you understand the unfamiliar word? First, the sentence indicates the parents' arguing is having some effect on the children. Second, from the detail "difficulty sleeping at night," it is easy to conclude that the arguing is having a harmful effect. Finally, you can infer (make an educated guess based on the information presented) that *pernicious* means something like harmful. And that is a reasonable definition of *pernicious*.

The key difference between defining words in isolation and defining words in context is that context stimulates you to combine the information presented with prior knowledge and experience to make an educated guess as to the meaning of an unfamiliar word. While you may not know a particular word, you may very well understand the situation or circumstance in which it is used. You use your understanding of this larger context to decipher the meaning of the unknown word. It is, in fact, rare to encounter new words in isolation, so vocabulary knowledge does not have to be an either/or situation of known or unknown. Understanding unfamiliar words and expanding word knowledge is very much a consequence of the wise use of prior knowledge and experience to comprehend the meaning of the context in which such words are found. If you are still at a loss to define any of the words in the exercise above, check your dictionary.

Examining Concepts

Look at the next set of words. Again try to define each word in isolation first, and then attempt the same from the sentences provided.

1. *geothermal* ____

   ____

2. *hydrodynamics* ____

   ____

3. *impressionism* ________________________________

____

4. *plate tectonics* ________________________________

____

5. *sectionalism* ________________________________

____

Now try defining the word by reading these sentences.

1. "Old Faithful" geyser in Yellowstone National Park is a famous example of geothermal activity.
   geothermal ________________________________

   ____

2. Our investigation of the river's hydrodynamics suggested the best place for building the dam to generate electrical power.
   hydrodynamics ________________________________

   ____

3. Monet is best known for his contribution to impressionism as a distinct art form emphasizing light and color.
   impressionism ________________________________

   ____

4. The study of plate tectonics offers a logical explanation for earthquakes, mountain-building, and related geological changes around the world.
   plate tectonics ________________________________

   ____

5. At least one cause of the Civil War was the increasing sectionalism that gripped the states in the years prior to the war.
   sectionalism ________________________________

   ____

How well did you do? Perhaps you had some appropriate prior knowledge that allowed you to define some of the words in isolation. Perhaps close examination of the sentences helped in some instances. But, in general, it is likely that you had more difficulty with this exercise than the previous one. And there is a good reason.

Certain words in your vocabulary are part of the general vocabulary you have accumulated as a consequence of speaking English and sharing common learning experiences. In reading, the meaning of a common word is immediately recognized, whereas an unfamiliar word may require further thought. If you try to pronounce an unfamiliar word when you see it, you may recognize the word as common to your listening and speaking vocabulary. It is only unfamiliar momentarily in the context of reading. Once "heard," the word is understood.

When you see an unfamiliar word in a sentence, you sometimes skip over it, trying to understand the context in which it is used. At first, you may not know the meaning of a word like *pernicious*, but you do recognize the context, a harmful situation. So your word knowledge is extended by your comprehension of the context and your new understanding of an initially unfamiliar word. Your general vocabulary may be more or less developed depending upon your experience, especially in educational settings, and your interest in language. A broad vocabulary helps you communicate clearly and persuasively in daily life. Moreover, your knowledge of vocabulary is crucial for understanding others. Your college courses offer you an important opportunity to expand your general vocabulary.

You may occasionally find that general vocabulary, prior knowledge, and associating the known with the unknown fail to unravel the meaning of an unfamiliar term. This is likely to be the case with words like *geothermal* or *impressionism*, because they are specialized conceptual terms developed to represent complex ideas or abstract thoughts in particular areas of knowledge and inquiry (geology and art history).

In a subject area that is new to you, the number of new concepts in your textbooks may seem overwhelming. You may find there is no easy way to substitute a common word for a specialized word. Even reference to a dictionary may be of little help. Knowing that impressionism is an artistic style of using color and light represented by the works of Monet doesn't actually demonstrate or explain how color and light are used to create illusion in an impressionistic painting; illustrations are needed. Furthermore, impressionism as a particular artistic style may only make sense when compared and contrasted with another artistic style such as representational art. In fact, difficulty deciphering the meaning of unfamiliar terms or concepts is frequently associated with the specialized use of language within various academic disciplines. Without the necessary prior knowledge and experience, most of the words presented in the previous exercise require special study for their meaning to become clear.

The important point here is that coming to understand specialized terminology or concepts that represent complex information requires a special strategy somewhat unlike the strategies used for understanding general vocabulary.

Summary and Prediction Questions

1. Summary: What is the difference between general vocabulary and specific concepts, and how does that difference determine how to approach unfamiliar words?
2. Prediction: What steps are suggested for a systematic approach to understanding and retaining both general vocabulary and specific concepts?
3. Prediction: What is "semantic mapping" and how can it help concept development?

A STRATEGY FOR LEARNING

Throughout this book you have read about how an active learner engages the learning process with specific strategies in mind. Developing vocabulary and concept knowledge is no different. Learning begins with a purpose, follows a sequence of steps, employs careful monitoring to determine progress, and concludes with an evaluation of ability to retain the knowledge gained.

Intent to Learn

Any approach to vocabulary development begins with the intent to learn. You begin learning concepts with the determination, or motivation, to deal with problems arising from subjects that are complex and unfamiliar. But motivation is not enough. You must also recognize that individual words and complex ideas are only understood and retained to the extent that they make sense. Approach study not with a particular assignment in mind, but with the goal of coming to know—to understand—something you didn't know before.

Prior Knowledge

A primary way to link your desire to learn with the goal of making sense is through recalling prior knowledge and experience. Look at how two forms of prior knowledge—knowledge of the world and knowledge of how to attack unfamiliar words—are used to explore the meaning of *prominent* in the following description.

> Harry Owen had been involved in the social and political life of the town since anyone could remember. He always coordinated the annual 4th of July celebration. He led the church choir during the Christmas pageant. He was elected mayor during the town's most difficult period of growth. And he represented the town for 25 years in the State Legislature. He will probably be recorded in the history books as the town's most prominent figure.

First, consider how prior knowledge of the world can assist your understanding. Here is a person, Harry Owen, with a lifetime commitment to his town. He coordinates activities, leads events, and represents the people. Quite simply, he's a leader. He stands out as someone special in his community. So, what does *prominent* mean? It means to "stand out," of course. Deciphering the meaning of *prominent* thus involves substituting a common idea, "to stand out," for the perhaps unfamiliar term, *prominent*. Next consider how prior knowledge of how to attack unfamiliar words might help.

A Common Approach to Unfamiliar Words

The initial response to an unfamiliar word is usually an attempt to pronounce it. In some sense you know instinctively that your oral language experience is likely to be more wide ranging than your written language experience. To pronounce the word *prominent* may trigger recall of the word knowledge necessary from your listening vocabulary. In addition, to see and say an unfamiliar word at the same time may cause you to search your memory more deeply for meaning, in the same way that you sometimes try to remember how you met someone or know him or her by looking at the person or his or her picture and repeating the person's name at the same time.

Using the context of an unfamiliar word is also a common approach that depends heavily on prior knowledge and experience. As noted earlier, the manner in which a word is used is often a clue to its meaning (the harmful situation of parents arguing serves as a clue to the meaning of *pernicious effect*). Rereading the sentence containing the unfamiliar word, or a few sentences preceding or following, may be especially helpful for determining the meaning of a word. In fact, using context is the preferred method for most people.

If an unfamiliar word is long, you might attempt to divide it into parts (syllables) in order to determine its meaning. Frequently, common prefixes (word beginnings), root words (central word parts), and suffixes (word endings) help make sense of things. To learn how to use word parts to identify words, see Figure 8.1 and the next "Brief Exercise."

Figure 8.1 lists a selection of important prefixes, roots, and suffixes, all of which contribute to the meaning of the words they form. Recognition of word parts should not be an exercise in memorization. Rather, your familiarity with word parts should grow as you become aware of them in words that you read, and as you begin to use them to determine the meaning of unfamiliar words.

Consider a simple word like *recall*. It has two parts, the prefix *re* meaning "back" or "again," and the root word *call* meaning "to speak" or "to summon." The meaning of recall is, quite simply, "to speak again" or "to summon back." In either case, the meaning of the parts creates the meaning of the whole.

A Brief Exercise

Using the information from Figure 8.1, Word Parts, determine the meaning of the following words. For example, *unfamiliar* means *not* (un) *known* (familiar). If you need assistance, refer to your dictionary.

1. *admire* means ______________________________
2. *antinuclear* means ______________________________
3. *unacceptable* means ______________________________
4. *enliven* means ______________________________
5. *multicultural* means ______________________________
6. *disqualify* means ______________________________
7. *absolve* means ______________________________
8. *graduation* means ______________________________

Prefixes

Prefix	*Meaning*	*Example*
ab-	away from	absent
ad-	to, toward	advise
anti-	opposed to	anticrime
auto	self	autonomy
bene-	good	benevolent
com-, con-	together	combine
de-	from, away	decline
dis-	apart, away	discomfort
en-	in, into	engage
ex-	out of	exchange
inter-	between	interstate
multi-	many	multicolor
non-	not	nonallied
pre-	before	preregister
re-	back, again	return
trans-	across	transport
un-	not	unprepared

Roots

Root	*Meaning*	*Example*
act	do, move	active
close	close, end	foreclose
dict	to speak	dictionary
grad	to step	graduation
man	hand	manual
phon	sound	microphone
port	carry	portage
quest	ask	question
script	write	descriptive
temp	mix, time	temporary
volve	to roll	revolve

Suffixes

Suffix	*Meaning*	*Example*
-able	capable of	manageable
-al	relating to	rational
-ation	process of	fascination
-ative	nature	formative
-ence	condition	prominence
-ful	full of	beautiful
-ic	pertaining to	prolific
-ism	practice	socialism
-ist	one who does	scientist
-less	without	homeless
-ology	study of	sociology
-ous	having, full of	wondrous

Figure 8.1 Word Parts

9. *phonetic* means ____________________

10. *closure* means ____________________

11. *temporal* means ____________________

12. *prescription* means ____________________

13. *knowledgeable* means ____________________

14. *valueless* means ____________________

15. *odorous* means ____________________

16. *eminence* means ____________________

17. *audiologist* means ____________________

18. *pragmatism* means ____________________

19. *admiration* means ____________________

20. *climatic* means ____________________

In the case of a word like *prominent*, analyzing the word parts may be of little help. So what's the next step? Seeking help from the dictionary is always an option for defining words. A quick look at *Webster's Ninth New Collegiate Dictionary* defines *prominent* as "standing out," "readily noticeable," and "widely and popularly known," all definitions applying to the activities of Harry Owen, the small town's leading citizen described in the passage earlier. The dictionary is very useful in this case, providing both specific and appropriate definitions. But because the dictionary frequently presents more than one definition for a word, selecting the correct definition will depend on your understanding of the word's context. Try to grasp the meanings of words from their contexts before going to the dictionary, and take care not to overuse the dictionary. Looking up too many words actually interferes with reading comprehension by breaking your concentration and causing you to lose focus. Moreover, definitions from the dictionary tend to be quickly forgotten, unless you note them deliberately in the margin of the text beside the unfamiliar words. A dictionary is a useful source of information, but it must be used properly. Take some time to familiarize yourself with a good dictionary and the resources it has to offer.

1. Try to pronounce the unfamiliar word aloud and listen for something similar in your listening or speaking vocabulary.
2. Reread the sentence containing the unfamiliar word, or perhaps a few sentences preceding or following, to determine if the meaning can be derived from the context.
3. Consider using word parts to decipher the meaning of an unfamiliar word. The meaning of specific prefixes, root words, or suffixes may offer some clue to meaning. Word parts can be especially useful for certain specialized fields such as nursing.
4. Use a dictionary when necessary, if the effort is likely to resolve a problem quickly and not interfere with your comprehension. If you use the dictionary, make note of the definition in the margin of the text near the word.
5. Decide whether it is possible to skip the word. Again the effect of the decision on your reading comprehension is the key issue here. Skip the word if it seems inconsequential. Don't skip it if any confusion is likely to result.

Unfamiliar words are ultimately understood through a variety of experiences. Therefore, if you want to steadily improve your word knowledge, read frequently with the active intent to learn new words.

Figure 8.2 A Common Approach to Unfamiliar Words

There is also one further option for managing unfamiliar words. You might decide quite reasonably to skip the word. Think about the Harry Owen excerpt again. All of the information suggests he's an important political and social leader in his town. Is it likely that the final sentence in the paragraph says anything different? If you didn't know that *prominent* means "standing out," can you still reasonably comprehend the paragraph? To skip an unfamiliar word, at least in this instance, may be a sound decision. You may eventually want to know the word *prominent*, but during reading it may be that comprehension does not demand it. (See Figure 8.2 for a brief overview of a common approach to unfamiliar words.)

Elaboration and Integration

Since the majority of new words students encounter reading textbooks are concept words or specialized terminology, your approach to these words must vary from common word attack strategies. Learning new concepts requires the use of good reading comprehension strategies and some additional strategy for working with the concepts as ideas. The approach suggested here is semantic mapping. Semantics is typically defined as the study of meaning in language. For you the task is to understand the meaning of a new word or concept. Mapping is one method by which you achieve that goal. Therefore, the technique is called semantic mapping, a technique that allows you to elaborate on specific aspects of a concept and to integrate that information with personal experience and knowledge. It is somewhat similar to the mapping technique presented in Chapter 7 but is more specialized.

Semantic Mapping

Semantic maps have as their focus a central word or concept (for example, the concept of short-term memory is central to Figure 8.3). Extending from that focus are four types of information—definition, examples, differences, and personal experience—some of which are found in the text and some of which are drawn from prior knowledge and experience.

The first type of information involves defining the concept. As a reader you usually derive such information directly from the text, though you probably break it down into meaningful parts while translating it from the text to the map.

For instance, discussing the concept *short-term memory*, the text may indicate that it is a "temporary working memory" of "limited capacity" that "requires some rehearsal to retain information." Include that information, then, under the label, Define the Concept.

Next, the map identifies examples of the concept. It's important to remember here that most textbooks organize information in a fairly standard way. The textbook author introduces the new concept, defines it, and explores its meaning by discussing examples and illustrations. Just as you read the introductory text for the definition of a new concept, also explore the discussion for examples of the concept. In the case of short-term memory, examples might include: "listening to someone speaking," "retaining a telephone number for immediate use," and "identifying an unusual sound."

Third, drawing more directly on your prior knowledge, decide how the concept you are mapping differs from similar concepts or ideas you have studied previously. This may be somewhat difficult, especially if the text discussion doesn't suggest differences, but it is a way to make sure you

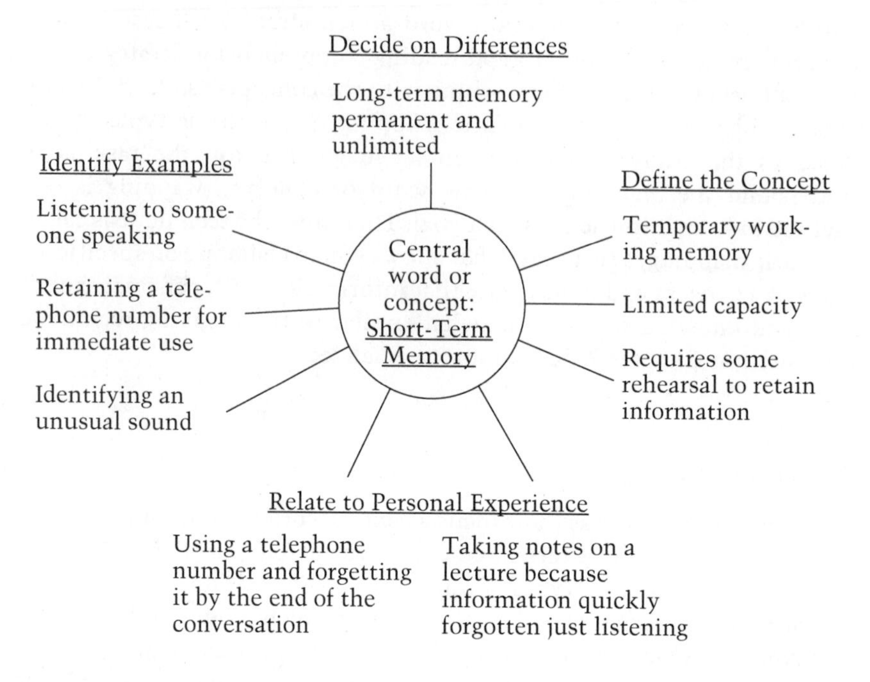

Figure 8.3 Semantic Mapping

understand new concepts. Often you can figure out what new ideas mean if you think about what they do *not* represent. For instance, short-term memory is clearly quite different from "long-term memory," which is essentially "permanent and unlimited" in capacity.

Finally, think about how the concept you are studying relates to your personal experience. Reflect on your past reading or actual experience, considering it in light of the new information. Then think about how to use the new information either to understand other topics or to plan for future activities. The point is to personalize the learning experience, to integrate new concepts or specialized language with your existing knowledge. Then you will be in a much better position to understand the information and retain it for later use. For instance, you will find the concept of short-term memory familiar if, when making a semantic map of the concept (see Figure 8.3), you think about "using a telephone number and forgetting it by the end of the conversation." Or knowledge of short-term memory may be useful for thinking about study practices such as the importance of "taking notes on a lecture because information is quickly forgotten just listening."

Semantic mapping clarifies new concepts by elaborating on their meaning through definition, example, differences, and personal experience.

A Closer Look at Mapping

To look more closely at how semantic mapping clarifies textual information read the following selection on the use of collage to illustrate children's literature.[1] Then study the sample semantic map shown in Figure 8.4 to see how to examine the selection in order to learn the concept *collage* by means of semantic mapping.

Collage—a word derived from the French word *coller*, meaning "to paste" or "to stick"—is a recent addition to the world of book illustration. Pasting and sticking are exactly what artists do when using this technique. Any object or substance that can be attached to a surface can be used to develop a design. Artists may use cardboard, paper, cloth, glass, leather, metal, wood, leaves, flowers, or even butterflies. They may cut up and rearrange their own paintings or use paint and other media to add background. When photographically reproduced in a book, collages still communicate a feeling of texture.

Eric Carle, a popular artist of picture books for young children, develops his collages through a three-step process. He begins by applying acrylic paints to tissue paper. Next, he uses rubber cement to paste down the paper into the desired designs. Finally, he applies colored crayon to provide any needed accents. Carle is known for his striking, colorful storybooks. *The Very Hungry Caterpillar* won the American Institute of Graphic Art's award for 1970. Carle's painted collages add vibrant colors to *Twelve Tales from Aesop*. In addition to brightly colored collage illustrations, his most recent books include pop-ups or other features that encourage children to interact with the book. For example, readers work tabs that move a honeybee's wings, stinger, and tongue in *The Honeybee and the Robber*.

Note that the semantic map in Figure 8.4 takes the primary definition and examples from the text excerpt. Identifying key elements of the definition and examples and representing them in an abbreviated fashion draw into play two important comprehension processes. First, identifying important information for the map makes the details more distinctive. A group of sentences becomes three key points: "type of illustration," "cut and paste objects of design," and "creates feeling of texture." Second, rephrasing the information for the map causes you to process the key points more fully and, therefore, makes them more memorable.

In addition, by tying the new material being studied to prior knowledge either by identifying how this new concept differs from others you have learned or by relating it to personal experience, you succeed in integrating this new material with your existing knowledge. In this manner you begin

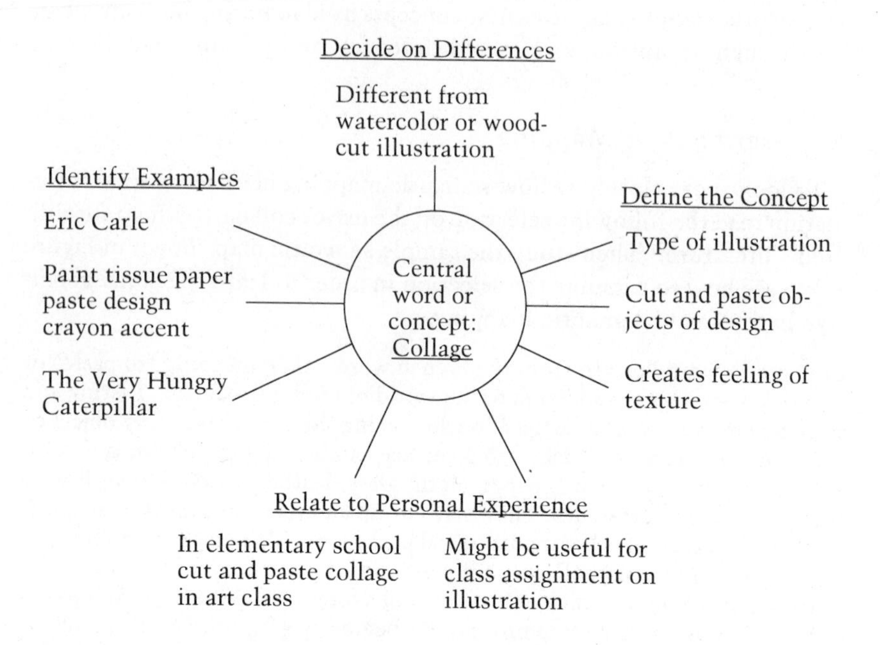

Figure 8.4 Sample Semantic Map

to "make sense" of new information. These are substantial benefits for such a fundamental approach to concept development.

Exercises in Semantic Mapping

Following are two reading selections that introduce and discuss specific concepts. One selection examines migration,[2] and the other examines ethnography.[3] First read the selection on migration and create your own semantic map for the selection. Then compare your map with the sample in the appendix. Second, read and map the selection on ethnography. Then compare your map with the sample in the appendix. There may be differences between your maps and the samples, especially with prior knowledge and personal experience, but the basic information for definitions and examples will probably be similar.

Migration is usually defined as a regular seasonal movement from one place to another, with a later return to the first place, usually on an annual cycle and involving a departure from and return to a breeding area. Birds are the best-known migrants, but certain insects (especially butterflies); fish such as salmon, eel, and herring; and mammals including bison, caribou, and whales migrate long distances.

The reason so many forms of life have evolved migration as part of their life cycle is that their environments cannot support them all year—this usually means there isn't enough food to go around. Since most migratory birds withdraw after breeding from areas that become colder, many people assumed that it was the cold itself that birds sought to escape; however, it now seems clear that birds leave colder areas only because the seasonal change in climate eliminates most of the food on which they depend. Even birds that spend only the warmest months of the year in North America and winter in the tropics can survive a cold and snowy winter if they have enough food; with the increasing popularity of bird feeders have come many new records of usually tropical-wintering birds, like the Northern Oriole, spending the winter dependent on a feeder in northern states. . . .

Compare your semantic map on migration with Figure 8.5 in the appendix. What are the similarities? How do the two maps differ? Continue with the next selection, on ethnography.

An **ethnography** is a description, based on direct observation, of customary behavior in a particular society or setting. Ethnographers spend a long time observing and interacting with the people they are studying. They participate in daily activities. They gossip. They conduct formal and informal interviews. They may collect individuals' life histories; ask people to explain an event they have just witnessed; present them with hypothetical situations and ask how they would respond. Ethnographers note who talks to whom, who makes decisions, and who settles disputes. They compare people's ideals with their actual behavior. In this way they learn the routines and capture the rhythms of daily life. What is special about ethnography is that the observers become active participants in the social world they are observing. They use themselves as research instruments.

Compare your map with Figure 8.6 in the appendix. What are the similarities and differences?

You should use good judgment in deciding whether or not to use semantic mapping as you study. Not all concepts require such an extensive effort. Sometimes concepts are readily understood and easily remembered. Common study practices will provide you with the necessary tools for success. Other times concepts are found to be extremely difficult to understand and one concept might be linked to another. It is in these difficult times that semantic mapping is most useful. So recognize your options, and use your knowledge of the learning process effectively.

Summary and Prediction Questions

1. Summary: Why does prior knowledge and experience play such an important role in vocabulary and concept development?
2. Summary: What is semantic mapping and how can it help concept development?
3. Prediction: What techniques reinforce language learning?

Up to this point, you have read about the importance of having an intention to learn, the usefulness of applying prior knowledge as an aid to understanding, and the benefits of semantic mapping for elaborating on and integrating new information. The next section explains how to study new words or concepts for long-term learning.

Rehearsal and Reinforcement

Language learning is primarily a consequence of repetition. That is probably obvious to you. If you are reading an article and you stop to look up an unfamiliar word in the dictionary and then go back to reading, by the time you finish the article you will probably forget both the word and its definition. If, on the other hand, you make note of this word and its meaning, encounter it repeatedly in your reading, and begin using it yourself, you learn its meaning quite readily.

The assignments in your college courses require that you master new information and new language quickly. To do so you need a planned approach to learning new terms and ideas. Three strategies are suggested here: using semantic maps, creating a word collection, and working with cooperative learning.

Semantic Maps

The logic of using semantic maps is probably obvious. In mapping meanings of new terms you clearly note definitions and specify examples, linking them to personal experience, so all of the critical information is present. The maps thus serve the purpose of review, rehearsal, and self-testing.

A review of a semantic map is simply a rereading of the information it summarizes, perhaps guided by questions. For example, consider your semantic map on migration. The first question is, "What concept is considered?" The answer is, "Migration." The second question is, "What defines migration?" The answer is, "Seasonal movement, from one place to another. . . ." The questions and answers emerge from the information on the map and prepare you for the next two steps.

Rehearsal is the active oral recitation of information. Speaking aloud about the idea allows you some direct verbal experience. Without looking back at the map, you ask yourself, speaking aloud, "What defines migration?" and you answer that question aloud. Then you ask, "Give two [any number is appropriate] examples of creatures that migrate." And so forth. Verify your responses by looking at the map to find out how well you're progressing. Continuous verbal rehearsal reinforces learning.

Finally, you are ready for self-testing. In this case, though, you design tests based on the semantic maps you created while reading your assignments for the course. You might, for example, list concepts and definitions from ten different maps, recording the information in mixed order on two sheets of paper, one for concepts and the other for definitions. You then test yourself by matching words with their definitions. You might do the same with examples. Or you might create an opposites test: "True or False: Migration is not staying in one place year round." The activities grow naturally from your semantic map information.

A Word Collection

Collecting new terms on 3″ × 5″ index cards is a useful way to review, rehearse, and self-test vocabulary development. You can carry such "flash cards" in your pocket for quick review.

The layout is simple. On one side of a card write the word or concept. On the other side, note key phrases from the definition and a couple of examples. When you're waiting for a class to begin, riding the bus, or just sitting around, pull out your cards and review them. Talk to yourself mentally about what a concept means, how to illustrate it, and why it is important. Or test yourself by making a list of examples and matching the word or concept side of the card with the appropriate example.

Practice with your word collection on a regular basis. Gradually incorporate the words into your own life by listening for them and using them in your own speech, or by being alert to them in your reading and incorporating them in your writing.

Cooperative Learning

In courses that appear overwhelming because of their extensive use of new concepts or specialized terminology, it's not uncommon for students to organize informal study groups to tackle these problems. Still, formalizing this type of cooperative learning may make it more productive.

Working together in pairs or in small groups offers many benefits with regard to vocabulary and concept development, if activities are well organized and specific roles shared.

For example, to organize the study of concepts, establish tasks: defining terms, identifying examples, explaining the usefulness of the concept, and practicing the word in appropriate contexts. To begin the tasks student A asks student B to define the first concept. Student B then asks student A to give an example to clarify the definition. In turn student A asks student B to use the concept in a sentence, and follows up B's response by asking B to clarify the concept in an additional sentence or two. With the next concept, the students reverse roles to give each the full range of experience.

Studying in groups is valuable for learning specialized terminology not only because it gives you a chance to practice but also because it helps you clarify difficult concepts through experience. Study groups can create a variety of learning exercises such as crossword puzzles or charades that reinforce vocabulary and concept development. In sum, cooperative learning is an excellent tool for active learning.

Each of the reinforcement strategies suggested here is further supported by the study activities and memory techniques presented in Chapters 4 and 9.

Self-monitoring

Self-monitoring is crucial to learning vocabulary and concepts. To check on your progress, answer the questions below.

A Self-monitoring Checklist

_____ Do I have a clear intent to learn new vocabulary and concept words?

_____ Am I making a conscientious effort to use my prior knowledge and experience?

_____ Do I use a standard approach to unfamiliar vocabulary, including pronouncing the word, examining the context, analyzing word parts, and looking it up in the dictionary?

_____ Are my semantic maps helping to clarify difficult concepts?

_____ Am I including definitions, examples, differences, and personal experiences in my semantic maps?

_____ Do I allot time regularly to rehearsal and reinforcement activities?

_____ Do I use semantic maps, a word collection, and cooperative learning to promote my mastery of concepts?

_____ Am I encountering any specific difficulties with vocabulary or concept learning?

_____ Do I need to try some other approach to learning concepts?

_____ How successful are my efforts, according to the results of quizzes, exams, and so forth?

Periodic review of these self-monitoring questions will refocus your attention on the total process of vocabulary and concept development and help you to identify areas of difficulty.

Evaluation

Concluding the application of any learning strategy is evaluation. For the vocabulary and concept development strategy the evaluation considers three factors: understanding, remembering, and ease of application.

Understanding is the primary objective of learning new vocabulary. Therefore, judge your progress not simply on the basis of "learning new words" but on the basis of how well you are now able to understand new material. Think about the exercise on ethnography. On the one hand, there is a new idea to be learned. On the other hand, mastery of the concept increases your understanding of what sociology is and what sociologists do. From this example you can see that wider understanding is the goal of learning new concepts.

Remembering is the second concern. Since knowledge is cumulative, you must judge the success of your semantic mapping and rehearsal and reinforcement in terms of your ability to remember material. How well do you retain specific facts and ideas? Understanding is the foundation for meaningful efforts at memorizing material. Understanding and memory intertwine each supporting the other.

Finally it is important to evaluate the ease of application of the new learning methods and your new knowledge. Do newly learned words begin to come naturally to you? Initial efforts using new concepts can be halting and awkward, but practice promotes ease of application. Periodic self-monitoring helps you to maintain a systematic approach to learning

1. Begin with an intent to learn.
2. Use prior knowledge to search out the meaning of an unfamiliar word, including the steps in Figure 8.2, "A Common Approach to Unfamiliar Words."
3. Develop an understanding of concepts by the elaboration of detail (including aspects of definition and specific examples) and by the integration of prior knowledge (including aspects of difference and personal experience) by visual representation of semantic mapping.
4. Promote memory through rehearsal and reinforcement using semantic maps, a word collection, and cooperative learning.
5. Self-monitor with a checklist of questions.
6. Evaluate the results through self-tests and review.

Figure 8.7 A Systematic Approach to Vocabulary and Concept Development

and regular experience helps to make the approach a natural part of learning. A systematic approach to vocabulary and concept development is critical to academic success. Regular use of the approach outlined here will improve your skill as an active learner. (For a review, see Figure 8.7, "A Systematic Approach to Vocabulary and Concept Development.")

A Brief Exercise

Practicing a new strategy is probably the best way to become comfortable with it and to gain insight into its effectiveness. To further your own experience, select one of your textbook assignments and carefully apply the strategy presented here.

1. Have a clear intent to learn.
2. Draw upon your wealth of prior knowledge.
3. Elaborate on word meaning and integrate with your prior knowledge through the use of semantic mapping.
4. Use rehearsal and reinforcement to enhance your memory of vocabulary and concept meaning.
5. Self-monitor in order to check the effectiveness of your efforts and the strength of your performance.
6. Evaluate the results of the strategy by your degree of understanding, the memorability of the information, and the increasing ease with which you apply the strategy.

Integrate this strategy into your active learning process.

Summary and Prediction Questions

1. Summary: What techniques reinforce language learning?
2. Summary: What steps are suggested for a systematic approach to understanding and retaining concepts?
3. Prediction: How can vocabulary and concept learning be readily integrated with the active learning process?

INTEGRATION WITH ACTIVE LEARNING

Throughout this chapter the discussion of vocabulary and concept development has focused on making the learner an active participant in the learning process. Active involvement, use of specific strategies, and an emphasis on understanding unfamiliar ideas are the basic principles for integrating vocabulary and concept development with active learning.

Value the Incidental

A great deal of learning is incidental. That is, your learning is a natural consequence of daily experience. Think about how much you have learned from simply becoming involved in certain activities at the gym of the local YMCA or in the political campaign for your favorite candidate. These experiences are one reason why your listening vocabulary and even your speaking vocabulary tend to be broader than your reading or writing vocabulary. To engage in daily life is to learn about uncommon characters, exotic places, extraordinary events, and original ideas. You can put such experience to good use in more formal learning.

Reading provides similar incidental learning, especially in literature. By engaging the language of experience in a variety of formats—newspapers, magazines, novels, poetry—you "incidentally" learn the meaning of the language used to convey the experience. To some extent, the conclusion is simple. The more time you spend reading, thinking, conversing, and experiencing, the greater the range of your knowledge and understanding. Daily experience and regular reading expand your vocabulary and conceptual knowledge incidentally and quite naturally if you are sensitive to the value of such experience.

To extend your systematic efforts at language learning and to exploit the natural consequences of incidental learning, it is necessary to integrate new language and learning into your daily life. When reading or listening, be alert for new words, their explanation, and their potential use. Try to use an ever increasing range of words in your general vocabulary to express feelings, describe experiences, and explain ideas. Might a new word describe more precisely an event or an idea? Incorporate vocabulary and concept learning into your writing. Consider how particular words or concepts clarify your thinking and communicate ideas more clearly. Make vocabulary and concept development an integral part of your learning, not just to pass a course but to better understand the nature of your experience.

The effective integration of general vocabulary and specific concepts with your existing store of knowledge is a consequence of the intent to learn a systematic approach to understanding and retaining such information so that it ultimately becomes, for the future, part of your "prior" knowledge and experience.

Review Questions

1. What is the difference between general vocabulary and specific concepts, and how does that difference affect your approach to unfamiliar words?
2. Identify each of the steps used with a systematic approach to understanding and retaining both general vocabulary and specific concepts.
3. Why does prior knowledge and experience play such an important role in vocabulary and concept development?
4. How can vocabulary and concept learning be readily integrated with the active learning process?

CHAPTER REVIEW

To complete this chapter, answer the following questions. When you are finished, review the chapter to check your answers.

1. True or False: A semantic map should be developed for each new concept studied.
2. True or False: Relating some personal experience to the understanding of a new concept helps to increase your familiarity with the concept.
3. True or False: Vocabulary development is partially a consequence of incidental learning.

4. True or False: Virtually every word can be understood by a careful reading of its context.

5. Semantic mapping is especially useful for concept development because
   a. it requires a careful reading of the text.
   b. it includes a common approach to unfamiliar words.
   c. it defines the concept in detail.
   d. it elaborates on specific details and includes prior knowledge.

6. Which of the following is not a technique suggested for reinforcement and rehearsal?
   a. semantic maps
   b. dictionary study
   c. a word collection
   d. cooperative learning

7. Identify each of the five steps in Figure 8.2, "A Common Approach to Unfamiliar Words," and explain how they are used while reading.

____

____

____

____

____

8. On a separate sheet of paper, create a sample semantic map showing the relationship of each part to the central concept.

9. Discuss how to integrate learning vocabulary and concepts with an active learning process.

____

____

____

____

10. How does the intent to learn influence the likelihood of success in vocabulary and concept development?

___

___

___

___

NOTES

1. Donna E. Norton, *Through the Eyes of a Child: An Introduction to Children's Literature*, 2nd ed. (Columbus: Merrill, 1987), p. 121.
2. Roger F. Pasquier, *Watching Birds: An Introduction to Ornithology* (Boston: Houghton Mifflin Company, 1977), pp. 192–193.
3. Michael S. Basses, Richard J. Gilles, and Ann Levine, *Sociology: An Introduction* (New York: Random House, 1980), p. 167.

9

Memory

Preview Exercise

Preview the chapter. Look closely at the various subheadings. Then create a "map" of the chapter following the procedure presented in Chapter 7. Use "Memory" as the central focus of your map, and use the major and minor subheadings as the branches. Notice how this initial map provides an overview of the chapter and a quick start for note-taking.

PURPOSE FOR READING: ______________________________

____

____

"Uh, do I feel stupid."

"Why Mike, what makes you say that?"

"Well, you know that test I studied so hard for last week?"

"Sure, you spent all week on it."

"It didn't matter. When I took the test, I couldn't remember half the material. And I know I studied it. I just forget it."

"Maybe it was just a hard test."

"No, I don't think so, I even remember studying a lot of the information. I just forgot everything."

Memory. How often does memory seem to fail just at the wrong moment? Or does it? Memory is a fascinating subject—much studied by psychologists, much desired by students, and much misunderstood by many.

The purpose of this chapter is to explore the subject of memory from the perspective of information processing, to discuss specific techniques for identifying, storing, and retrieving important information, and to present a systematic strategy for remembering what you learn.

Guiding Questions

1. What are the three stages of memory suggested by an information-processing perspective?
2. Why is a functional approach useful for memory improvement?
3. How can the encoding, storage, and retrieval processes each be improved?
4. What are the five steps in the strategy for remembering?
5. How does self-monitoring help improve the memory process?

MEMORY AS A PROCESS

There are several ways to look at memory. One is an information-processing model.[1] From this perspective, learning and remembering occur in three basic stages: activation of the sensory register, transfer to short-term memory, and storage in long-term memory.

Sensory Register

The first stage is activating the sensory register. This is the starting point when you take in information from the environment. Information is gathered through your senses. You see it, or hear it, taste, touch, or smell it, and it registers ever so briefly in the mind. If you are reading, for instance, words are the stimulus that begin the memory process, activating the sensory register.

This initial process is brief and the storage so momentary that a second process must be triggered. Information must be transferred to short-term memory or it will simply be lost.

Short-Term Memory

Short-term memory is a temporary storage place much limited in its capacity to hold information. The classic example of short-term memory is remembering a telephone number. Say you look up a number in the telephone book. That is the stimulus that activates the sensory register. To retain the number, you repeat it to yourself, thereby shifting it to the short-term memory. Without that rehearsal the shift of information from the sensory register to short-term memory will fail and you will have to look up the number again.

During reading, the process of locating important information, identifying it, and thinking about its meaning trigger the shift of information from the sensory register to the short-term memory. Yet, because short-term memory is limited in capacity and duration, information is quickly forgotten. Therefore, a further stage is required—long-term memory.

Long-Term Memory

Committing knowledge to long-term memory is a critical stage in the learning process because it provides the opportunity to store large, perhaps unlimited, amounts of information permanently. But such storage and retention require an intent to remember as well as repetition, or practice.

Consider the telephone number again. If you intend to use it only one time, the information is quickly lost from short-term memory. Further use requires another look at the telephone book. If, though, you wanted to remember the number, you might repeat the number a few times to shift it over to long-term memory. That rehearsal, plus periodic use of the number, would help store the information in your memory for future use. The long-term memory stores information that is meaningful and is reinforced through repetition.

Unfortunately, a variety of factors influence the memory process in ways that cause memory to fail. Such memory failure may be a consequence of poor storage caused by lack of attention, interference from the environment, or inappropriate strategies for study. Or memory failure may be a consequence of difficulties accessing and retrieving information from storage. The question is, How can you improve your memory?

Summary and Prediction Questions

1. Summary: What are the three stages of memory suggested by an information-processing perspective?

2. Prediction: Why is a functional approach useful for memory improvement?
3. Prediction: How can the encoding process be improved?

IMPROVING MEMORY

A parallel perspective for exploring the memory process refers to function: encoding, storage, and retrieval.[2] While this approach corresponds somewhat with the information-processing model, it also extends it. Encoding—taking in information—is somewhat like the sensory register, where information is taken in and registered. The storage process focuses on retaining information and, therefore, is a process that parallels the shift of information from the sensory register to short-term memory and from short-term memory to long-term memory. The retrieval process is linked to long-term memory; it is the process through which information is retrieved from the final point of storage. The functional approach is useful because it focuses attention on specific techniques for improving memory.

The Encoding Process

Focusing Attention

Focusing attention, or concentrating on the activity at hand, is the first step in encoding. Establishing a purpose—"to understand the three stages of an information-processing perspective," for example—for reading, or listening, or writing, or any other activity helps focus attention. And the focus identifies information for memory.

Meaningful Activities

Making an activity meaningful also promotes encoding. Imagine doing an assignment simply because you are told to do it. You don't know why. It doesn't make any sense. And you have more important things to do. The result is that you are just going through the motions—taking a course rather than truly learning a subject. Instead, if an activity is meaningful, you think "That's an intriguing idea; let me see what I can find out about it," then you are much more likely to remember it. To improve memory, you must begin with a purpose, and make your learning meaningful.

Interesting Activities

In a similar sense, activities that you find interesting, you are likely to learn much more readily than activities that you do not. The question is, What do you find interesting? Some interests develop naturally from your previous experience or your academic or career goals. Other interests develop as your sense of confusion about a subject declines and your knowledge increases. One reason for a general education is to offer experiences in learning that stimulate new interests. Think about this. Imagine a sport, basketball for instance, that you really love. How much do you know about it? A lot? Now imagine another sport, tennis perhaps, in which you have no interest. How much do you know about it? Much less? Knowledge and interest frequently go hand in hand. So when you are beginning something new, think about it as an adventure from the unknown to the known, search for the meaning it has for you, and make the subject interesting. You'll learn more.

Organization

Encoding is also aided by organization, an idea that is repeated throughout this book. Bits and pieces of information scattered about generally fail to make much of an impression on your mind. But an organized view of any subject promotes both understanding and memory. Imagine a long list of numbers 1 784 619 4128 that someone asks you to remember in order. At first glance that looks like quite a task, right? Now, let's give the list some meaning and some organization. For meaning, imagine it's a long distance telephone number. Then use your knowledge of telephone numbers to give the list organization: 1-784-619-4128. Eleven items of little meaning have become four items that make a lot of sense.

An intent to remember, an interest in the subject, a clear sense of organization, each provide a powerful motivation for learning. (See Figure 9.1 for review.)

A Brief Exercise

For each of the following sample assignments describe, on a separate sheet of paper, how you could promote encoding by making the material potentially more meaningful or more interesting.

1. Prepare a brief paper explaining how the study of music history may help a student become more fully educated.

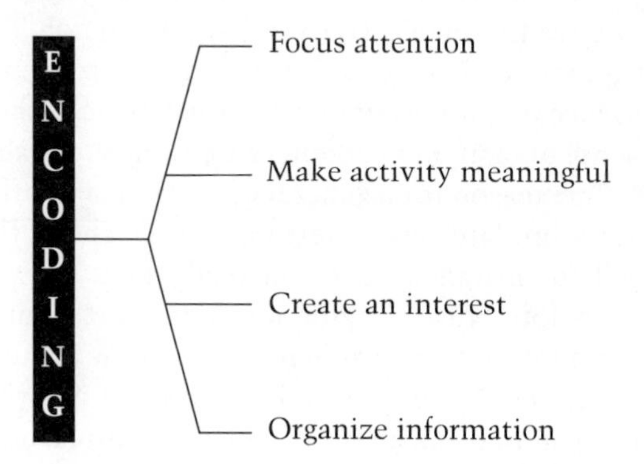

Figure 9.1 The Encoding Process

2. Read Chapter 16 and be prepared to discuss the major causes for crime in urban, suburban, and rural areas.
3. Prepare for Friday's exam by paying special attention to the distinguishing characteristics of the major geographic regions of the United States.

Summary and Prediction Questions

1. Summary: Why is the functional approach useful?
2. Summary: How can encoding be improved? Identify each technique.
3. Prediction: How can the storage process be improved?

The Storage Process

Failure to store information effectively is probably the major reason for forgetting. However, certain techniques can greatly improve your memory.

Repetition and Rehearsal

Repetition and rehearsal are guiding forces in the storage process. To regularly repeat or rehearse a point of information or an activity will increase your ability to retain such information. You are surely familiar with the technique of saying things over and over to yourself until you can remember them. You are also aware that people who are successful at something—playing tennis, acting in theater or television, selling products—regularly practice their activity. So repetition and rehearsal are clearly valuable tools for the retention of information. Get in the habit of practicing what you wish to learn.

Manageable Chunks

Organizing information into manageable chunks is also an important principle of learning. In earlier chapters, you read about organizing study periods into segments of intense study with frequent breaks, and you learned how to divide textbook chapters into subsections and study the material a step at a time. Organizing, or reorganizing, material into manageable chunks also aids storage and retention.

It is also worth noting that information is more fully remembered if you make it more distinctive—so that it creates a special impression. On the one hand, identifying what is important in readings, notes, and lectures helps make certain facts and ideas distinctive. On the other hand, specific techniques for storage add to the distinctiveness of the information, enhancing retention. Techniques such as acronyms, acrostics, imaginative stories, and systems of association, all frequently referred to as *mnemonics*, organize material into manageable chunks and make information more distinctive.

ACRONYMS. One approach to chunking is the use of acronyms. This is a familiar method of using the first letter of each word of a phrase to make a code word that is easy to remember. For example, you are probably familiar with the acronym *NASA*, the common reference for the National Aeronautics and Space Administration. NASA is easy to remember because it can be pronounced as a word rather than separate letters. Another agency of the United States government, the Occupational Health and Safety Administration, is commonly known by its acronym, OSHA. If you were studying about the three branches of government in a political science class, you might well create an acronym code for the information, JEL, for the judicial, the executive, and the legislative branches. Acronyms do not apply to every type of learning, but they are useful for many storage activities.

ACROSTICS. A variation of acronyms is acrostics, the art of creating imaginative sentences based on the first letter of each new word of an idea or fact to be learned. These sentences can serve as a general code to the information or they can follow a specific sequence of events.

Let's assume you are taking an introductory course in environmental science in which you are studying the plant communities of land. These communities are called biomes, and the major land, or terrestrial, types are identified as deserts, grasslands, tundras, coniferous forests, deciduous forests, and rain forests.

Of course, you can always use a basic rehearsal technique with this information, but making it more distinctive with a creative sentence makes it more memorable. Assume you want to remember both the concept of biomes and the types. Your sentence might look like this: Basically, drifters gather tin cans from decaying fences and rotten floors.

The image you create is of drifters gathering cans, but the translation is: biomes, deserts, grasslands, tundras, coniferous forests, deciduous forests, and rain forests. Acrostics is both an entertaining and a workable technique.

A Brief Exercise

To have an opportunity to experiment with the acrostic, or creative sentence, technique, create an acrostic for the following list of "major elements necessary for life."[3] For each element, think of a common word substitute beginning with the same letter, and create an imaginative sentence to aid you in storing and retrieving the elements list. One sample sentence is provided to help you think about how to create a sentence of your own.

Major Elements Necessary for Life

carbon	calcium
hydrogen	sulfur
oxygen	magnesium
nitrogen	chlorine
phosphorus	micronutrients
sodium	iron
potassium	

Sample acrostic sentence: Charlie held onto Niki Pearson so Penny could stop marking cans made improperly.

Your acrostic sentence: ______________________________

IMAGINATIVE STORIES Requiring somewhat more effort than either acronyms or acrostics, imaginative stories serve the same functions: organization and distinctiveness. Whereas acronyms are useful as codes for key concepts, acrostics are useful for memorizing lists of information. Imaginative stories may help you especially to draw together large amounts of information into a more easily memorable form. Again, specific information is "coded" into the story, and the story images cause you to remember and eventually recall the key ideas. Consider an example.

Classes in psychology and child development frequently discuss the work of Jean Piaget, a psychologist most well known for his investigation of children's cognitive development. Piaget suggests there are four major stages of development, each distinguished by a characteristic way of thinking and each occurring during a certain age range. The first period, the sensorimotor period, occurs from birth until about 2 years and is characterized by thinking associated with physical activity. The second, or preoperational, period occurs from 2 to 7 years and is characterized by the child learning to represent objects symbolically through language. Toys, for instance, can be rearranged to represent something else. The third period, the period of concrete operations, occurs from 7 to 11 years and is characterized by the child's ability to perform logical analysis, to develop empathy, and to understand cause and effect. The final period, the period of formal operations, begins about age 12 and is characterized by the development of logic, symbolic representation, and hypothetical thought.

Obviously, Piaget's ideas are much more complicated than this, but they are very influential in educational psychology and other disciplines. Students asked to learn the four periods of cognitive development might compose the following imaginative story as an aid to memory.

A Story of Cognitive Development

Cognitive Development was quite a thoughtful person when I first met him. But he said that it had taken him some time to develop his thinking ability. It had all started many years before.

When Cognitive was very young, from the time of his birth until about age 2, his mother said he was a very physical person. He spent most of his time looking around and grabbing, or chewing, or kicking things. He used all his senses and kept active like a little motor.

From the time Cognitive was 2 until he was about 7, he not only continued to be physically active but he also began to talk about everything. And he gave everything a name, and he could use his toys in different ways by giving them different names. Cognitive was always operating on his environment, even though he was still a preschooler.

The more experience Cognitive had the more he learned, and between 7 and 11, Cognitive was very concrete with his thinking. If he needed to solve a problem, he would analyze it logically. When he read about someone who had a different life from his, he tried to empathize with their experience. And always he tried to reason through why things happened the way they did. He was always thinking about the cause or the effect.

Cognitive believes that he was about 12 when a really fascinating change took place. He was trying to solve a particularly difficult problem in a very formal way when he realized that he could represent the problem with symbols, be very logical in thinking about it, and guess at the possible answers. This was the first time he thought hypothetically. And he has continued to be quite a thinker ever since.

There are, of course, many ways to represent information through stories. They can be simple tales, humorous episodes, or complicated sketches. The point is to weave an informative text into a memorable story that serves as a system for storing information efficiently. The imaginative story is one option you can use for storing information. It is a creative, less boring alternative to repetition and rehearsal.

ASSOCIATION Many systems of association are used to enhance memory. Frequently suggested are rhymes or songs. The student associates the new information with different parts of a well-known rhyme or song, so that singing or reciting a known phrase or verse triggers memory of the new word or idea associated with it. Many people can remember the correct order of the alphabet only by singing or humming the "alphabet song," for example. Frequently, the association between something known and something unknown is further increased because the information is also very visual.

Another system of association that students find useful is the key-word method. Often used in the study of foreign languages, the key-word method takes a new word and associates it with a similar-sounding common word. The purpose is to create a visual image that draws the two words together.

For example, imagine you're studying about the gas sulfur dioxide. Associate the term with the similar-sounding phrase *silly old ox.* Imagine that silly old ox pulling a cart with a bottle of gas labeled sulfur dioxide. The sound and the image help you remember the name for that colorless gas.

Visual Imagery

Translating information from one form to another helps increase the distinctiveness of information being stored. Translating information into both a verbal and visual form combines the dominant modes of thinking to enhance the memory effort. This use of visual images may be locational, representational, or transformational. Each plays a role in the storage process.

LOCATIONAL. Visualizing information from a locational perspective is an age-old technique called "method of loci." The idea is to associate information to be remembered with some path of familiar objects or places such as the furniture in your house or landmarks on the path to school.

For instance, you might take the five steps in problem solving and link them to objects on an imaginary path to school. Your first stop is the corner stop sign, so there is the first step in problem solving: stop and identify the problem. As you continue along, you pass a grocery store. This will be the second step: select a strategy. The next stop is the entrance to the campus. Here is the point for trying out the strategy. As you walk up the path, you pass the administration building. This triggers the evaluation stage. Finally, you approach the building with your first class. This is the spot for revision. When you want to remember the five steps in problem solving, just retrace your walk to school.

REPRESENTATIONAL. Visualizing information is a fairly common experience. You quite naturally form mental pictures of what you hear and read. To some extent using representational images requires simply that you be more conscious about how you represent ideas and events in your mind. Imagine, for instance, reading about a person who is not paying attention while driving. Distracted by some thought, he accidentally drives up on the sidewalk, hits a fire hydrant, and is totally shocked to see water spewing everywhere. Surely that's an image to be remembered.

But representational images of informational text might also be consciously created with the mapping technique discussed in Chapter 7 or simply by drawing an illustration representing the text.

Remember the example of acrostics used to learn biomes? Well, suppose that you need to remember not only the different plant communities but also their characteristics. Here's where mapping can help. First, the subject is terrestrial biomes. Extending from this central subject are the various plant communities such as deserts and grassland. Each commu-

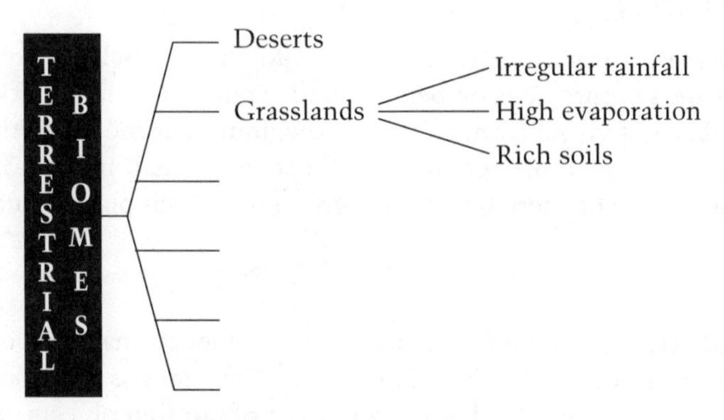

Figure 9.2 Mapping Categories

nity branches into its distinguishing characteristics. Grasslands, for instance, are characterized by irregular rainfall, high evaporation rate, and rich soils. The map creates a visual image of the information and the relationship of one point to another. (See Figure 9.2.)

Drawing a sketch to represent informational text is also useful. Illustrating a point forces you to think about the information under study and helps you to understand it. Suppose you are studying the root structure of plants. You read that roots transport food and water to a plant. The system is made up of the xylem, which carries water, the phloem, which carries food, and the additional structures of endodermis, cortex, and epidermis. A representational illustration helps make this information meaningful and therefore more memorable. To solidify the learning of these new words, you might also create an acronym—EXCEP—as a code for storing the information: epidermis, xylem, cortex, endodermis, and phloem. The representational image clarifies the information and the acronym aids in storage. (See sample Figure 9.3.)

TRANSFORMATIONAL. In addition to locational and representational images, there are transformational images, which translate information from the text into some contrived image that triggers the recall of appropriate material. You might think of the way political cartoonists illustrate current events on the editorial page of the newspaper. Ideas are remembered through the unique image created. Transformational images are also associations, similar to the key-word method, which created some exaggerated view, or transformation, of the text simply to make it more memorable. Imagine, for instance, creating an illustration to represent

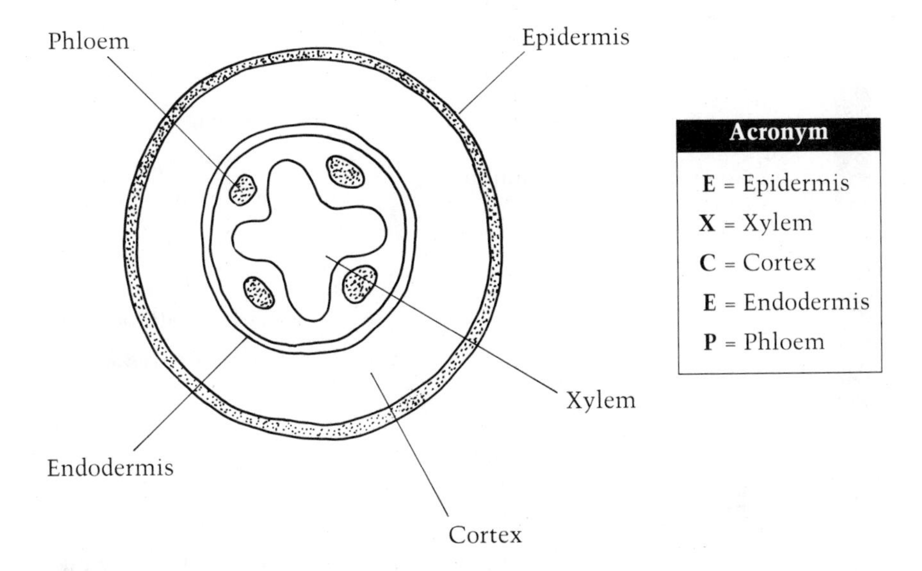

Figure 9.3 Root Structure

cognitive development and the four stages—perhaps a cartoon character climbing a ladder of developmental stages. Use your imagination.

Spaced Study

Finally, the storage of information is greatly facilitated by planning spaced study periods. Organize active study periods that are relatively short, 45 minutes, perhaps, and followed by 5- or 10-minute breaks. Or divide lengthy study assignments into smaller blocks of time spaced throughout the day. Plan to avoid fatiguing extended periods of study because fatigue interferes with concentration and retention.

Regardless of what techniques you employ to increase your store of information and no matter how effective those techniques, information overload can undermine all your efforts. By organizing information, using effective storage techniques, and spacing study periods with alternative activities, you can build your store of information systematically. Even a good night's rest will aid your memory, simply because it allows your mind time to integrate new information with existing knowledge, and to sort out the confusions of the moment. Then once the information

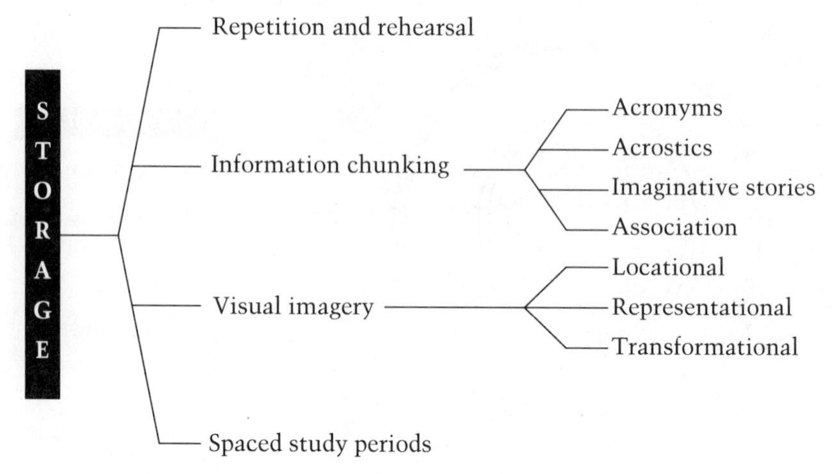

Figure 9.4 The Storage Process

is effectively stored, you can get on with the subject of retrieval. (See Figure 9.4 for review.)

A BRIEF EXERCISE

As a review of the storage process, create a representational map of the techniques discussed. Then use that information to make up a creative sentence, or acrostic, for storing the information. Practice associating the sentence with the storage techniques; then test yourself to determine the results.

Summary and Prediction Questions

1. Summary: How can storage be improved? Identify each technique.
2. Prediction: How can the retrieval process be improved?

The Retrieval Process

Difficulty with retrieving facts learned is often related to improper storage, but retrieval can be a problem itself. Assume, for instance, that you had taken a good deal of time to store information using a number of the techniques previously discussed. Yet, when you finally took the exam, your memory failed you: "My mind just went blank." The question is,

Why? The answer is probably failure to practice retrieving information or failure to use retrieval techniques in the appropriate circumstance. Both suggest a closer look at retrieval is worthwhile.

Self-testing

Self-testing is the major study activity for improving retrieval. Do you recall the saying, "Practice makes perfect"? Well, self-testing is the practice activity for improving retrieval. If you want to know whether or not you have facts and concepts stored in memory and readily accessible, test yourself with a common question-and-answer technique. For example, "What are the four basic aspects of the storage process?" Answer: "Repetition and rehearsal, information chunking, visual imagery, and spaced study periods." The results are easy to check.

Self-testing has a number of benefits. First, it simulates the actual test situation, providing you with practice in taking tests. Second, it allows you to check your responses and monitor your progress in storing and retrieving information. In this sense, self-testing helps guide your review activities. Third, self-testing is a progressive activity in the sense that practice actually helps improve your retrieval ability. Finally, self-testing complements the repetition and rehearsal process because it helps evaluate your efforts and judge when you're done.

Cooperative Learning

Cooperative learning also has a role to play in self-testing. You can enhance learning by exchanging roles with others for understanding and remembering new information. With a partner, try playing the roles of "Question" and "Answer" to facilitate self-testing, switch roles as you work through the material. Working together, you can quiz each other, add or clarify information, and more effectively monitor the accuracy of self-testing. Cooperative learning is an important source of feedback and a useful alternative to working alone.

Reversing Storage

Retrieval also involves "reversing" storage activities, using acronyms, acrostics, imaginative stories, and association techniques to recall specific information. If, for instance, you create an acronym to remember the basic elements of the root structure, you must practice using the acronym to retrieve this information. In this sense, storage and retrieval are interactive; they work together. To spend time creating an imaginative story, then not practice using it to retrieve the information would be a waste of time.

The same holds true for visual imagery. To make visual imagery work, you must create vivid images with memorable clues to store information. Then you must practice mentally recreating those images to establish them as useful retrieval techniques. You might, for instance, take some time each day to practice recreating visual images and judging how effective they are for recalling information. Imagery, like any other activity, requires practice to be effective.

Overlearning

Another technique that promotes successful retrieval is overlearning. Overlearning is worthwhile because it tends to reinforce and strengthen initial learning and the firmness, or tenacity, with which memory holds information learned. Information "decays" rather quickly in memory, and it is surprising how quickly you can forget. Regular practice to the point of overlearning is one way to combat forgetting.

Imagine you read an article titled "Ten Techniques for Improving Memory." It's not hard to guess that a quiz would ask you to list, or describe, those ten techniques. Wisely, you decide that a little verbal rehearsal is in order. Then you test yourself. Perhaps the first self-test results in only seven of ten items, so you do a bit more verbal rehearsal. Your next test results in ten out of ten items. You have successfully stored and retrieved the ten techniques. But don't stop. Test yourself a couple more times. Impress the information in memory by overlearning, and the list will stay with you much longer.

Periodic Review

Combine overlearning with relearning through periodic review. Information is relearned rather quickly and better maintained in memory if it is subject to periodic review. Actually, this is a commonsense notion. Through reading and study you learn new information, and through storage and retrieval you develop a memory for that information. Then by periodic review you reinforce that initial learning, creating a store of information that is more secure, more steadfast, and, therefore, more memorable. Your ability to retrieve information is greatly influenced by the frequency with which you use the information. Periodic review reinforces both storage and retrieval.

Problem Solving

A few common problem-solving techniques are useful to overcome retrieval failures.

ALPHABET. One of the most common techniques is to use the alphabet. Imagine taking a test in literature and finding yourself unable to recall the name of an important character. Rather than becoming anxious or frustrated, carefully work your way through the alphabet. You see, your mind is on the subject, but it is having difficulty accessing a particular piece of information. A certain letter in the alphabet may be just the access code your mind needs in order to recall the character's name.

RETRACE STEPS. Retracing your steps is another common technique. The effectiveness of this technique is suggested by the use of locational maps as a storage technique. To gain the benefits of storage, you must retrace your steps, retrieving the stored information. Retracing the steps in some activity or process also promotes recall of information that wasn't purposely stored with locational maps. For instance, you might use your recall of steps in a science experiment to remember the results of the original activity. In other words, you retrace your steps to increase your memory of past events and to solve a problem of "lost" information.

ASSOCIATION AND BRAINSTORMING. You might also consider free association techniques or brainstorming techniques. Fairly similar in nature, these techniques allow your mind to work *for* you rather than against you. Sometimes overattention to recalling a bit of information seemingly forgotten actually gets in the way of remembering. If you have difficulty accessing some bit of information, just let your mind wander through your mental storehouse of information looking for items stored under the subject category.

Imagine that question on the exam in speech class is, "Describe the characteristics of an effective delivery." You remember that five points were discussed in class, but you can remember only three of them. A brainstorming approach suggests that you take a few moments to list as

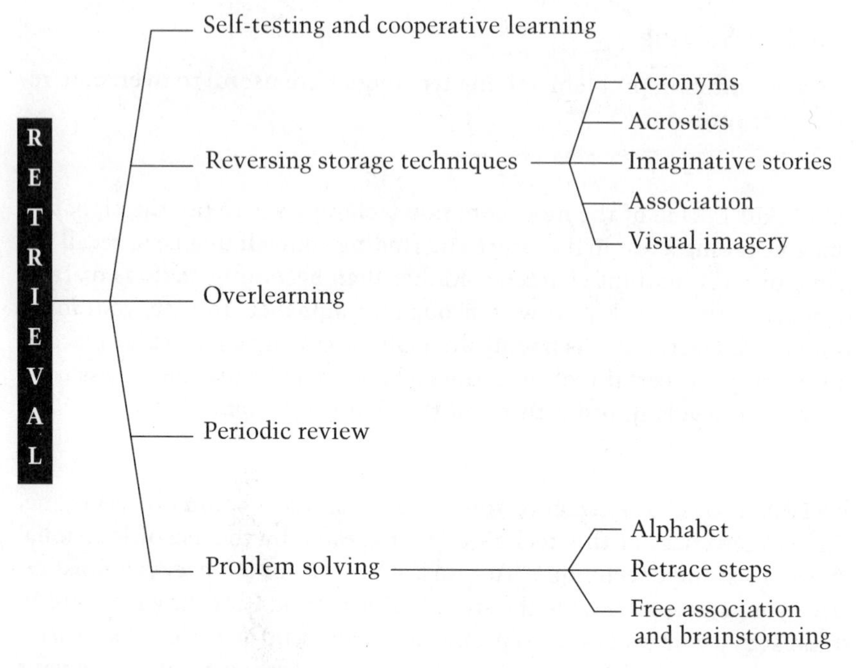

Figure 9.5 The Retrieval Process

many points as you can for making good speeches. The characteristics of effective delivery will emerge from your list. You may find that the information was never stored, but chances are it was stored and can be retrieved through free association or brainstorming.

Remember, retrieval efficiency is increased by continuous practice and monitored most effectively with self-testing.

Encoding, storage, and retrieval, these are the basic stages in the memory process. Learn how to use each of these stages to your advantage and your memory will be enhanced. (See Figure 9.5 for review of retrieval.)

A Brief Exercise

Complete each of the following incomplete sentences about retrieval of information stored in memory.

1. Self-testing is an excellent way to practice retrieval because

____

2. To talk about reversing storage techniques means to

____

3. Imagine that you've been studying a history assignment in preparation for a quiz. Your self-testing indicates that you have pretty well mastered the material but you have decided to try a couple more self-tests because the principle of

____

suggests that

____

4. If you draw a blank while trying to remember something, you might try

______________________, ______________________,

or ____

Summary and Prediction Questions

1. Summary: How can retrieval be improved? Identify each technique.
2. Prediction: What are five steps in the strategy for remembering?

A STRATEGY FOR REMEMBERING

Once you have a basic understanding of how to improve encoding, storage, and retrieval, a working strategy for remembering information will tie everything together. Suggested here is a five-step strategy to guide your memory activities:

1. Know your task.
2. Plan your approach.
3. Apply techniques flexibly.
4. Monitor your activities.
5. Evaluate your success.

Know Your Task

To be successful with an endeavor you need to understand your purpose; knowing your task is the first step in this strategy. Key questions like "What is it that I wish to accomplish?" and "What information is necessary for me to remember?" will help you decide on your purpose. Be sure to ask the instructor what information is important (actually you are asking what is *most* important, and whether you can study selectively); also inquire how you will be tested (so you can organize self-test practice sessions). Add to this some assessment of your own prior knowledge and interest. It may be that a major issue for you is to make the activity more meaningful in order to increase your attention. Or perhaps the amount of new information requires breaking it into chunks. Or you may prefer to handle the situation with the help of others through cooperative learning.

Plan Your Approach

Knowing your task is integrally related with planning your approach. As you decide what you want to accomplish, you also begin planning how to accomplish your task. That is, you want to design some step-by-step approach. Remember the planning model in Chapter 2, on active learning? Use that four-step model to assess the situation, but use the memory process as the focus of your attention. (Suggestions for planning are presented in Chapter 4, on purposeful study.) For example, visual images may be especially helpful for remembering information in a literature class; imaginative stories may help to organize the large number of new concepts in a psychology class; overlearning may be the key to retaining the many procedures presented in a machine design class. Ask yourself, "What procedure should I follow, what techniques should I use, to accomplish my goal?"

Be Flexible

Next, you want to apply the various memory techniques in a flexible fashion, and you probably don't want to over-rely on any one or two techniques. If you can accomplish a task with the simple use of verbal rehearsal, do it. If the material is fairly complex, consider using a locational or representational mapping technique to help you visualize items. And if you find science class overwhelming you with new terms, try inventing an acrostic to remember some of them. Whatever the case, become familiar with the variety of memory techniques and use them flexibly. That way you have some choices and are not stuck with the same approach all the time.

Self-monitor

As you already know, self-monitoring helps you guide your learning. Keeping track of what you are doing and how well you are doing it is also critical for developing a sound memory. Obviously, self-testing, a major aspect of retrieval, is a primary method for monitoring your progress. In addition, the feedback you receive from others through cooperative learning is an excellent source of information concerning your progress.

Still, you also need to look at how you're handling the total activity. Consider whether or not your task is clear, particularly as you become more involved in the material. Consider your plans and whether or not the techniques, the schedule of activities, and the results of your efforts are working toward the accomplishment of your goal. Consider the possibility of alternative strategies if problems arise. Know exactly where you are going in the memory process.

Evaluate Your Success

Finally, any strategy requires an evaluation of success. Once you formally take an examination, carry out an experiment, program a computer, or complete an assignment, take time to evaluate the results. How well did you do? Were the results what you expected? Were your plans effective in accomplishing your goal? How effective and efficient were your techniques? Are any alternative approaches necessary? Is there any way to improve your strategy? These are the sorts of questions you may use to evaluate your success and to begin reconsideration of your efforts.

A Brief Exercise

Apply the five steps that of "A Strategy for Remembering," to one of your assignments. Then evaluate the results of your experience. What is your reaction to the strategy?

Summary and Prediction Questions

1. Summary: What are the five steps in the strategy for remembering?
2. Prediction: How can self-monitoring help improve the memory process?

SELF-MONITORING

Monitoring the memory process is a matter of judging whether or not you are using the appropriate techniques at the appropriate time and in the appropriate circumstances. It's important to know, for instance, whether or not you approach an assignment with an intent to remember. It's also important to know if your learning is readily accessible through retrieval. The following checklist can help you monitor your activities.

SELF-MONITORING CHECKLIST

_____ Do I have a clearly established purpose to guide my memory activities?

_____ Do I approach each task with the intent to remember, with an interest in learning, and a concern with organization?

_____ Am I planning each memory activity from encoding to storage to retrieval?

_____ Am I using repetition and rehearsal to store information; dividing material into manageable chunks by means of acronyms, acrostics, imaginative stories, and forms of association; and applying the techniques of visual imagery?

_____ Do I apply my knowledge of memory techniques flexibly, linking information to appropriate techniques?

_____ Am I giving enough attention to the retrieval process, especially self-testing, but also to cooperative learning, regular practice, overlearning, and problem solving?

_____ Do I continually monitor my efforts in order to judge both the progress of my efforts and the effectiveness of my activities?

_____ Am I evaluating the results of my activities, especially with my plan of study and the results of the exam, and making any necessary changes to improve my strategy?

Summary Question

How can self-monitoring help improve the memory process?

SUMMARY

Memory increases with knowledge and practice. Study the techniques to improve memory. Understand them and use them to your benefit. As you progress, reward yourself for a job well done. Don't see difficulties as failures. See them as problems to be resolved through the effective use of technique and strategy. Build on your self-confidence as you build on your ability. Remembering what you learn is a critical step in achieving success as an active learner.

Review Questions

1. What are the three stages of memory suggested by an information-processing perspective?
2. Why is a functional approach useful for memory improvement?
3. How can the encoding, storage, and retrieval process each be improved?
4. What are the five steps in the strategy for remembering?
5. How does self-monitoring help improve the memory process?

CHAPTER REVIEW

To complete this chapter, answer the following questions. When you are finished, review the chapter to check your answers.

1. True or False: A major factor in memory improvement is the intent to remember.
2. True or False: Acronyms are an important encoding technique.
3. True or False: Repetition and rehearsal are common but not necessarily the most useful storage techniques.
4. True or False: Retracing steps sometimes helps retrieve lost information.
5. Which of the following explains the storage technique, acrostics?
   a. making up creative sentences that serve as a code for remembering important information
   b. developing a variety of visualization techniques that create mental pictures of information.
   c. looking for a relationship between what is studied and personal interests in order to make activities meaningful
   d. creating key-word associations between new terms and common words to store information in memory.
6. Which of the following is not a retrieval technique?
   a. self-testing
   b. overlearning
   c. retracing steps
   d. monitoring information

7. Design a strategy for memorizing the following information. Practice the techniques of your strategy until a self-test indicates 100 percent recall of the information.

   The artistic techniques used for illustrating children's picture books are:

   watercolor painting,
   oil painting,
   pen and ink illustration,
   woodcuts in black and white, and color,
   collage,
   stone lithography.

8. List the five steps of a strategy for remembering.

   ____

   ____

   ____

   ____

   ____

9. After practicing the techniques suggested for encoding, storage, and retrieval, state which are most useful for you and explain why.

   ____

   ____

   ____

   ____

10. Discuss how the various techniques for improving memory might be integrated with the strategy for studying textbooks in Chapter 6.

    ____

    ____

    ____

    ____

NOTES

1. Lester A. Lefton, *Psychology* (Boston: Allyn and Bacon, 1979).
2. Morris K. Holland and Gerald Tarlow, *Using Psychology: Principles of Behavior and Your Life*, 2nd ed. (Boston: Little, Brown, 1980).
3. Charles K. Levy, *Elements of Biology*, 3rd ed. (Reading, Mass.: Addison-Wesley, 1982), p. 123.

10

Taking Tests

Preview Exercise

Carefully preview the chapter with special attention to Predicting Test Questions and A Strategy for Taking Tests. Compare these topics with the strategies you currently use to prepare for and take tests. Look for similarities and differences.

PURPOSE FOR READING: ______________________________

____

____

Taking tests is a central feature of academic life. Tests, in their many forms, are the means instructors use to evaluate their students' learning. Successful strategies for reading, studying, and remembering are judged by tests. Consequently, successful test-taking strategies deserve close attention.

This chapter is divided into three parts. First, a method for predicting and practicing test questions is offered. Second, the problem of text anxiety, along with some possible solutions, is discussed. Finally, strategies for taking tests are examined in detail.

Guiding Questions

1. How can test questions be predicted and practiced?
2. How can test anxiety be avoided or overcome?
3. What general strategy can be used for taking tests?
4. How can the test-taking process be monitored?

PREDICTING TEST QUESTIONS

Learning begins by listening to lectures and taking notes, and by reading textbooks and completing assignments. The goal of studying is to identify which information is important to understand, to decide which is necessary to remember, and to apply useful memory techniques with periodic review. Previous chapters have explored these ideas in depth. Now it is time to consider how to predict test questions and to practice them in preparation for an exam.

Sources of Information

Sources of information for predicting test questions are many. Obviously, lecture notes and reading assignments provide most information. The more often you identify certain information as important, the more likely that material is to appear on a test. If, for instance, you read a chapter assignment in sociology on the causes of crime among youth, and your lecture notes also cover the same subject, it's a good guess that the topic of crime among youth will show up on an exam. Your identification of such information then leads you to predict a question on the topic—for example, "What are the causes of crime among youth?"

Instructors are also a good source of information. Many times their lectures indicate what to study. A lecturer might say, "This is especially important," or "That idea may be on the exam," or "Don't forget how that type of problem is solved." Many instructors also provide a review session or give direction on preparing for exams. They may specify what to study or which topics deserve special attention, and maybe even which ones they regard as less important. Finally, don't be afraid to ask the instructor for information. Ask questions like: "Is there anything special that should be reviewed?" "Should some topics be given more attention than others?" "What type of test is it?" and "How many questions?" The more information you have about the exam, the easier it is to form a plan of study.

Rethink lectures and class discussions. Important points tend to be repeated. Therefore, be aware of repetition. Instructors give clues to important points. An instructor might say, "Remember the discussion of . . . ?" or "Notice how this point of view appears in each of these arguments." Ask yourself, "What was given special attention in class?"

Students also help one another by exchanging information about instructors—what they expect of students, how they test, and how they grade. Clues about how to prepare for exams come from other students. Someone may say, "Watch out for the true–false questions. They're really tricky." That's important information.

A Brief Exercise

Take a few moments to think over your prior experience preparing for exams. Then, on separate paper, describe what sources of information you used and how you might plan to approach things in the future.

Practice Questions

Practice questions are one useful approach to preparing for exams. Once you have identified important information and predicted some questions, practicing your responses is the final preparation for the exam.

Remember the discussion of retrieval in the memory chapter? Retrieval of information is what exams require. Successful retrieval is a matter of practice. Like becoming a better basketball player, or a better salesperson, or a better writer, successful test-taking requires practice, plus a review of that practice and a desire to improve.

Practice questions offer you experience retrieving information, and they aid your memory because you spend additional time with the material.

Assume that you are taking a course on the environment.[1] In the course, the origins of agriculture are discussed. You learn that early in history humans survived by hunting for animals and gathering plants found in their immediate surroundings. Then about 12,000 years ago in the "fertile crescent" of Asia, the agricultural revolution began. People discovered that they could cultivate plants they found growing wild by planting seeds from the wild crops. They plowed fields and planted the seeds of wheat and oats and barley. Now they could provide a steady supply of food and establish more permanent settlements.

Assume that both you and your instructor decide this information is important enough for an exam. What questions might be predicted?

True–false questions are useful for studying specific facts, especially if you know the instructor uses true–false. For example,

True or False: The agricultural revolution began about 12,000 years ago.

That is a true statement. Yet, asking the question is better preparation than reading or memorizing alone, because it is practice for the test.

True–false questions also help you think about the importance of certain facts. For example,

True or False: Finding a steady food supply made life more stable for human society.

This statement is true although the point is not made specifically in the text. Its truth can be pieced together by thinking about how society might look today if people still went out each day to gather plants in order to eat. Furthermore, this type of question is good preparation for an essay question like, "Why was the agricultural revolution important to the development of human society?" Piecing information together helps interrelate facts and leads to greater understanding.

The factual information also suggests possible multiple choice questions. For instance,

Three sources of seed used in early agriculture were

a. beans, oats, and corn.
b. wheat, oats, and barley.
c. wheat, corn, and oats.
d. tomatoes, corn, and beans.

In this case (b) is the answer, with (c) only slightly incorrect (wheat and oats were used) and (a) and (d) clearly incorrect (tomatoes, corn, and beans were not discussed). Two points are of interest here. One is that sometimes very specific information is desired by an instructor. If you know that to be the case, creating a test question with very specific information is good practice. Second is that practice creating a few good multiple choice questions makes you aware how some responses can be fairly similar, such as (b) and (c), whereas others can be easily eliminated because of your experience with the text.

Look at how multiple choice questions might also stimulate thinking about a subject. For example,

Which of the following seems the most likely reason for the beginning of the agricultural revolution?

a. Hunting and gathering were no longer effective means of survival.

b. Human society probably learned about agriculture by closely observing nature and planting wild seeds.
c. Around 12,000 years ago, people decided that they wanted a more permanent source of food.
d. The agricultural revolution probably began as an historical accident.

This is an interesting question simply because it requires some thought. The best choice for a correct answer is (b). The possibility of raising food by planting wild seeds was surely learned by observing nature. Response (c) seems like a good answer, but a permanent source of food may include a good supply of animals for hunting, or access to good fishing waters, not necessarily agriculture. Learning to plant seeds and raise food successfully points toward agriculture.

Response (a) may be true, but no information presented suggested it as a reason. It may be that the rise of agriculture gave people a choice. Finally, response (d) doesn't really provide a reason; it's just a statement. You have to think further for the reason behind the "accident."

Finally, essay questions are predictable from the discussion of agriculture. There are some fairly brief questions such as "When did the agricultural revolution begin?" or "How did human society benefit from the agricultural revolution?" These questions require knowledge of facts. And some questions require more thought to link factual information with an understanding of its implications—such as "Why was the agricultural revolution such an important development in the history of human society?" or "Describe how the agricultural revolution most likely began." Essay questions frequently require that you not only recall information you have stored in memory, but also that you be able to think about it—analyzing, synthesizing, and evaluating information—and use it in many different ways.

Of course you wouldn't want to spend time predicting and practicing responses to all these questions for only a small amount of information. Decide what's important and how you'll be tested. Then practice accordingly. If you decide the agricultural revolution is a likely topic for the exam, and if you know the instructor gives multiple choice exams, then you also know your course of action: to create multiple choice questions about the agricultural revolution. The point is to predict and practice asking and answering questions in preparation for exams.

A Brief Exercise

Imagine studying the management of a small business such as a hardware store. First, you read to identify important information. Second, you predict likely test questions. And third, you practice answering those questions. Read the selection below, and write two true–false questions, two multiple choice questions, and two essay questions. Then identify or write out the correct response.

> Management of a small business such as a hardware store requires considerable effort. One primary concern for a manager is directing the activities of employees to make the business a success. In general, three steps guide the manager's plans: (1) The first step is to establish standards—what's expected of employees; (2) the second step is to compare an employee's performance with these standards—how well are things going; and (3) the third step is to correct any problems that arise—how to solve a particular problem.
>
> To be specific, a manager might decide that a certain employee must inventory paint supplies once a week to be sure there is a good supply of everything for the weekend. That's a standard. After three weeks the manager decides to check on the inventory to see if it's done on time. This comparison of the performance with the standard shows that sometimes the inventory is not complete because the employee has been busy with other projects. So that's a problem. In response the manager decides to ease the employee's workload to allow more time for the inventory. That's one approach to correcting a problem that should bring the inventory standard and the employee performance into line and make the business a success.

Now write the questions and the appropriate responses on a separate sheet of paper. Then compare your questions with the sample questions in the appendix.

Summary and Prediction Questions

1. Summary: How can test questions be predicted (identify sources of information) and practiced (discuss the different types of questions)?
2. Prediction: How can test anxiety be avoided or overcome?

OVERCOMING TEST ANXIETY

Every student probably experiences some anxiety when it's time to take a test. There's a certain tightening of the stomach muscles, a queasy feeling, an edginess or irritability in behavior, maybe a bit of a headache that suggests trouble ahead. Such anxiety is a response to those "internal" questions: "Am I ready for this test?" "Did I study the right material?" "How difficult are the questions?" "Will I pass?"

Some anxiety can be accepted as normal, a natural response to a challenging situation like an exam. Too much anxiety can be damaging, especially as that "challenging" situation becomes a "threatening" situation. When anxiety becomes overburdening, it must be overcome. At times it may be hard to distinguish between the anxiety of a challenge and the anxiety of a threat. So it's probably best to approach each new situation from a position of strength.

Careful preparation for a test is one important step toward taking tests successfully. Read the text. Take good notes. Study systematically. Review periodically. Predict questions and practice responses. All these activities provide the foundation for successful test-taking. A test at this point is merely one measure of success in a long process of active learning, so it is easily seen as a challenge, not a threat.

A positive attitude builds on careful preparation, and the two are mutually reinforcing. Think about those times when you've done your best preparing for a test, when you've felt confident about the challenge of the exam, and when the results of the tests rewarded your efforts and reinforced that attitude of success.

There are other times when for any number of reasons success slips out of reach. The only questions asked should be "Why?" or "How can I improve next time?" Even difficult times are challenges, not threats. They are a challenge to reexamine the what and why of the problem, and to replan for success. Perhaps you planned to study for an exam, but someone in your family became ill and you were too busy to get to the books. In the immediate, such situations are unavoidable. In the long run you might better plan for the unexpected by trying to stay ahead of a tight schedule. To respond that you have no time to study, or that you are a poor student, or that it doesn't matter anyway does nothing to solve the problem. A positive attitude is more likely to ease the pressure of a difficult situation and to promote a realistic assessment of how to solve the problem.

Many college counselors recognize that test anxiety limits students' performance. More and more frequently exercises in progressive relaxation are recommended to ease pressures and lower anxiety. The technique allows many students to perform more fully on an exam, rather than have their anxiety overburden their thoughts.

Progressive Relaxation

Progressive relaxation techniques are frequently used in conjunction with visualization activities. Since stress creates physical tension, progressive relaxation uses that tension to create a fuller awareness of it and to promote the experience of a progressive, gradual shift from tension to relaxation. The emphasis of the technique is on tensing and relaxing various muscles. Use the following exercise for practice in progressive relaxation.

An Exercise

Find yourself a quiet place to sit or lie down. Then simply follow each of the tension–relaxation steps listed below. As you follow the steps, remember to inhale as you tighten each muscle; exhale as you release and relax.

Step 1 Tighten your right fist; feel the tension build. Now release the fist. Let your hand go limp; feel the relaxation.
Next tighten your left fist; feel the tension. Now release; feel the relaxation.

Step 2 Bend your right arm, tightening your fist and your biceps. Hold it tight and feel the tension in your arm. Now release the tension and let your arm hang loose; feel the relaxation.
Next bend your left arm, tightening your fist and your biceps. Hold it tight and feel the tension in your arm. Now release the tension and let your arm hang loose; feel the relaxation.

Step 3 Straighten out your right arm until it feels stiff as the triceps tightens. Now release the tension and let the arm hang loose.
Next straighten out your left arm until it feels stiff. Then release the tension and let the arm hang loose.

Step 4 Close your eyes tight; feel the pressure mount. Now open your eyes and relax the tension.
Next clench your teeth; feel the pressure in your jaws. Now release your jaws and feel the relaxation.

Step 5 Inhale deeply and hold the breath tight in your lungs. Now release and feel the flow of relaxation.
Again, inhale; hold it. Exhale. Relax.

Step 6 Now tighten your stomach muscles; hold the tension. Now release the muscles and relax.
Again, tighten the stomach muscles; now relax.

Step 7 Straighten your legs and tighten your thighs, let the tension build. Now release the tension, let your legs lie loose, and feel the relaxation.
And again, straighten your legs and tighten your thighs. Now release the tension.

Step 8 Straighten your feet and tighten your calves. Now let your muscles go loose.
And again, tighten your calves; then release your muscles and feel the relaxation.

Step 9 Now relax your body completely, allowing it to lie limp. Feel the total relaxation that comes from a lack of tension.

When you feel tense, practice these exercises so that you learn how to approach difficult situations with a sense of relaxation and self-confidence. Taking tests is made easier when approached in a calm, self-confident manner.

Positive preparation, a positive attitude, and practice with progressive relaxation all help overcome test anxiety. Yet, sometimes such anxiety does not appear until the last moment, when the test is about to begin. At that point a quick fix is necessary, and a simple breathing and fist tighten–release exercise may help.

Since it is so important to begin a test with a good feeling, eliminate anxiety at the start. Begin by taking two or three slow, deep breaths to slow down the pace of events. Then hang your arms down straight, tighten your fists, and inhale deeply. Hold that position for a moment. Then release your fists and exhale, letting the tension flow out the ends of your finger tips. Repeat that procedure two or three times, and then continue with the exam. It's better to release anxiety, and the tension it creates, through a few simple exercises than to hide it or fight it and let it interfere with successful test-taking.

Summary and Prediction Questions

1. Summary: What action can you take to avoid or overcome test anxiety?
2. Prediction: What are the steps of a general strategy for taking tests?

A STRATEGY FOR TAKING TESTS

Successful test-taking requires a good deal of preparation. That point is clear. But successful test-taking also requires a strategy for taking the test itself. Think about that for a moment. Do you have a plan of attack when you sit down to take a test?

A strategy for test-taking is a plan that can be followed step by step, with each step increasing the likelihood of success. (See Figure 10.1.)

Follow Directions

First to be considered are the test directions. A successful test-taker must know what is to be done. Perhaps the directions are simple ones:

1. Read test directions twice; know what's required.
2. Preview the complete test; become familiar with the test and understand its purpose.
3. Plan a course of action; consider the number and type of questions, the number of points and times available, the best approach and where to begin.
4. Put the plan into action; with multiple choice tests, read the question completely, choose the best response, use a process of elimination, and be test wise; with essay tests, understand the question, outline a response, write clearly, and review briefly.
5. Briefly review the exam to be sure that it is complete.
6. Evaluate the test results; use the results as feedback to prepare for the next exam.

Figure 10.1 A Strategy for Taking Tests

"Below are 50 multiple choice questions. Read each question carefully and circle the letter of the correct response." The directions are clear and to the point: multiple choice questions, read carefully, circle the letter. Some directions are more complex. Perhaps the test is in two parts and some questions are worth more points than others: "This test is divided into two parts. The first part includes 10 short-answer questions worth 5 points each. The second part includes three lengthier essay questions worth 15 points each. Answer all questions clearly and completely." The directions here are also clear and to the point: two parts, 10 short answers worth 5 points each, three lengthier essays worth 15 points each. But this test is more complex than the first and requires more planning to do a successful job.

Read test directions at least twice. Read them first simply to find out what's required of you. Then read them a second time to be sure you understand the directions and to plan your approach to the test.

Preview the Exam

The next step is to preview the exam. Become familiar with the exam; try to understand its purpose. For instance, a 50-question multiple choice exam may ask mostly factual questions: "Long-term exposure to tobacco smoke causes (a) . . . , (b) . . . , (c) . . . , (d) . . . ." Recall of specific facts answers the question. However, perhaps the preview shows that many of the questions require more thought. Take a sample question from a business class: "Assume that there has been a slowdown in the economy causing sales to decline in your business. The six-month outlook is positive, but immediate costs must be cut. Which of the four cost-cutting strategies is most effective in bringing costs down while maintaining the morale of employees. (a) . . . , (b) . . . , (c) . . . , (d) . . . ." Obviously a question like this requires both specific knowledge and careful reflection. Previewing helps you plan how to divide your time between factual questions, which are answered quickly, and thought-provoking questions, which require more time for thinking.

A preview also offers the opportunity for developing a plan for completing the test. How many questions are there? What type of questions are asked? How difficult are the questions? Which questions offer the most points? How much time is available? Where is a good place to begin? What's my best approach?

Imagine, for instance, that a test is divided into two parts. The first part requires that two of three short-answer essays be completed, and the second part requires that one of three lengthy essay questions be done. Perhaps the preview indicates that each of the three short-answer questions is fairly easy, but the lengthy questions all seem fairly difficult. That assessment will surely affect how you plan for the exam, determining which questions to answer first and how much time to allot to each. Furthermore, if the directions indicate that the complicated essay is worth half the points on the test, by all means plan to devote at least 50 percent of your time to that question.

Reading the directions focuses your attention on the test. Previewing the questions provides you with the facts you need to plan an approach.

Plan Your Approach

The third step is a plan of action. Every test probably requires its own plan of action, but there are some useful strategies to keep in mind. To begin a test identify two or three questions that seem easy, and answer them first. That makes the initial experience positive and gets things started. You can even begin with question 1. Just don't start with questions that are confusing or create apprehension, or uneasiness, about the test.

Once you have a comfortable start, try to accumulate points quickly. Success is invariably based on total score, so work from the easiest questions to the most difficult. Skip problematic questions and return to them later. Some questions that seem difficult at first may be easier to answer once you have thought through other questions on the exam. And remember to pace yourself. Create a schedule for the test and try to keep it. Finally, leave some time at the end of the test to review your answers. If some questions are still unanswered, make some response. If there's no penalty for guessing with multiple choice or true–false, then guess. If you're unsure about an essay question, sketch some sort of reasonable response to show that you've at least thought about the question. Don't leave questions unanswered. Take chances and try your best.

Put the Plan into Action

The fourth step is putting the plan into action. Now the question is how to tackle individual questions. With multiple choice there are four steps of attack. First, read the question and each of the possible responses completely. Be sure to understand the question and the choices. Second, choose the best response. Don't jump to conclusions. Sometimes one answer is slightly better than another, so be careful. Third, if in doubt about an answer, use a process of elimination. Usually some choices can be readily eliminated, thereby narrowing the number of possibilities. Finally, consider the issue of "test wiseness." Correct responses are frequently longer than other choices. Compare the "stem," the initial part of the question, with the choices and consider each as a true–false question. Look at the grammar of the question, or the way a question is asked, as a clue to the answer. Consider the possibilities of "all of the above" or "none of the above" if those choices are listed. And use common sense. Don't answer a question with a response that doesn't make any sense.

Imagine, for instance, that you've been studying recycling as one solution to the problem of solid waste disposal, and the test question is multiple choice. Without any additional information, how would you answer this question:

The value of recycling as a response to the problem of waste disposal and pollution is

a. that it's a fairly easy process.
b. that it eliminates the problem of pollution.
c. that it converts waste back into usable commodities.
d. that it's a fairly inexpensive process.

Notice that the question can be restated: "How is recycling a response to waste disposal?" Then look at the responses. Response (a) indicates it's an easy process, but that doesn't tell you how and it may not be true. Response (b) initially appears as a likely answer, but it exaggerates the issue. There are many forms of pollution, and recycling will not solve all of them. Response (d) is a bit like (a). It may be true, but it doesn't really answer the question. That leaves (c). Response (c) is correct because it answers the question by providing an explanation. Furthermore, think test wise. The answer is most complete, slightly longer, and it makes sense. Multiple choice questions are a challenge that can be answered with the right strategy.

True–false questions are commonly used to test retention of details. Typically, true–false questions are statements of fact taken from a reading assignment or lecture notes. For instance, a true–false question might state that "The first step in a strategy for taking tests is to read the directions twice." The statement presents specific information and is true according to the information presented in this chapter. But you must be mindful of the exact wording for each question. Consider the statement, "Effective test-taking requires a written plan of action." It is true that effective test-taking requires a plan of action; but it's probably not one that's written, so the statement is false.

Because true–false questions appear to be simple statements, it is important to approach them with care. Consider the exact wording of the statement. Compare the wording with what you have studied. Be sure your response makes sense. And be alert to absolute words like "all," "only," "always," and "never," which are likely to make a statement false, and words like "some," "many," "sometimes," "usually," "often," and "generally," which suggest a statement is true. The best attack for true–false questions is to prepare fully, read carefully, and use good judgment.

Essay questions also require four steps of attack. First, understand the question. Key words like "define" or "list" suggest short-answer questions with a specific goal of defining a term or creating a list. Key words like "compare" and "contrast" give directions about how to organize information. To compare and contrast, you examine the similarities and differences of two things. Words like "explain" require a discussion of why or how something occurs. A word like "summarize" requires that you identify the salient (important) facts about a subject and present them in a brief, yet well-organized fashion.

The second step in attacking a lengthy essay is an outline. You need an outline to organize information as you think through a question. If your response will include three major points, the outline lists the points in order of presentation, with their supporting examples. Organizing an outline often brings to mind ideas that might otherwise have been overlooked.

The third step of attack is to write the essay clearly, logically, and completely. Introduce the subject first. Use organization words such as "The main point is . . . ," "Also," "In addition." And be sure to provide the necessary explanation or illustration to support each idea. (See Chapter 13 for a further discussion of writing.)

Finally, when you are finished writing, skim over your essay to be sure you've made your point and answered the question fully.

Take a close look at the example below. Imagine a business course where you are introduced to Frederick Taylor, the originator of "scientific management."[2] You learn that Taylor was concerned with a lack of standards between "a fair day's work" and a fair wage. His question was, "How can a job be done most efficiently?" His solution to this problem, which he believed was a great waste of resources, was to systematically analyze a particular job. He wanted to identify each aspect of a job (such as in his classic study of a man moving pig-iron) to determine how the best performance might be achieved and to prescribe the pace of each aspect of the job. Once clear standards were established not only would efficiency improve but also cooperation between management and labor since both would know what was expected.

Now imagine an essay question that directs you to: "Discuss the origin of scientific management." First, get your thoughts together with an outline. For example,

I. Frederick Taylor, originator, concerned with lack of standards and waste.
II. Analyzed jobs to see how they could be done more efficiently—prescribe pace of each activity.
III. Believed efficiency and worker–management cooperation would improve.

Next, write the essay following your outline. Note how the outline helps to identify important information and creates the organization for the essay.

Scientific management began with the work of Frederick Taylor. Taylor was concerned that there was a great deal of waste in business because of a lack of standards between a fair day's work and a fair wage. Therefore, Tay-lor began to systematically analyze specific jobs to determine how each activity could be done more efficient-ly. This analysis was then used to pre-scribe the pace of each activity. Tay-lor believed that a scientific approach to the management of the work place would promote efficiency in production and cooperation between management and labor. Taylor's early efforts estab-lished the foundation for a new ap-proach to management in the early twentieth century.

Finally, you want to briefly review the essay to be sure that you have included the information necessary to fully answer the question.

Briefly Review the Exam

Take time to briefly review your exam responses before turning in the exam paper or booklet. Be sure you have answered all questions according to the directions and to the best of your ability. Make sure you don't leave any questions unanswered unless there is a penalty for guessing. A brief review is usually all that is needed if you have planned carefully and followed through completely. But it's always wise to double-check your work to avoid overlooking any questions or directions. Then you can hand in the exam with the confidence that you've done the best job possible.

Evaluate the Results

Reviewing the results of an exam is also a useful way to prepare for future exams. Evaluate each item carefully with an eye both to strengths and to weaknesses. Did you follow directions? Was your plan well designed? Did you complete the exam? Do your errors suggest a specific problem that needs to be solved? Can you refine your approach to testing to save time, or be more relaxed, or review more carefully? Exam results are not merely a grade indicating your degree of success. They are also valuable feedback that can be used to prepare for future exams. Use such information wisely.

A Brief Exercise

Read the following selection an "the historic role of unions."[3] Then predict three questions—one true–false, one multiple choice, and one essay—that identify important information. Practice the appropriate response.

> The historic role of unions was to balance the economic power of the employer. The employees, through their elected representatives, negotiate the terms of employment with company officials. The agreement thus reached by "equals" becomes the accepted mode of conduct between the parties for a contracted period of time.
>
> The union is much more than an economic institution. It has political characteristics, seeking to use its political power and public opinion to accomplish its goals. Even collective bargaining is a more complicated concept than it appears on the surface. Broadly speaking, *collective bargaining* refers to a process by which employers and employee representatives attempt to arrive at agreements governing the conditions under which employees will contribute and be compensated for their services.

Next review Figure 10.1, "A Strategy for Taking Tests." Finally, take the brief quiz that follows and compare your answers with a review of the selection.

Quiz

Directions: Answer each of the following questions as accurately as possible.

1. True or False: The historic role of unions was to balance the economic power of the employer.

2. True or False: The unions were only equal in a relative sense.

3. Unions are more than economical institutions because
   a. they bargain collectively.
   b. they decide how a business is run.
   c. they seek to improve working conditions.
   d. they seek to influence the political process.

4. Define the term "collective bargaining."

   ____

   ____

5. Explain how a union may benefit employees.

   ____

   ____

Summary and Prediction Questions

1. Summary: What are the steps of a general strategy for taking tests?
2. Prediction: How can the test-taking process be monitored?

MONITORING THE TEST-TAKING PROCESS

A Brief Exercise

Throughout this book checklists of questions are used to monitor various learning processes. The test-taking process can be monitored in the same way. Your task now is to review the major issues discussed in this chapter and create a list of questions to use as a self-monitoring checklist. Do this exercise on a separate sheet of paper. Then compare your list with the suggested list immediately below.

A Self-Monitoring Checklist

_____ Do I check important sources of information in preparation for an exam?

_____ Am I using practice questions with important information, emphasizing true–false, multiple choice, or essay questions according to the type of exam given?

_____ Am I careful to prepare fully and approach test-taking with a positive attitude?

_____ Do I use my progressive relaxation technique, if necessary?

_____ Am I approaching my exams in a systematic way,

- _____ reading directions?
- _____ previewing the test?
- _____ planning my approach?
- _____ putting the plan into action?
- _____ briefly reviewing?
- _____ evaluating the results?

_____ When evaluating the results of an exam, am I careful to distinguish between errors that relate to the material studied and errors that relate to my test-taking strategy?

_____ Am I having difficulty with any specific aspect of the test-taking process?

_____ Is any corrective action necessary?

_____ What else can I do to improve my test-taking ability?

Monitoring the test-taking process is crucial to academic success, and evaluating your test results requires distinguishing between errors due to inadequate study and errors due to test-taking. Suppose you erred on a multiple choice question. To evaluate the error, ask yourself two questions, "Is the answer wrong because I forgot something, was confused, or overlooked something while studying?" *and* "Was the error caused by misreading the questions, failing to consider all possible choices, or overlooking the question?" If you cannot identify the source of the problem, make an appointment to see your instructor and ask for some advice. Determining the cause of an error is crucial for taking the appropriate corrective action. Careful self-monitoring allows you to assess your learning and take control of your potential for success.

Summary Question

How can the test-taking process be monitored?

SUMMARY

Each step in the test-taking process from careful preparation to active self-monitoring is an important step on the road to academic success. Overcoming test anxiety and applying a systematic approach to taking tests places you in control of learning. A detailed evaluation of test results provides you with the feedback for refining your strategies whether that involves creating more practice questions or reading the exam questions more carefully. Each experience helps you become a more skillful test-taker and a more successful learner.

Review Questions

1. How can test questions be predicted and practiced?
2. How can test anxiety be avoided or overcome?
3. What general strategy can be used for taking tests?
4. How can the test-taking process be monitored?

CHAPTER REVIEW

To complete this chapter, answer the following questions. When you are finished, review the chapter to check your answers.

1. True or False: Outlining your response to an essay question is usually too time consuming for a lengthy test.
2. True or False: Practice test questions should only be used if the instructor has identified the important information to be studied.
3. True or False: Self-monitoring of the test-taking process is only helpful once the test results are available.
4. True or False: A planned approach to test-taking increases the likelihood of success.
5. Which of the following steps immediately precedes turning in an exam?
   a. a brief review of the test
   b. a careful evaluation of the questions
   c. a rereading of the directions
   d. a review of the plan of action
6. Practice questions
   a. improve your chances of success.
   b. provide you with practical test-taking experience.

c. increase your awareness of test questions.
d. do all of the above.

7. List the six steps in a strategy for taking tests.

____

____

____

____

____

____

8. Discuss how you might deal with the problem of test anxiety.

____

____

____

____

9. How will you use self-monitoring in preparing for your next exam?

____

____

____

____

10. Evaluate your own efforts to create practice test questions. What difficulties do you encounter? What benefits are gained? Do you feel that practice questions give you an advantage on exams?

____

____

____

____

____

____

NOTES

1. Adapted from W. Norman Richardson and Thomas H. Stubbs, *Evolution, Human Ecology and Society* (New York: Macmillan, 1976), pp. 57–58.
2. Adapted from James H. Donnelly, Jr., James L. Gibson, and John M. Ivancevich, *Fundamentals of Management: Functions, Behavior Models*, 4th ed. (Plano, Texas: Business Publications, 1981), pp. 43–44.
3. Robert M. Fulmar, *The New Management*, 2nd ed. (New York: Macmillan, 1978), p. 189.

11

Studying Science and Math

Preview Exercise:

Before your preview, make a list of techniques that you use to study science and math. Which approaches have been useful to you in the past? As you preview the chapter, compare the topics introduced with your methods of study.

PURPOSE FOR READING: ______________________________

____

____

Science and math are subjects many students try to avoid. Sooner or later, however, degree requirements or career goals are likely to demand the study of science and mathematics. Even students who like science and math—who enjoy carrying out experiments, solving problems, seeking to discover the unknown—find reading textbooks in these areas tough going.

Why do so many students find the study of science and math so difficult? For most students the problems center on language (new concepts and specialized terminology), on the information load (most science and math texts fill each page with a wealth of information and sometimes it seems too much), and on a method for bridging the gap between the known and the unknown (how to extend understanding the commonsense meaning of a "rock" to a geological knowledge of "rocks," for example).

The purpose of this chapter is to explore some of these issues with an emphasis on strategies for studying textbooks, learning new concepts, solving problems, and remembering important information in science and mathematics.

Guiding Questions

1. What strategies can be used to study science textbooks?
2. How are new concepts systematically learned?
3. What steps can be followed to solve science and math problems?
4. How can new information from science and math be mastered for remembering?
5. What questions are used to monitor the study process?

STUDYING TEXTBOOKS

The organization of science textbooks is not unlike that of textbooks in other subjects. Students typically find the material more formidable because they have little prior experience with it or because the language of science is less familiar.

Mathematics books tend to look different from other textbooks because they follow a sequential pattern of development (presenting a series of steps that develop into a mathematical understanding of a topic) and because they emphasize formulas and problems (creating a text where symbols and problem solving are substituted for the common language of explanation and illustration). A close look at a math text is presented later in the discussion of problem solving.

Chapter Previews and Graphic Overviews

As you well know by now, study of any textbook chapter should begin with a preview of it. Previews give you an idea of the scope of the chapter and sequence of information. Moreover, previewing chapter-end questions focuses your attention on specific types of important information.

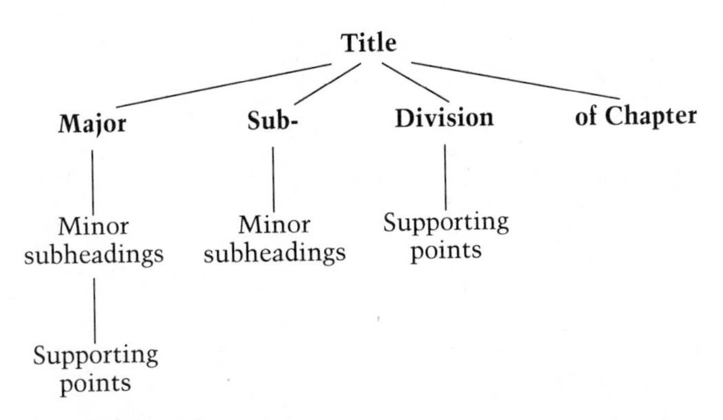

Figure 11.1 Graphic Organizer

This preview process can be taken a step further to help you organize the information and, thereby, make it more meaningful and manageable. This form of organization is referred to as a "graphic organizer" or "graphic overview.[1]"

In Chapter 7 you studied a note-taking procedure called mapping. In Chapter 9 the previewing exercise called for a map of the chapter based on the various subheadings. A graphic organizer is a similar method for organizing textbook information into an easily understandable form.

Look at the typical textbook chapter; it undoubtedly begins with a boldly lettered title. Make this title the title of the graphic organizer. As you proceed through the chapter, notice that some subheadings are in larger or bolder print than others. These differences indicate the subdivisions in the chapter. The major subdivisions usually have the largest subheadings; minor subheadings or supporting points usually have smaller subheadings within major subdivisions. By organizing major subdivisions under the main heading and supporting points under major subdivisions, a graphic overview is created. (See Figure 11.1.) This overview then helps you keep in mind the relationship among ideas within the chapter and establishes a useful organization for keeping track of the numerous details presented in each discussion.

Consider the following example from a geology text.[2] The title of the chapter is "The Materials of Geology—Rocks." That title becomes the heading of the graphic organizer. Proceeding through the chapter, three major subdivisions are identified: "Sedimentary Rocks," "Igneous Rocks," and "Metamorphic Rocks." So there are three major subdivisions on the chart. The minor subdivisions, or supporting points, under "Sedimentary Rocks" include "Cementation," "Characteristics of Sedimentary

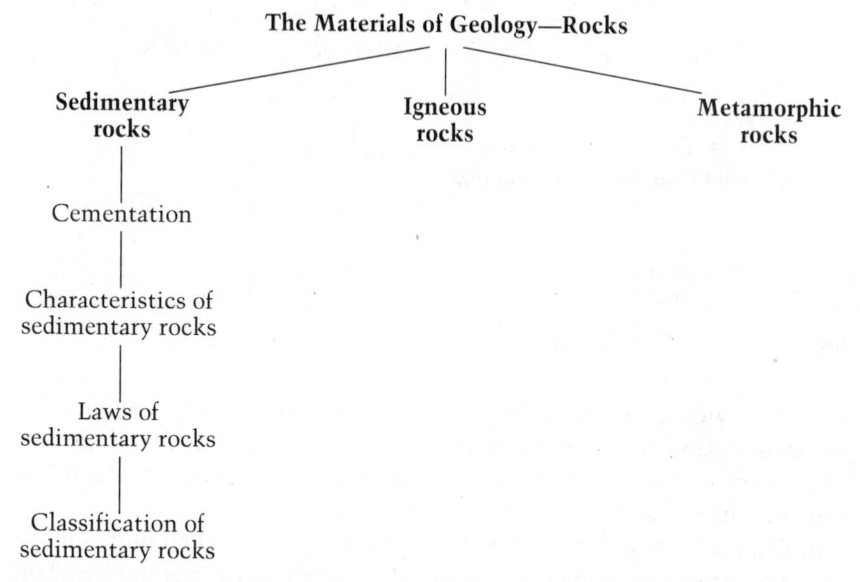

Figure 11.2 Graphic Organizer—Geology

Rocks," "Laws of Sedimentary Sequences," and "Classification of Sedimentary Rocks." A graphic organizer of this information presents the distinct subdivisions of a chapter, an understandable organization for studying information, and a clear indication of what is required to master the chapter. (See Figure 11.2.)

The organization of a graphic organizer, such as the one on rocks, identifies quickly the important information to know and the important distinctions for organizing detailed information. In addition, the subdivisions under sedimentary rocks focus study ("What are the characteristics of sedimentary rocks?"). And they predict test questions ("Identify and discuss the laws of sedimentary sequences"). Moreover, since science chapters are typically filled with detail, this graphic overview keeps the basic organization as a guide for keeping details in their proper places.

A Brief Exercise

Select a chapter from a science text—physical science, biology, oceanography, nursing—and make a graphic organizer. Use the subheadings of the chapter as the subdivisions of the organizer. (More complex chapters require more space than one sheet of notebook paper, but the organization still follows the same logical subdivisions.)

Once you've completed your graphic organizer, identify the major subdivisions and think about how they might help you with a plan of study. Notice how subheadings focus your reading efforts. And predict some likely test questions. Graphic organizers create an excellent foundation for study.

Following the Organization

Science writing, like other forms of writing, uses a number of different patterns such as those discussed in Chapter 6, "Reading Textbooks." Yet, there is also a typical pattern of organization that is useful to know because that pattern suggests an approach to reading and studying.

The pattern is actually quite easy to follow. First, the text introduces an idea. For instance, in a textbook discussion of how plants respond to their growing environment, the concept of "photoperiodism"[3] is introduced. Second, the text defines the idea. In this example, the text notes that plants respond to the length of light in a 24-hour period, which changes throughout the year and is fairly regular. Third, quite often the text's author clarifies the definition by specifying examples that make an abstract idea more concrete and therefore easier to grasp. In this case, the clarifying sentence is: "Photoperiodic responses in plants include initiating dormancy, flowering, germination, and stem and root development." Fourth, the discussion elaborates on the idea, usually laying the groundwork for the next step in the discussion. The text on photoperiodism continues with an explanation of how the light-absorbing pigment in plants works.

So a typical pattern is established: introduction, definition, clarification, and elaboration. A careful reader is aware of what to look for while reading and of how previously unknown information may begin to make sense.

The pattern also suggests certain questions. In one way, the introduction of a new idea poses a question to guide reading—in the example: "What is photoperiodism?" In another way, the pattern also suggests a way to check your comprehension: "Define photoperiodism and explain how it works." Asking yourself such questions as you read creates a more active involvement with the material.

Finally, notice that since chapter discussions usually explore concepts through detailed examination of specific information, linking ideas to one another, learning is again a cumulative process. Each stage leads to the next. Therefore, identifying new ideas, asking questions, examining points of definition and clarification, checking your comprehension, and following the author's presentation to the next stage is a beneficial approach to reading science.

A Brief Exercise

As you read the following selection from a biology text,[4] answer each of the following questions as you progress through the selection.

The idea introduced is ______________________________

It can be defined as ______________________________

______________________________.

Examples are ______________________________

______________________________.

The authors elaborate on the idea by discussing the difference between

______________________ and ______________________.

> All the diverse substances that occur naturally on earth are alike in two respects: they occupy space and have mass. All contain one or more types of about ninety naturally occurring **elements**, which are materials that cannot be decomposed into substances with different properties.
>
> By international agreement, a one- or two-letter chemical symbol stands for each element, regardless of the element's name in different countries. For example, what we call *nitrogen* is called *azoto* in Italian and *stickstoff* in German. But the symbol for this element is always N. Similarly, the symbol for the element sodium is always Na (from the Latin *natrium*).
>
> * * *
>
> Different elements combine in proportions that are fixed and unvarying to form **compounds**. For example, the compound water has a fixed proportion of two elements: 11.9 percent hydrogen to 88.1 percent oxygen by mass. Compounds are unlike **mixtures**, in which two or more elements can be present in varying proportions. Seawater is a mixture. It consists of sodium, chlorine, potassium, calcium, sulfur, magnesium, and other substances dissolved in water, but the percentage of each substance varies from place to place. The compound water is 11.9 percent hydrogen and 88.1 percent oxygen no matter where you find it.

After reading the passage, write out two or three questions you predict an instructor might ask about the material. Compare your questions with those in the appendix.

Use of Illustration

Science textbook writers make considerable use of illustrations to help clarify the complex information presented in the text. In fact, many writers assume that a reader works back and forth between text and illustration until some complex thought is clearly understood.

For instance, a geology book's elaborate discussion of plate tectonics and continental drift becomes much more meaningful with an illustration of how the continents may have fit together ages ago. Or, in a discussion of plants, the details of how water is absorbed by the root structure of a plant may quickly make sense with an illustrated cross section of the root structure.

Figure 11.3 presents a typical science text illustration used to clarify how volcanism contributed to the changing Earth's atmosphere.[5] The illustration creates a visual understanding of how a volcanic explosion "contributed large quantites of water, carbon dioxide, and other gases to the air and materials to the land." Careful attention to illustrations, on the part of the reader, contributes greatly to clarifying complex ideas more difficult to understand through text alone.

Illustrations help clarify a text when the two are approached interactively. Read the text and study the illustration. Then work your way back and forth between the two until you can say to yourself, "Now I've got it."

A Brief Exercise

In a science text locate two or three passages where the discussion is supported by a detailed illustration. Then read the selection and study the illustration. Unless it is a required assignment, don't try to achieve total mastery. Just focus on how the illustrations help clarify certain points or make certain relationships more obvious. Think about how more attention to illustration could help you with your reading comprehension and retention.

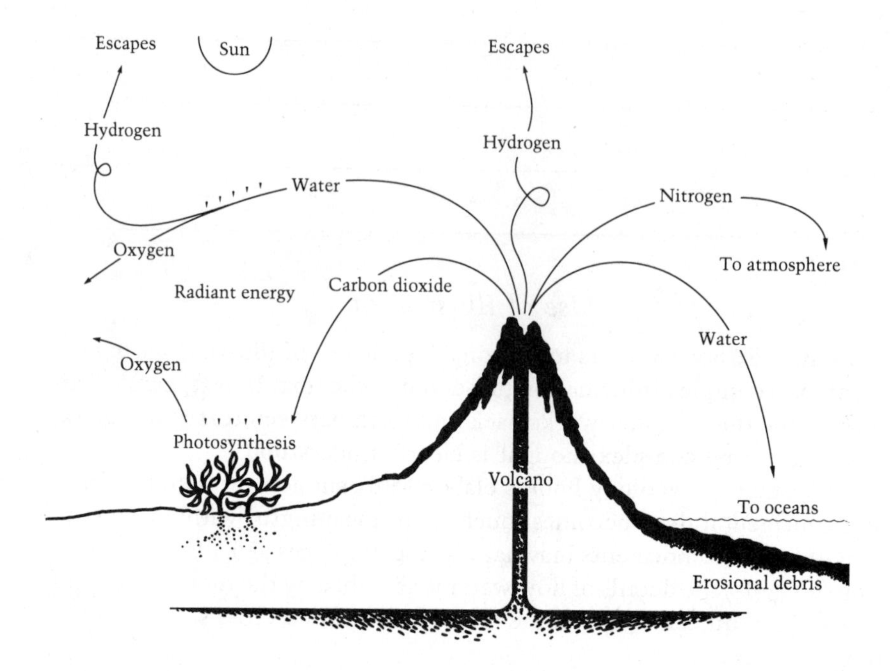

Volcanism has contributed large quantities of water, carbon dioxide, and other gases to the air and materials to the land.

Figure 11.3 A Typical Science Text Illustration

Summary and Prediction Questions

1. Summary: What strategies can be used to study science textbooks?
2. Prediction: How are new concepts systematically learned?

LEARNING CONCEPTS

In science, as in other subjects, reading is a search for meaning. Typically, though, the sciences introduce a large number of new concepts. Since learning any new subject proceeds more smoothly with a systematic approach to study, three guiding principles will help you to learn concepts from science: (1) Approach reading as a search for understandable explanations. (2) Use prior knowledge and experience to translate new information into meaningful form. And (3) apply specific techniques of study for remembering information.

First, consider how the search for understandable explanations is a useful guide. Read the next two sentences about the "Earth's axis of rotation."[6] Then briefly note what you learn.

The largest of the terrestrial planets, Earth revolves around the Sun in an orbit that deviates from a circle by just over 3 percent. Were it not for the 23° 27′ inclination to the plane of its orbit of Earth's axis of rotation, there would be, at each latitude, only a 7 percent variation of temperature during the year—either eternal spring, summer, fall, or winter.

You might notice first that the orbit of the Earth around the Sun is just about equal to a circle, deviating only 3 percent. But there is an angle of the Earth's axis of rotation that has some influence over things like temperature.

Continue reading to see what else you can find out about this axis.

Like many things about the Earth, the axis of rotation is not fixed but slowly changes its direction among the stars. Thus the axis's northern end, which points roughly in the direction of the pole star, is drifting very slowly away from that direction. In about 26,000 years, it will once again point in its present direction. The reason for this so-called precession is pull exerted on the Earth by the Sun and the Moon.

Some very specific information is presented here. First, the axis of rotation is not fixed, but changes slowly. Second, its cycle of change is about 26,000 years. Third, the reason is the pull on the Earth by the Sun and Moon, called precession.

How does prior knowledge help you understand the new information and make it more meaningful? You may already know that the Earth rotates on an axis that is at an angle to the Sun. That's one primary reason for the change of seasons. In this case, such prior knowledge makes reading easier because the facts are familiar. Keeping in mind what you already know makes learning a new term like "precession" easier.

Now read the next four sentences. Look for a further explanation of precession and think about how this discussion helps clarify your understanding the axis of rotation.

The Earth is slightly oblate so that it has, like some of its inhabitants, a bulge at its equator. The precession motion is essentially like the wobble of a spinning top, the wobbles occurring 26,000 years apart. It has been calculated that if only the Sun were producing the precession of the Earth's axis, the period would be nearly three times longer. Actually, the axis of rotation is not exactly fixed with respect to the surface, and so the true north pole and south pole wander a little in the region, as do the magnetic poles.

Much of this discussion is about precession and its influence on the axis of rotation. And the material is translated into a common language for you. For the Earth to be oblate is for it to have a bulge at its center, like some overweight people. The rotation effect created is like the wobble of a spinning top. Visualizing these two points mentally increases your understanding. You also learn that the axis of rotation on the Earth may shift a bit. In this case, the most obvious benefit in reading for understandable explanations is that the text itself attempts to tap your prior experience to translate ideas of science into a common language.

Now read the two final sentences, which will modify further your understanding of the shape of Earth, suggesting why the axis of rotation is not a fixed phenomenon.

Precise measurements of the orbits of the innumerable artificial satellites that circle the Earth have shown that it is slightly pear-shaped, the North Pole being some 20 meters higher than the average surface and the South Pole correspondingly lower. Also, the equator is not exactly circular, projecting 60 meters in the vicinity of the eastern Pacific and having an 80-meter depression in the Indian Ocean.

Here you learn the Earth is somewhat pear-shaped and the equator is not exactly circular, factors that you can guess affect the axis of rotation.

Notice how, over the course of the material, information is accumulated about the axis of rotation. Notice also how both your search for understanding, plus the value of translating ideas on the basis of prior knowledge, directed your comprehension of the text.

Consider how this material might be organized for study. A traditional note-taking form would emphasize topic plus detail. For example:

Earth's axis of rotation

1. revolves around sun about equal to a circle
2. axis is at an angle (23° 27′)
3. axis changes slowly (26,000 years)
4. affected by pull of sun and moon, called precession
5. Earth oblate, so rotates like the wobble of a spinning top
6. influenced by pear-shaped Earth and noncircular equator

The problem with this approach is that the emphasis is probably on memorizing a long list of items, which may appear at first to contain over-

Front Side

Earth's

axis of rotation

Back Side

revolves around sun at an

angle like wobble of a

spinning top (precession =

pull of Moon & Sun) affected

by oblate, pear shape

Figure 11.4 A Flash Card

whelming detail. Concept understanding becomes a task of memorizing a list of details. A more selective approach, and a common one, would be to make up "flash cards."

The benefit of a flash card is its convenience. A concept can be identified on one side of a 3″ × 5″ note card, and a selection of important ideas can be listed on the reverse side. Figure 11.4 is an example.

The flash card approach emphasizes the selection of critical information that is easier to practice and more memorable. Note that the information is translated from scientific terminology into common English. Certain details can be added (such as the specific angle of rotation) if that information is necessary for some reason. Flash cards are useful for the

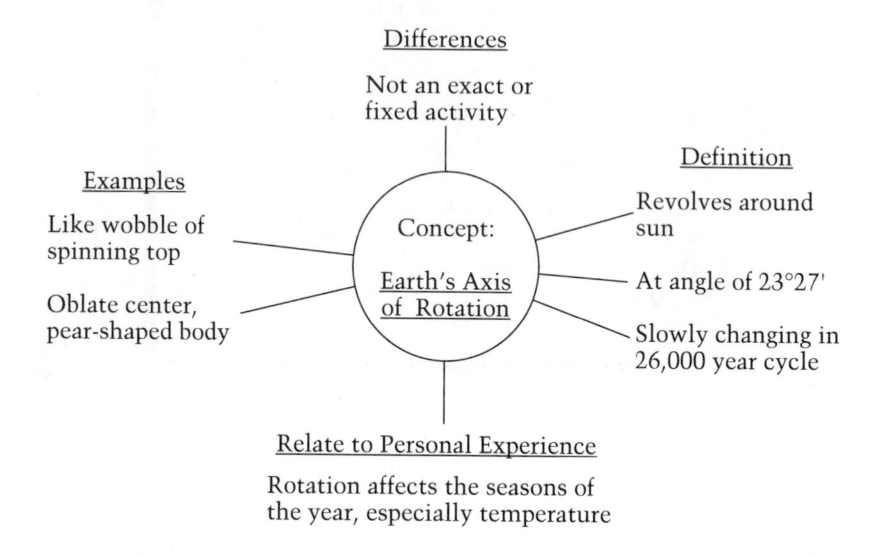

Figure 11.5 Semantic Map

study of new concepts because information is selectively identified and precisely stated.

A third technique, perhaps even more useful, is the approach to concept development discussed in Chapter 8. This approach is more graphic than the flash card approach and identifies an array of information more clearly. For an example, see Figure 11.5.

Clearly this semantic map provides more detailed information than a flash card would, looking at the concept from various perspectives. It is best used as a model to aid understanding. It considers definitions, examples, and prior knowledge and experience, and it invites reflection on what a concept is *not*. Gaining such understanding should precede trying to memorize the facts. Yet, it is also a useful model for enhancing memory because it clearly delineates various elements and can easily be used for self-testing. Most of all, remember that a semantic map is designed to assist instruction. When a full understanding and thorough recall of complex information are necessary, it's an extremely useful tool. If it is overused, it may become a time-consuming overemphasis on detail. Use it selectively to your benefit. (See Chapter 8 for a review of this approach.)

A BRIEF EXERCISE

Read the following selection on "skeletal muscle."[7] Follow the three strategies for learning concepts: (1) Approach reading as a search for understandable explanations. (2) Use prior knowledge and experience to translate new information into meaningful form. And (3) apply specific techniques of study for remembering information—in this case use semantic mapping. A sample map is provided in the appendix.

> Skeletal muscle, as its name implies, is connected by tendons or other connective tissues to the bones and cartilage of the skeleton and to some of the body's fleshy parts, such as the face and the tongue. The action of skeletal muscle maintains body posture, brings about movement of the skeleton by exerting pull on bones across joints, and allows us to speak and change our facial expression. These are complicated tasks and account for the fact that skeletal muscle comprises about 40 percent of total body weight in men and 25 percent in women. Skeletal muscle is sometimes referred to as *voluntary muscle* because it controls our voluntary actions and is hence under our conscious control.
>
> Skeletal muscle tissue forms what people commonly refer to as their muscles. A typical skeletal muscle is composed of *muscle cells,* also called *muscle fibers,* and noncontractile connective tissue elements that serve to organize the muscle cells into an effective mechanical unit.
>
> * * *
>
> The connective tissues of a muscle serve to connect the muscle with other types of connective tissue to which the muscle is attached. For example, the connective tissues of skeletal muscles that move bones are continuous with tendons at the ends of the muscles; the tendons, in turn, attach to bones by merging with the periosteum.
>
> In addition to muscle cells and connective tissues, skeletal muscle tissue contains nerves that stimulate it to contract and capillaries that provide it with oxygen and necessary nutrients.

Summary and Prediction Questions

1. Summary: How are new concepts systematically learned?
2. Prediction: What steps can be followed to solve science and math problems?

SOLVING PROBLEMS

The process of solving problems in math and science is an important one. It is common to hear scientists talk about the scientific method, a step-by-step way to investigate the natural world. The approach is an ideal model that creates a formal method for solving problems. The steps are (1) making observations of a particular phenomenon such as acid rain, (2) formulating a hypothesis about how it affects a specific environment, (3) designing and conducting an experiment to investigate the impact of acid rain, (4) analyzing the results of the experiment and drawing some conclusions, (5) evaluating the initial hypothesis on the basis of the results, and (6) formulating a theory based on the investigation. Applying this method furthers scientific understanding of the natural world and builds the knowledge base for further study.

Problem solving is the fundamental way students of math and science understand the knowledge currently available to mathematicians and scientists. The chemist may want students to understand how a certain chemical reaction is achieved in the laboratory. A biologist may want students to understand the evolutionary process of genetic diversity from the perspective of cell division. And a math instructor may want students to understand the logic of a number system. Whatever the case, each activity involves a careful understanding of a step-by-step, or sequential, approach to a particular problem.

With reference to the study of science and math, a basic five-step approach to problem solving is useful. First, it is imperative to identify important information. This information is usually presented in a very specific way. Second, recognize how this information is translated into scientific language (H_2O) or a specific mathematical formula ($A = p(1 + r)^n$ is the compound interest formula). Third, study any sample problems. Fourth, take this information and apply it to practice problems in order to understand and carry out the procedure whether through an experiment, with sample problems, or chapter questions. Fifth, repeat the steps, particularly 3 and 4, until mastery of the material is achieved.

Consider how this process might work with an examination of stream erosion in a geology text.[8] Among the points of important information are (1) that a stream can be studied by looking at the elevation of the stream from its source to its mouth, or base level, and charting the changes on a "longitudinal profile," and (2) that erosion conditions vary according to amounts of sediment carried and the slope of the stream; additionally, (3) the longitudinal profile of many streams is represented by a mathematical equation.

The important points are translated into the mathematical equation.

The equation can be derived by assuming that the tendency of a stream to erode at any particular point along its profile is directly proportional to the height of a stream above base level. Thus let

H = elevation above base level

X = distance downstream from source

a and b = positive constants

If the tendency of a stream to erode (dH/dx) is proportional to its elevation above base level, then,

$$\frac{dH}{dx} = bH \quad \text{or} \quad \frac{dH}{H} = -b\,dx$$

thus

$$\ln H = bx + a \text{ and } H = ae^{-bx}$$

This equation leads to a set of curves . . ."[9]

Note that whether or not you can understand all the elements of the equation, its basic purpose is clear. It establishes a basis for determining when streams are in equilibrium, or "graded." Next, you could study any supporting illustrations presented in the text to see how the equation created a longitudinal profile or read further for a discussion of specific examples.

Now, if you had to solve a problem regarding stream erosion, you would practice applying the equation to the data until you mastered the process. Clearly, this is not a simple task, but the strategy offers specific direction and repetition of the practice problems will ultimately lead to success.

A Brief Exercise

For practice applying the five basic steps suggested for solving problems in math and science, read the following selection from a math text.[10] As you read, (1) identify important information, (2) locate the translation of information to scientific language such as a formula, (3) study any sample problems offered as examples, (4) apply this information to the practice exercise, and (5) repeat the process if necessary.

Empirical or Experimental Probability

Empirical probability is based on past experiences and is used to determine what "probably" will or will not occur in the future. Empirical probability is used in manufacturing, educational tests and measurements, genetics, weather forecasting, insurance, investments, opinion polls, and other areas where present-day data are used to predict future trends.

Empirical probability can only suggest what should happen on the basis of present-day knowledge. It cannot guarantee that an event will or will not occur. Old Faithful, a geyser at Yellowstone National Park, has erupted about once every hour since records of its activities have been kept. It will "probably" continue to erupt once every hour today and for many years to come. However, the fact that it has always erupted in the past is no guarantee that it will continue to erupt in the future.

The empirical probability of an event is the relative frequency of the event. . . . The empirical probability of event E, symbolized by $P'(E)$, is based on actual observations and is determined by this formula.

$$P'(E) = \frac{\text{number of times event } E \text{ has occurred}}{\text{total number of times the experiment has been performed}}$$

A probability will always be a number between 0 and 1, inclusive, and may be expressed as a decimal, a fraction, or a percent. An empirical probability of 0 indicates that the event has never occurred. An empirical probability of 1 indicates that the event has never failed to occur.

Example 1

George Montgomery threw 960 strikes out of 1430 pitches. Find the empirical probability of his throwing a strike when he throws a pitch.

Solution

Montgomery threw 960 strikes in 1430 attempts.

$$P' (\text{Montgomery throws a strike}) = \frac{960}{1430} = 0.67. \square$$

List important information from the selection:

____

____

____

____

Write the formula for computing empirical probability:

____

Give the probability of the sample exercise:

Practice Exercise: If a pitcher has pitched 16 of the last 50 games, what is the empirical probability of him pitching the next game?

$$P'(\qquad\qquad) = \qquad = .$$

Repeat the process if necessary. Answers are located in the appendix.

Approaching problem solving in math and science is made easier if it is done systematically.

Summary and Prediction Questions

1. Summary: What steps can be followed to solve science and math problems?
2. Prediction: How can new information from science and math be mastered for remembering?

REMEMBERING INFORMATION

Developing an understanding of science or math requires incorporating new ideas into your current store of knowledge in memory. Using a variety of strategies to gain an initial understanding contributes to memory activities simply because understanding and familiarity make the information meaningful. And meaningful material is more readily stored in memory. Moreover, a working knowledge of the fundamentals in science and math lays the groundwork for investigating more complex ideas.

To promote memory, traditional techniques such as verbal rehearsal and active recitation—talking yourself through information—can be very useful for increasing familiarity. For instance, the formula for converting the temperature scale Fahrenheit to Celsius is $C = 5/9\ (F - 32)$. Verbally repeating the formula to prepare for its use on an exam is a useful adjunct to working practice problems. The formula must be remembered to solve the problem.

In addition, specific techniques such as acronyms or acrostics (creative sentences) are useful for learning lists of facts. Imagine, for instance, that you wanted to remember the names of the planets in the solar system. A creative sentence might begin, "*M*any *v*isitors *e*arned *m*oney *j*umping . . . ." The translation is, "*M*ercury, *V*enus, *E*arth, *M*ars, *J*upiter. . . ." The assumption behind acrostics as a memory tool is that the sentence image is relatively easy to store and will stimulate an association with the planet list, making it retrievable from memory.

Visualizing information and sketching pictures of information also promotes storage and retrieval of information. The semantic mapping technique for concept development is partially based on creating a visual image of the relationship among ideas. Furthermore, science and math frequently explore systems of information that are not usefully learned with traditional techniques because of the complexity of information. First, a visual approach relies on special attention to the textbook's illustrations to clarify ideas. If, for instance, a geology text explores the importance of volcanism in the history of the earth, a careful study of supporting figures may provide a more complete overview or a more identifiable integration of process. Illustrations frequently present information wholistically—as a package—while a text discussion proceeds sequentially. Illustration, thereby, clarifies.

Second, using a visual approach also means creating your own visual aids for study. For example, introductory biology texts frequently discuss cell structure and invariably use illustrations to clarify the discussion. To become more familiar with cell structure and to practice storage and retrieval of new information, try drawing cell structures. See Figure 11.6, for a sample sketch of a cell structure.[11] The value of this drawing as an aid to memory is that the initial act of creating the figure increases familiarity with the material. In addition, for later study, the labels can be covered for practice in identifying parts and then uncovered for immediate feedback. A working memory is developed through active involvement with the material. This type of activity is readily applicable to any study of biological systems such as the heart or brain where identifying parts and understanding their function is important.

A Brief Exercise

Find a textbook for an introductory course in biology, or chemistry, or physical science. Locate some discussion that uses both written text and illustration to explain organization of a complex system such as the human brain and identify its parts. Read the text and study the illustrations. When you are ready, create your

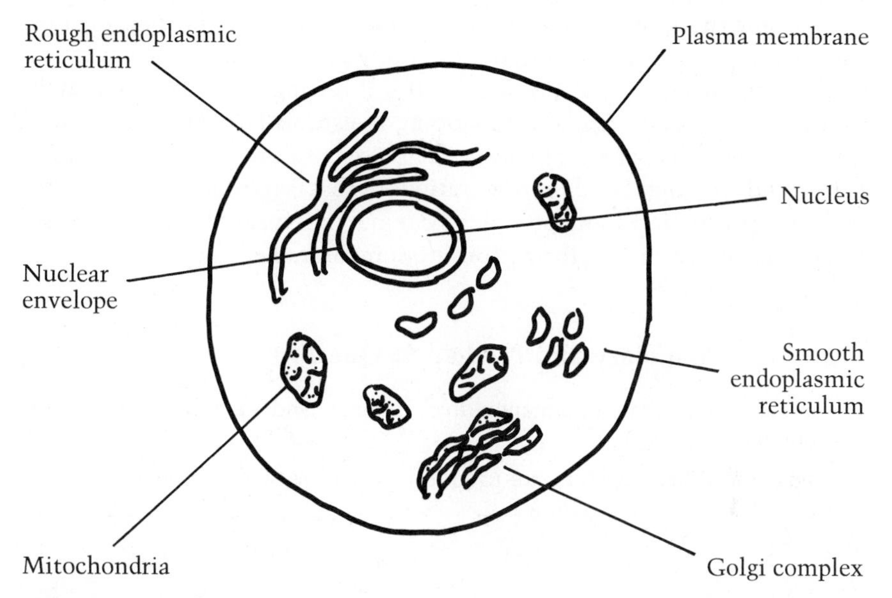

Figure 11.6 A Cell Structure

own illustration identifying important information as in Figure 11.6, "A Cell Structure." Practice identifying the parts with your illustration. Finally, assess your efforts, asking yourself: "Did the study of the text illustration help increase my understanding?" "Does creating practice illustrations improve my familiarity with the material?" "Is practice identifying parts a benefit to recall of important information?" "Will the technique be helpful in my studies?"

Science and math courses provide many opportunities for developing memory in their equipment and design. As noted earlier, textbooks regularly provide questions, sample problems, and suggested activities at the end of each chapter. Your efforts to answer these questions and solve the problems provide an excellent opportunity to monitor your progress, identify areas of difficulty, and increase your familiarity with the material. In addition, the glossaries frequently included in a text are helpful for quick reference regarding definitions or as an answer for your own practice tests.

Study guides and laboratory manuals are also important opportunities to practice answering questions or to review experiences in a laboratory setting. Reviewing with laboratory manuals is especially useful for courses that require considerable lab work since examinations are bound to reflect those activities.

Choosing the appropriate memory techniques depends on a number of considerations, from your purpose for studying a subject to the nature of the material itself. Verbal rehearsal and self-testing are easily integrated into any study plan. Semantic mapping is especially useful for understanding concepts. Problem-solving exercises are the basis for learning math. And creating visual representations of text is most useful for studying new information about complex systems. Careful application of these techniques makes any information more memorable.

Summary and Prediction Questions

1. Summary: How can information from science and math be studied for memory?
2. Prediction: What questions are used to monitor this study process?

SELF-MONITORING

A review of the various strategies presented in this chapter identifies the topics from which specific questions can be developed to monitor the process. For instance, a review of the strategies suggested for studying a science text indicates the value of previewing a chapter and creating a graphic overview, following the typical pattern of organization, and studying supporting illustrations. Self-monitoring questions are then based on these strategies.

A Brief Exercise

Based on the strategies suggested for studying a science text, develop a list of questions that could help you keep track of these activities while you are studying. Then compare your list with the first few questions of the following checklist.

Self-Monitoring Checklist

A good self-monitoring checklist follows the sequence of strategies suggested for a particular study activity. A self-monitoring checklist of activities discussed in this chapter may include the following:

_____ Do I carefully preview each chapter and create a graphic overview of important information?

_____ Am I alert to the pattern of organization used to present information?

_____ Have I studied the supporting illustrations for clarification of the text?

_____ Am I reading in search of explanations and using my prior knowledge to promote understanding?

_____ Do I use note-taking, flash cards, or semantic mapping to study important new concepts?

_____ Am I applying a systematic approach to problem solving that emphasizes working practice problems?

_____ Have I used specific techniques such as verbal rehearsal and creative sentences to promote memory?

_____ Do I apply techniques such as semantic mapping and visual illustration with more complex material?

_____ Am I careful to identify any learning problems during study, so I can seek some solution to the problem?

_____ How successful are my study procedures?

While you may wish to create a slightly different list of monitoring questions, these will serve to guide your efforts initially.

Summary Question

What activities should be the focus of self-monitoring questions?

SUMMARY

In many ways studying science and mathematics is no different from studying any other subjects, so the general principles of learning discussed throughout this book apply to these specialized areas. Yet, it is also important to recognize that certain strategies discussed in this chapter are especially helpful in managing the complexities of math and science. Effective strategies combined with a positive attitude toward learning lead to active learning and a successful experience. Knowledge is readily accessible to a systematic approach.

Review Questions

1. What strategies can be used to study science textbooks?
2. How are new concepts systematically learned?
3. What steps can be followed to solve science and math problems?
4. How can new information from science and math be mastered for remembering?
5. What questions are used to monitor this study process?

CHAPTER REVIEW

To complete this chapter, answer the following questions. When you are finished, review the chapter to check your answers.

1. True or False: Prior knowledge and experience can be helpful translating new information into an understandable form.
2. True or False: Working with practice problems is an absolute must for mastering science and math.
3. True or False: Illustrations have a special role to play in science because they offer a visual understanding of complex ideas and a practical method for remembering the material.
4. True or False: Semantic mapping tends to be less useful in science study than in other disciplines.
5. A useful method for organizing text information as preparation for study is
   a. the graphic organizer.
   b. the use of prior knowledge.
   c. the study of illustrations.
   d. all of the above.
6. A useful self-monitoring question for the study of math is:
   a. Have I used creative sentences to promote memory?
   b. Am I applying a systematic approach to problem solving that emphasizes working practice problems?
   c. Do I have a sincere interest in the material being studied?
   d. Have I tried semantic mapping as a practical alternative to practice problems?
7. Describe the organization of a graphic overview and explain its potential value. Discuss your reaction to the procedure.

8. List the steps of a basic approach to solving problems in math and science.

9. Locate an introductory science text. Then identify a particular part of the text that develops some new concept and provides supporting illustrations. Study the selection and then, on a separate sheet of paper, create your own visual illustration as an aid to memory. Discuss how such illustrations could improve your success on an exam.

10. Which of the strategies presented in this chapter seems to offer the most benefit to your study of science and math? Why?

NOTES

1. Judith N. Thelen, *Improving Reading in Science*, 2nd ed. (Newark, Del.: International Reading Association, 1984).

2. James Gilluly, Aaron C. Waters, and A. O. Woodford, *Principles of Geology*, 4th ed. (San Francisco: W. H. Freeman, 1975), pp. 36–49.

3. Gil D. Brum and Larry K. McKane, *Biology: Exploring Life* (New York: John Wiley & Sons, 1989), p. 370

4. Cecie Starr and Ralph Taggart, *Biology: The Unity and Diversity of Life*, 5th ed. (Belmont, Calif.: Wadsworth, 1989), pp. 36–37.

5. Frank Press and Raymond Siever, *Earth*, 3rd ed. (San Francisco: W. H. Freeman, 1982), p. 15.

6. Roman Smoluchowski, *The Solar System: The Sun, Planets, and Life* (New York: Scientific American Books, 1983), p. 54.

7. William DeWitt, *Human Biology: Form, Function, and Adaptation* (Glenview, Ill: Scott, Foresman, 1989), p. 119.

8. John J. W. Rogers and John A. S. Adams, *Fundamentals of Geology* (New York: Harper & Row, 1966), pp. 248–251.

9. Ibid., p. 250.

10. Allen R. Angel and Stuart R. Porter, *A Survey of Mathematics: With Applications*, 2nd ed. (Reading, Mass.: Addison-Wesley, 1985), p. 474.

11. Adapted from Starr and Taggart, p. 68.

12

Reading Literature

Preview Exercise

Reading literature differs from reading informational text. Take a few moments to think about how you read fiction. Is your experience different from other types of reading? Now look over the chapter. What topics are the focus of discussion? How might your reading of fiction benefit from this chapter?

Purpose for Reading: ______________________________

____

____

Reading literature for pleasure is quite common, and most readers truly enjoy a good book. Reading literature for a course of study is also quite common, but the requirements of study are more rigorous. Bridging the gap between pleasure and study is one good reason for developing a better understanding of literature.

Reading literature with understanding requires, first, a knowledge of the elements of fiction, four of which are discussed in this chapter—plot, setting, theme, and character. Reading literature with attention requires, second, the use of specific reading strategies such as asking questions and visualizing characters and events. Reading literature for analysis and discussion requires, third, the use of organizing strategies such as summarizing the plot, analyzing the characters, and identifying the theme. Reading literature for study requires, finally, the use of a self-monitoring strategy. Each of these points is discussed in this chapter.

Guiding Questions

1. What are the major elements of fiction and why are they important to understanding fiction?
2. What reading strategies are especially useful for reading fiction?
3. How can specific organizing strategies help analyze fiction and aid memory?
4. What questions are most useful for monitoring the process of understanding fiction?

ELEMENTS OF FICTION

Character

Reading fiction and understanding the elements of fiction are interrelated activities. Character, for instance, is one crucial aspect of fiction and is central to story development. Characters are understood in a variety of ways, such as through what they say and how they act. Successful reading usually requires identification with story characters. And perhaps the best way to understand character is to apply the same standards you do in everyday life. How do you learn about, and make judgments about, family members, friends, fellow employees, social acquaintances, or strangers? You listen to them, observe their behavior, consider the reactions of others, and compare their beliefs with your own sense of morality, ethics, or justice. Characters in fiction are considered in a similar fashion. Remember, of course, that writers offer only so much information in their stories and that will influence your reaction to character. Story characters are designed to create a response on the part of the reader.

A BRIEF EXERCISE

Read the following selection to see what you can find out about Hattie in Saul Bellow's introduction to "Leaving the Yellow House."[1]

> The neighbors—there were in all six white people who lived at Sego Desert Lake—told one another that old Hattie could no longer make it alone.

> The desert life, even with a forced-air furnace in the house and butane gas brought from town in a truck, was still too difficult for her. There were women even older than Hattie in the county. Twenty miles away was Amy Walters, the gold miner's widow. But she was a hardier old girl. Every day of the year she took a bath in the icy lake. And Amy was crazy about money and knew how to manage it, as Hattie did not. Hattie was not exactly a drunkard, but she hit the bottle pretty hard, and now she was in trouble and there was a limit to the help she could expect from even the best of neighbors.

Describe Hattie: What sort of character is she?

Hattie is growing old and can no longer care for herself, at least that is what you're told. She apparently drinks too much, is having some trouble in her life, and can't expect too much from her neighbors. From this short paragraph, much is learned about Hattie. Yet, further information about Hattie—her past, perhaps, and her future—will undoubtedly develop as the story continues. Remember, this short paragraph "tells" you about Hattie. To better analyze her character, you would read the story to "see" how she acts, to "listen" to what she says, and to "discover" her motivation. Understanding character is central to understanding fiction.

Setting

Setting also plays an important role in fiction. Most simply, setting is a descriptive aspect of stories suggesting when and where events happen. An author may be very specific with a setting, wishing to identify the atmosphere and surroundings of an event. Crime stories, for example, frequently take place in urban settings. Stories of human tragedy and personal triumph in the United States frequently have a regional flavor, taking place in such areas as the rural South or the plains of the Midwest. The circumstances of such stories are very specific. But authors may also leave settings vague, so that the story could happen almost anywhere. The stories take on a universal quality.

A Brief Exercise

Read Shirley Jackson's introduction to "The Lottery."[2] Notice how the description opens the story to the reader.

> The morning of June 27th was clear and sunny, with the fresh warmth of a full-summer day; the flowers were blossoming profusely and the grass was

> richly green. The people of the village began to gather in the square, between the post office and the bank, around ten o'clock; in some towns there were so many people that the lottery took two days and had to be started on June 26th, but in this village, where there were only about three hundred people, the whole lottery took less than two hours, so it could begin at ten o'clock in the morning and still be through in time to allow the villagers to get home for noon dinner.

Now describe the setting or your reaction to this description in your own words.

Jackson writes of a warm summer day, blossoming with the beauty of new growth. The "village" suggests a small town, rural environment. People are gathering for a lottery. Simple enough. As setting is established, a mood is created. But as the story develops, the scene may very well change. And the setting of events surely influences how readers react to a story.

Plot

Plot is also central to fiction. It is the sequence of events in a story—the "what happens." Some stories follow a simple sequence from beginning to end. Others may begin in the middle of a sequence, relate earlier events through a "flashback," and then continue to the finish. A few stories may actually begin at the "end" and then proceed to examine the events that led to this end. Plot is the way a story happens.

Fundamental to plot is the problem, or "conflict," faced by the characters. This conflict creates the events of a story and, when resolved, creates the resolution, or ending. In a way, conflict is the source of the plot while characters are the source of the conflict.

A plot has certain basic elements that create the sequence of events of any story. These elements may vary as authors explore various techniques for story telling, but there is a common pattern of development.

A typical plot begins with an introduction, usually presenting character and setting. Conflict becomes apparent as the plot continues and some difficult situation arises to embroil the central character or characters in the story. As the plot continues, the conflict leads to further problems, or complications. Frequently a crisis of events develops that leads to the climax of the story. The climax is the turning point in the story, when the conflict is confronted or the character overwhelmed. The sequence of events concludes when the conflict is resolved, and the events of the story draw to a close. Remember, the key to plot is "what happens." (For a discussion of the plot structure of the story by Richard Wright, "The Man

Who Was Almost a Man," read the sample lecture, "Understanding Plot Structure" in Chapter 5.)

Theme

Theme is commonly understood as the meaning of a story. Recall your reading as a child. In fairy tales such as "Sleeping Beauty," the typical theme is the triumph of good over evil. The theme is understood from resolution of the conflict among characters in a particular setting. In fairy tales, the characters, actions, and resolutions to conflict are fairly simple and straightforward. Therefore, the theme is easy to interpret. As stories become more complex, interpreting theme becomes more difficult. Fiction is a reflection of the human experience. Deciding why things happen the way they do in life—falling in love, becoming a victim of crime, experiencing the death of a loved one—is a complicated task. Interpreting the theme of a story is similarly difficult. Yet, by examining characters, considering events, and trying to make sense of some conclusion, an interpretation of the story's meaning is made. A theme emerges from an understanding of "why" something happens.

A Brief Exercise

Imagine a story about a happily married couple planning a summer party to celebrate their happiness with their friends. Imagine also that the wife has decided to surprise her husband with a special gift. But to carry out the surprise she needs the help of his friends.

Over the next few weeks, quite by accident, the husband sees his wife out with one of the friends on numerous occasions, but he keeps the information to himself. Slowly his surprise at seeing his wife with someone else grows to jealousy, and from jealousy to anger, ultimately from anger to despair. Throughout the experience, he speaks to no one about these events and is consumed by his feelings.

Finally, in a moment of jealous rage, he shoots his wife and friend, and then himself. The story ends in tragedy.

How might you interpret this story?

The theme may be that jealousy can become a self-consuming emotion with tragic consequences. That interpretation fits the specifics of the story. The theme may also be that reality is a tenuous truth, easily subject to misinterpretation, again with tragic consequences. Or the theme may be more general, suggesting that the sensibility of reason is vulnerable to the uncertainty of emotion, with potentially tragic consequences. Notice how, in each instance, the specific elements of a story can lead to a more universal interpretation, a theme that offers insight into the human experience beyond the story itself. How you interpret the various elements of a story determines the theme.

Summary and Prediction Questions

1. Summary: What are the major elements of fiction and why are they important to understanding fiction?
2. Prediction: What reading strategies are especially useful for reading fiction?

STRATEGIES FOR READING

Although numerous strategies are used to read fiction, four specific strategies are presented here. Each is designed to increase your involvement with a work of fiction.

Dividing the Text

First, approach fiction like any reading activity with an eye toward dividing the text into workable amounts of information. To be understood, a text is read, analyzed, and thought about. And such activities are more productive if considered as meaningful parts leading to the whole. For instance, short stories frequently begin with a two- or three-paragraph introduction. Consequently, it's useful to read that segment, consider the information presented, perhaps ask a few questions, and predict what might come next. As the reading continues, be alert to logical breaks in the text, such as when one character leaves a scene and another enters or when there's a shift in time or place. Attention to the progression of the plot can also help you determine when the text naturally shifts the scene. Such points are useful for considering what has occurred thus far and predicting what may come next.

Consider how the text of a story can guide the reader in logically dividing and analyzing a story. Herman Melville's "Bartleby, the Scrivener"[3] begins,

> I am a rather elderly man. The nature of my avocations, for the last thirty years has brought me into more than ordinary contact with what would seem an interesting and somewhat singular set of men. . . .

This initial information introduces the narrator, "a rather elderly man," and suggests you will meet some other "interesting" men. Further along in the paragraph, the narrator notes his intent to write especially about a character named "Bartleby," so the purpose of the story is becoming clear. This paragraph serves as the introduction.

The second paragraph begins:

> Ere introducing the scrivener, as he first appeared to me, it is fit I make some mention of myself, my employees, my business, my chambers, and general surroundings; because some such description is indispensable to an adequate understanding of the chief character about to be presented.

The narrator establishes his purpose for writing at this point and suggests the reader's purpose for reading. This paragraph and the next three describe the narrator's business as a lawyer and his place of business. This segment of the text might be considered the second division in the story after the introduction.

The sixth paragraph begins:

> At the period just preceding the advent of Bartleby, I had two persons as copyists in my employment, and a promising lad as an office boy.

This line suggests that three characters will be discussed next. Therefore, this segment might be considered the third division in the story after the introduction.

After describing each of the three characters, a number of paragraphs later, Melville writes:

> In answer to my advertisement, a motionless young man one morning stood upon my office threshold, the door being open, for it was summer. I can see that figure now—pallidly neat, pitiably respectable, incurably forlorn! It was Bartleby.

Note the shift away from the other three characters and to Bartleby. Again a logical division of the text is suggested. Similar divisions become apparent as the story continues.

At some later point, after completing the story, these divisions serve as an aid in analyzing how individual aspects of a story are interrelated to create a total story, offering an interpretation of human experience. Each segment is read, analyzed, and thought about until an understanding of the total work is brought together upon completion.

Asking Questions

Next, it's useful to approach fiction with a series of questions in mind, questions suggested by the elements of fiction.

For character, crucial questions might include:

Who are the characters?

How do they behave?

What attitudes or values do they represent?

What is their response to circumstances?

How believable are they?

Questions about character focus the reader's attention.

For setting, important questions may include:

Where does the story take place?

How detailed is the description?

When does the story take place?

How important is the time period?

Does the setting suggest an atmosphere that influences events?

What changes in time and place occur?

Authors focus on setting either more or less depending on the importance of setting to character and plot. Sometimes setting is very specific, sometimes it is left vague. Questions help determine the influence of setting in understanding a work of fiction.

For plot, questions focus on the sequence of events, and the issue of conflict. Questions may include:

How is the story introduced?

What is the conflict?

How is the conflict further complicated?

What is the crisis of events?

When is the climax reached?

What is the final resolution of the conflict?

Such questions identify points in the sequence of events that help to organize the presentation.

For theme, questions include:

What meaning can be derived from the story?

Why is the conflict resolved in this particular manner?

Are different interpretations possible?

What might be the author's purpose?

What universal truth is portrayed?

Since determining theme depends upon how readers interpret various aspects of a story, questions of theme require more thought than identifying the elements of the story. But analyzing the interrelationships among character, setting, and plot will offer evidence for an interpretation of theme.

While the questions presented thus far link the general elements of fiction with the specifics of the work being read, questions even more specific to a story enhance both comprehension and retention.

Take questions of character, for instance. It's surely important to approach a story with a question like, "Who are the characters?" But once involved in a particular story such as Washington Irving's "Rip Van Winkle,"[4] a more specific question like "Who is Rip Van Winkle?" identifies the character more fully. Additional questions of character are also suggested, such as "How does Rip behave when he's in the village with the boys?" "What is Dame Van Winkle's reaction to Rip's laziness?" or "Why does Rip go off into the mountains with his dog?"

This specific focus increases involvement in a story, creates greater familiarity with the piece, and aids retention of precise information for further analysis.

Similar questions for setting, plot, and theme have the same effect on comprehension. Consider a question of setting and atmosphere: "How does the setting of the 'Kaatskill Mountains' (the Catskills) help create an atmosphere of mystery and magic?" For plot a good question might be, "What conflict is introduced early in the story that causes Rip Van Winkle to venture into the mountains, and how is the conflict resolved on his return to the village at the end of the story?" For theme, a couple of questions come to mind. One is, "What may be Washington Irving's purpose in telling the story of Rip Van Winkle?" A second is, "How might the story be interpreted differently by a reader who likes Rip as a character than by a reader who dislikes Rip?"

The point is that general questions based on the elements of fiction guide the reader into a story and aid understanding; whereas, specific questions aid in the comprehension and retention of specific information.

Visualizing Characters and Events

Another useful strategy for reading fiction is to mentally visualize the characters and events of a story. Fiction is written to convey images of human experience, from the struggles of growing up to the tragedy of death. The extent to which any story can be pictured more vividly in the mind's eye is the extent to which that story can be more fully understood.

Practice in visualizing can greatly enhance a reader's response to literature. Begin, for instance, by looking at familiar objects, actions, or events. Take an orange and look at it closely. Close your eyes and recreate a picture of that orange in your mind. Think about its size, its color, its texture, and so forth. Then open your eyes and compare your image with the orange itself. Continue the practice with different objects, adding more and more to your picture.

Extend your experience by visualizing everyday scenes such as people riding on the bus, taking a break on the job, fixing a flat tire, or waiting for class to begin.

To link visualization to memory, think about some past event in your life. Take a few moments to talk with yourself about the experience. Ask "Where did it happen?" "Who else was there?" "Exactly what happened?" "Why is it an important memory?" Then close your eyes and recreate the scene in your mind. Look closely at the details of the event. Notice the setting—time, place, atmosphere. Notice the people involved—who are they, how do they behave, what is their purpose? Follow the sequence of events—what happened first, second, and so forth. Now think about why this particular event is a memorable experience.

Again, practice using visual memory both to examine past events and to strengthen your visual memory of precise detail.

Combining visualization and memory is a direct benefit to reading, understanding, and remembering fiction simply because it enables you to "see" better the images conveyed by language as you "see" everyday experience.

A Brief Exercise

Read the following excerpt from "Rip Van Winkle." The author offers the reader some insight into Rip's character. As you read, try to create a visual image in your mind of this character, Rip Van Winkle.

> In that same village, and in one of these very houses (which, to tell the precise truth, was sadly time-worn and weather-beaten) there lived many years since, while the country was yet a province of Great Britain, a simple good-natured fellow, of the name of Rip Van Winkle. He was a descendant of the Van Winkles who figured so gallantly in the chivalrous days of Peter Stuyvesant, and accompanied him to the siege of Fort Christina. He inherited, however, but little of the martial character of his ancestors. I have observed that he was a simple good-natured man; he was, moreover, a kind

> neighbor, and an obedient, henpecked husband. Indeed, to the latter circumstance might be owing that meekness of spirit which gained him such universal popularity; for those men are most apt to be obsequious and conciliating abroad who are under the discipline of shrews at home. Their tempers, doubtless, are rendered pliant and malleable in the fiery furnace of domestic tribulation; and a curtain lecture is worth all the sermons in the world for teaching the virtues of patience and long-suffering. A termagant wife may, therefore, in some respects be considered a tolerable blessing; and if so, Rip Van Winkle was thrice blessed.

Now describe what picture came to mind.

____

____

____

____

A Brief Exercise

Take the opportunity to visualize another scene from Rip's experience by reading the following excerpt introducing his venture to the mountains. Combine language and experience to create an image of the scene.

> In a long ramble of the kind on a fine autumnal day, Rip had unconsciously scrambled to one of the highest parts of the Kaatskill Mountains. He was after his favorite sport of squirrel shooting, and the still solitudes had echoed and reëchoed with the reports of his gun. Panting and fatigued, he threw himself, late in the afternoon, on a green knoll, covered with mountain herbage, that crowned the brow of a precipice. From an opening between the trees he could overlook all the lower country for many a mile of rich woodland. He saw at a distance the lordly Hudson, far, far below him, moving on its silent but majestic course, with the reflection of a purple cloud, or the sail of a lagging bark, here and there sleeping on its glassy bosom, and at last losing itself in the blue highlands.
>
> On the other side he looked down into a deep mountain glen, wild, lonely, and shagged, the bottom filled with fragments from the impending cliffs and scarcely lighted by the reflected rays of the setting sun. For some time Rip lay musing on this scene; evening was gradually advancing; the mountains began to throw their long blue shadows over the valleys; he saw that it would be dark long before he could reach the village, and he heaved a heavy sigh when he thought of encountering the terrors of Dame Van Winkle.

Now describe what picture came to mind.

___

___

___

___

If you find visualization somewhat difficult at first, keep in mind that it is a natural part of your experience. The difficulty may be a lack of experience combining visual imagery with written language. With practice, you'll gain greatly from the insight of imagery.

Personal Involvement

The three major reading strategies explained thus far—dividing the text, asking questions, and visualizing stories—promote an understanding of fiction. Yet there is a fourth strategy that should not be overlooked. Understanding and interpretation are greatly influenced by personal involvement in any learning activity. Understanding fiction demands the use of prior knowledge and experience for examining, analyzing, and interpreting any story. If you can identify with a particular character in a story, say a character struggling to achieve some goal, you will become more sensitive to his or her experience. If you recognize the conflict that provokes the flow of events, perhaps a secret from the past interfering with the happiness of the present, you become alert to the possibilities of resolving the conflict.

To compare and contrast the characters and events of fiction with your prior knowledge and personal experience makes reading a reality; when the story comes alive its details become more memorable.

Summary and Prediction Questions

1. Summary: Describe each of the four strategies suggested for reading fiction with understanding.
2. Prediction: How can specified organizing strategies help analyze fiction and aid memory?

ORGANIZING STRATEGIES

The study of fiction encompasses many activities, the most frequent of which are discussing the stories in class, writing papers of various sorts, and taking exams, usually essay exams. The common element to each of these activities is the need for an organized understanding of each piece which can be translated into an organized memory of important information. Once again the elements of fiction provide the framework for this organization.

Summarize Plot

First, summarize the plot. An overview of major events is the foundation for thinking about any work of fiction. Just as summaries identify important information in textbooks, summaries of plot structure organize the major aspects of a story. A summary tells simply and briefly what happens in a story. The elements of plot—introduction, conflict, complication, climax, and resolution—guide the organization of the summary.

Describe Character

Second, describe each major character. Since character is the central feature of fiction, noting and describing characters are important for discussing, interpreting, and remembering stories. Just as you recall memorable characters from your own experience, you learn to recall characters from story experience. The questions asked about character while reading provide the information necessary for this organizing process.

Identify Setting

Third, identify the setting. Again the issue is when, where, and under what conditions the story takes place. Remembering these key points influences how you ultimately interpret a particular piece or make connections between reality and fiction.

State Theme

Finally, state the theme of the story. Any interpretation of theme is a consequence of the interrelationship among plot, character, and setting.

Your organization of the other elements thus helps you think about the meaning of the story, or the variety of interpretations that can be made.

A Model Strategy

The following organizing strategy is based on an analysis of Mary E. Wilkins Freeman's "The Revolt of Mother."[5]

SUMMARIZE THE PLOT. Mary E. Wilkins Freeman's "The Revolt of Mother" is about a woman's desire to have the new house she was promised 40 years ago. The conflict arises over the fact that "Father" is starting another barn in the spot promised for the house, a barn that seems unnecessary to "Mother." Unable to dissuade Father from building the barn, Mother bides her time. Then while Father is away on a trip, Mother packs up the house, with the help of the children, and moves into the new barn, which she intends to use as a new house. Although the townfolk and children are uncomfortable with this "revolt of Mother" and fear Father's return, the story has a satisfying conclusion. Father, at first shocked by the turn of events, realizes his responsibility to Mother and the family. The barn will be the new house and he will make the necessary changes.

DESCRIBE CHARACTERS. Mother, Sarah Penn, is a hard-working wife and mother who has always accepted her responsibility to her family. But she is a strong-willed woman who accepts her role by choice. When she feels wronged, she works to accomplish what is right—having the new house—and is fully willing to accept the consequences.

Father, Adoniram Penn, is also a strong-willed, rather silent, character intent to play the person in charge. Unfortunately, he displays a narrow point of view and fails to recognize how his actions may be unfair to others. Throughout the story he is a stubborn character, but his conversion at the conclusion helps to humanize him in the readers' eyes.

Sammy and Nanny Penn are the children of the household. Their supportive role in the story helps the reader understand better the character of Mother and Father, and the roles created for men and women in the story's historical time period.

IDENTIFY SETTING. The story takes place at a farm in rural New England during the nineteenth century. Both the family and the farm are portrayed as typical of this period.

STATE THEME. On the one hand, the story comments on the subject of responsibility. The conflict arises because Father has failed to build the new house and instead builds another barn. On the other hand, the story suggests that individuals must assert their rights if they are to maintain their dignity. Independence and courage are valuable traits to emulate.

Having completed this process, you now have a well-organized package of information for review and analysis. You are prepared for a variety of activities typical of literature courses, from class discussion to test-taking.

A Brief Exercise

Select a short story from a magazine or a collection of stories. Read it through using the strategies suggested: (1) divide it into workable amounts, (2) ask both general and specific questions, (3) visualize characters and events, and (4) consider prior experience. When you have completed the story, organize the information by (1) summarizing the plot, (2) describing character, (3) identifying setting, and (4) stating theme. Finally, evaluate your efforts: How did the strategies work? Were you able to organize the information effectively? Do you have any problems?

Summary and Prediction Questions

1. Summary: How can specific organizing strategies help analyze fiction and aid memory?
2. Prediction: What questions are most useful for monitoring the process of understanding fiction?

MONITORING QUESTIONS

As with all learning activities, self-monitoring is necessary for reading and studying fiction. Again, questions are used to identify specific steps in the process and to check your progress with any story. Let the following list guide your monitoring efforts. Add any relevant questions that occur to you.

Self-Monitoring Checklist

_____ Am I dividing the text into manageable and meaningful parts and does that help me think about the story more clearly?

_____ Am I using guiding questions such as "Who are the characters?" and "What is the conflict?" to focus my attention on the elements of fiction as I read?

_____ Am I also using questions specific to a story to make myself more familiar with the story and to increase my memory of important elements?

_____ Am I able to visualize the characters, setting, and events of the story and do I use this mental imagery to promote my understanding?

_____ Do I look for common ground between my personal experience and the characters, setting, or plot structure of the story?

_____ For organizing the information, am I able to summarize the plot, describe character, identify setting, and state theme?

_____ Does this organization help me with discussions, papers, and exams? If not, what seems to be the problem?

_____ Is there any step in this approach to reading and studying fiction that causes me problems? If so, how can I solve the problem?

Remember that self-monitoring helps you keep track of the learning process and take corrective action as you identify problems.

Summary Question

Discuss the importance of using a self-monitoring checklist and identify the major points of concern in the checklist.

An Exercise in Reading a Short Story—Sarah Orne Jewett's "A White Heron"

The purpose of this exercise is to provide you with a guided experience in reading a short story[6] with a specific set of strategies for reading, analyzing, and organizing information. The appendix provides a sample of possible responses for each step in the exercise. The sample responses are a model of what might be done rather than "the correct" responses to particular questions. Look for similarities between your response and those in the appendix.

1. Read the introduction, the first three paragraphs. Think about these questions: "Who are the characters?" "Where does the story take place?" "How is the story introduced?"

I

The woods were already filled with shadows one June evening, just before eight o'clock, though a bright sunset still glimmered faintly among the trunks of the trees. A little girl was driving home her cow, a plodding, dilatory, provoking creature in her behavior, but a valued companion for all that. They were going away from the western light, and striking deep into the dark woods, but their feet were familiar with the path, and it was no matter whether their eyes could see it or not.

There was hardly a night the summer through when the old cow could be found waiting at the pasture bars; on the contrary, it was her greatest pleasure to hide herself away among the high huckleberry bushes, and though she wore a loud bell she had made the discovery that if one stood perfectly still it would not ring. So Sylvia had to hunt for her until she found her, and call Co'! Co'! with never an answering Moo, until her childish patience was quite spent. If the creature had not given good milk and plenty of it, the case would have seemed very different to her owners. Besides, Sylvia had all the time there was, and very little use to make of it. Sometimes in pleasant weather it was a consolation to look upon the cow's pranks as an intelligent attempt to play hide and seek, and as the child had no playmates she lent herself to this amusement with a good deal of zest. Though this chase had been so long that the wary animal herself had given an unusual signal of her whereabouts, Sylvia had only laughed when she came upon Mistress Moolly at the swamp-side, and urged her affectionately homeward with a twig of birch leaves. The old cow was not inclined to wander farther, she even turned in the right direction for once as they left the pasture, and stepped along the road at a good pace. She was quite ready to be milked now, and seldom stopped to browse. Sylvia wondered what her grandmother would say because they were so late. It was a great while since she had left home at half past five o'clock, but everybody knew the difficulty of making this errand a short one. Mrs. Tilley had chased the horned torment too many summer evenings herself to blame any one else for lingering, and was only thankful as she waited that she had Sylvia, nowadays, to give such valuable assistance. The good woman suspected that Sylvia loitered occasionally on her own account; there never was such a child for straying about out-of-doors since the world was made! Everybody said that it was a good change for a little maid who had tried to grow for eight years in a crowded manufacturing town, but, as for Sylvia herself, it seemed as if she never had been alive at all before she came to live at the farm. She thought often with wistful compassion of a wretched dry geranium that belonged to a town neighbor.

" 'Afraid of folks,' " old Mrs. Tilley said to herself, with a smile, after she had made the unlikely choice of Sylvia from her daughter's houseful of children, and was returning to the farm. " 'Afraid of folks,' " they said! I guess she won't be troubled no great with 'em up to the old place!" When they reached the door of the lonely house and stopped to unlock it, and the cat came to purr loudly, and rub against them, a deserted pussy, indeed, but fat with young robins, Sylvia whispered that this was a beautiful place to live in, and she never should wish to go home.

2. What specific questions can you ask about Sylvia or Mrs. Tilley (for instance, "What sort of person is Sylvia?") Write your questions and answers here:

____

____

____

____

____

____

How did you visualize the setting described in the introduction?

____

____

____

____

Have you experienced a similar situation or met a similar character?

____

____

____

____

3. Continue reading the next few paragraphs, again using questions to guide your reading: "What new character is introduced?" "How does Sylvia behave?" "Why?" "Is there further description of setting?"

The companions followed the shady wood-road, the cow taking slow steps, and the child very fast ones. The cow stopped long at the brook to drink, as if the pasture were not half a swamp, and Sylvia stood still and waited, letting her bare feet cool themselves in the shoal water, while the great twilight moths struck softly against her. She waded on through the brook as the cow moved away, and listened to the thrushes with a heart that beat fast with pleasure. There was a stirring in the great boughs overhead. They were full of little birds and beasts that seemed to be wide-awake, and going about their world, or else saying good-night to each other in sleepy twitters. Sylvia herself felt sleepy as she walked along. However, it was not much farther to the house, and the air was soft and sweet. She was not often in the woods so late as this, and it made her feel as if she were a part of the gray shadows and the moving leaves. She was just thinking how long it seemed since she first came to the farm a year ago, and wondering if everything went on in the noisy town just the same as when she was there; the thought of the great red-faced boy who used to chase and frighten her made her hurry along the path to escape from the shadow of the trees.

Suddenly this little woods-girl is horror-stricken to hear a clear whistle not very far away. Not a bird's whistle, which would have a sort of friendliness, but a boy's whistle, determined, and somewhat aggressive. Sylvia left the cow to whatever sad fate might await her, and stepped discreetly aside into the bushes, but she was just too late. The enemy had discovered her, and called out in a very cheerful and persuasive tone, "Halloa, little girl, how far is it to the road?" and trembling Sylvia answered almost inaudibly, "A good ways."

She did not dare to look boldly at the tall young man, who carried a gun over his shoulder, but she came out of her bush and again followed the cow, while he walked alongside.

"I have been hunting for some birds," the stranger said kindly, "and I have lost my way, and need a friend very much. Don't be afraid," he added gallantly. "Speak up and tell me what your name is, and whether you think I can spend the night at your house, and go out gunning early in the morning."

Sylvia was more alarmed than before. Would not her grandmother consider her much to blame? But who could have foreseen such an accident as this? It did not appear to be her fault, and she hung her head as if the stem of it were broken, but managed to answer, "Sylvy," with much effort when her companion again asked her name.

Mrs. Tilley was standing in the doorway when the trio came into view. The cow gave a loud moo by way of explanation.

"Yes, you'd better speak up for yourself, you old trial! Where'd she tucked herself away this time, Sylvy?" Sylvia kept an awed silence; she knew by instinct that her grandmother did not comprehend the gravity of the situation. She must be mistaking the stranger for one of the farmer-lads of the region.

The young man stood his gun beside the door, and dropped a heavy game-bag beside it; then he bade Mrs. Tilley good-evening, and repeated his wayfarer's story, and asked if he could have a night's lodging.

"Put me anywhere you like," he said. "I must be off early in the morning, before day; but I am very hungry, indeed. You can give me some milk at any rate, that's plain."

"Dear sakes, yes," responded the hostess, whose long slumbering hospitality seemed to be easily awakened. "You might fare better if you went out on the main road a mile or so, but you're welcome to what we've got. I'll milk right off, and you make yourself at home. You can sleep on husks or feathers," she proffered graciously. "I raised them all myself. There's good pasturing for geese just below here towards the ma'sh. Now step round and set a plate for the gentleman, Sylvy!" And Sylvia promptly stepped. She was glad to have something to do, and she was hungry herself.

4. What did you find out about Sylvia as the story progressed?

____

____

____

____

Describe the new character. What conflict appears to develop? How is Mrs. Tilley's reaction to the young man different from Sylvia's reaction? Can you predict what will happen next?

____

____

____

____

5. Continue reading with a thought toward gaining further background considering character and setting. What potential for conflict appears in the differing attitudes toward birds displayed by Sylvia and the ornithologist?

It was a surprise to find so clean and comfortable a little dwelling in this New England wilderness. The young man had known the horrors of its most primitive housekeeping, and the dreary squalor of that level of society which does not rebel at the companionship of hens. This was the best thrift of an old-fashioned farmstead, though on such a small scale that it seemed like a hermitage. He listened eagerly to the old woman's quaint talk, he watched Sylvia's pale face and shining gray eyes with ever growing enthusiasm, and insisted that this was the best supper he had eaten for a month; then, afterward, the new-made friends sat down in the doorway together while the moon came up.

Soon it would be berry-time, and Sylvia was a great help at picking. The cow was a good milker, though a plaguy thing to keep track of, the hostess gossiped frankly, adding presently that she had buried four children, so that Sylvia's mother, and a son (who might be dead) in California were all the children she had left. "Dan, my boy, was a great hand to go gunning," she explained sadly. "I never wanted for pa'tridges or gray squer'ls while he was to home. He's been a great wand'rer, I expect, and he's no hand to write letters. There, I don't blame him, I'd ha' seen the world myself if it had been so I could.

"Sylvia takes after him," the grandmother continued affectionately, after a minute's pause. "There ain't a foot o' ground she don't know her way over, and the wild creatur's counts her one o' themselves Squer'ls she'll tame to come an' feed right out o' her hands, and all sorts o' birds. Last winter she got the jay-birds to bangeing here, and I believe she'd 'a' scanted herself of her own meals to have plenty to throw out amongst 'em, if I hadn't kep' watch. Anything but crows, I tell her, I'm willin' to help support,—though Dan he went an' tamed one o' them that did seem to have reason same as folks. It was round here a good spell after he went away. Dan an' his father they didn't hitch,—but he never held up his head ag'in after Dan had dared him an' gone off."

The guest did not notice this hint of family sorrows in his eager interest in something else.

"So Sylvy knows all about birds, does she?" he exclaimed, as he looked round at the little girl who sat, very demure but increasingly sleepy, in the moonlight. "I am making a collection of birds myself. I have been at it ever since I was a boy." (Mrs. Tilley smiled.) "There are two or three very rare ones I have been hunting for these five years. I mean to get them on my own ground if they can be found."

"Do you cage 'em up?" asked Mrs. Tilley doubtfully, in response to this enthusiastic announcement.

"Oh, no, they're stuffed and preserved, dozens and dozens of them," said the ornithologist, "and I have shot or snared every one myself. I caught a glimpse of a white heron three miles from here on Saturday, and I have followed it in this direction. They have never been found in this district at all. The little white heron, it is," and he turned again to look at Sylvia with the hope of discovering that the rare bird was one of her acquaintances.

But Sylvia was watching a hop-toad in the narrow footpath.

"You would know the heron if you saw it," the stranger continued eagerly. "A queer tall white bird with soft feathers and long thin legs. And it would have a nest perhaps in the top of a high tree, made of sticks, something like a hawk's nest."

Sylvia's heart gave a wild beat; she knew that strange white bird, and had once stolen softly near where it stood in some bright green swamp grass, away over at the other side of the woods. There was an open place where the sunshine always seemed strangely yellow and hot, where tall, nodding rushes grew, and her grandmother had warned her that she might sink in the soft black mud underneath and never be heard of more. Not far beyond were the salt marshes and beyond those was the sea, the sea which Sylvia wondered and dreamed about, but never had looked upon, though its great voice could often be heard above the noise of the woods on stormy nights.

"I can't think of anything I should like so much as to find that heron's nest," the handsome stranger was saying. "I would give ten dollars to anybody who could show it to me," he added desperately, "and I mean to spend my whole vacation hunting for it if need be. Perhaps it was only migrating, or had been chased out of its own region by some bird of prey."

Mrs. Tilley gave amazed attention to all this, but Sylvia still watched the toad, not divining, as she might have done at some calmer time, that the creature wished to get to its hole under the doorstep, and was much hindered by the unusual spectators at that hour of the evening. No amount of thought, that night, could decide how many wished-for treasures the ten dollars, so lightly spoken of, would buy.

6. Describe your image of Sylvia and the ornithologist from what you've read so far. Are they somewhat similar or different to people in your life?

___

___

___

___

What potential for conflict exists?

___

___

___

___

What specific questions occurred to you as you were reading?

___

___

____

____

As the story progresses, what is likely to happen next?

____

____

____

____

7. Continue reading the next segment of the story. Consider how the characters develop and how the conflict becomes more complicated. What questions could you ask?

> The next day the young sportsman hovered about the woods, and Sylvia kept him company, having lost her first fear of the friendly lad, who proved to be most kind and sympathetic. He told her many things about the birds and what they knew and where they lived and what they did with themselves. And he gave her a jack-knife, which she thought as great a treasure as if she were a desert-islander. All day long he did not once make her troubled or afraid except when he brought down some unsuspecting singing creature from its bough. Sylvia would have liked him vastly better without his gun; she could not understand why he killed the very birds he seemed to like so much. But as the day waned, Sylvia still watched the young man with loving admiration. She had never seen anybody so charming and delightful; the woman's heart, asleep in the child, was vaguely thrilled by a dream of love. Some premonition of that great power stirred and swayed these young foresters who traversed the solemn woodlands with soft-footed silent care. They stopped to listen to a bird's song; they pressed forward again eagerly, parting the branches—speaking to each other rarely and in whispers; the young man going first and Sylvia following, fascinated, a few steps behind, with her gray eyes dark with excitement.
>
> She grieved because the longed-for white heron was elusive, but she did not lead the guest, she only followed, and there was no such thing as speaking first. The sound of her own unquestioned voice would have terrified her—it was hard enough to answer yes or no when there was need of that. At last evening began to fall, and they drove the cow home together, and Sylvia smiled with pleasure when they came to the place where she heard the whistle and was afraid only the night before.

8. Now answer the questions that guided your reading of this last segment. Consider how the characters respond to the circumstances of setting; what different points of view do they represent?

____

____

____

____

____

____

9. Continue reading. What questions come to mind as you read? What more do you learn about Sylvia?

II

Half a mile from home, at the farther edge of the woods, where the land was highest, a great pine-tree stood, the last of its generation. Whether it was left for a boundary mark, or for what reason, no one could say; the woodchoppers who had felled its mates were dead and gone long ago, and a whole forest of sturdy trees, pines and oaks and maples, had grown again. But the stately head of this old pine towered above them all and made a landmark for sea and shore miles and miles away. Sylvia knew it well. She had always believed that whoever climbed to the top of it could see the ocean; and the little girl had often laid her hand on the great rough trunk and looked up wistfully at those dark boughs that the wind always stirred, no matter how hot and still the air might be below. Now she thought of the tree with a new excitement, for why, if one climbed it at break of day, could not one see all the world, and easily discover whence the white heron flew, and mark the place, and find the hidden nest?

What a spirit of adventure, what wild ambition! What fancied triumph and delight and glory for the later morning when she could make known the secret! It was almost too real and too great for the childish heart to bear.

All night the door of the little house stood open, and the whippoorwills came and sang upon the very step. The young sportsman and his old hostess were sound asleep, but Sylvia's great design kept her broad awake and watching. She forgot to think of sleep. The short summer night seemed as long as the winter darkness, and at last when the whippoorwills ceased, and she was afraid the morning would after all come too soon, she stole out of the house and followed the pasture path through the woods, hastening toward the open ground beyond, listening with a sense of comfort and companionship to the drowsy twitter of a half-awakened bird, whose perch she had jarred in passing. Alas, if the great wave of human interest which flooded for the first time this dull little life should sweep away the satisfactions of an existence heart to heart with nature and the dumb life of the forest!

There was the huge tree asleep yet in the paling moonlight, and small and hopeful Sylvia began with utmost bravery to mount to the top of it, with tingling, eager blood coursing the channels of her whole frame, with her bare feet and fingers, that pinched and held like bird's claws to the monstrous ladder reaching up, up, almost to the sky itself. First she must mount the white oak tree that grew alongside, where she was almost lost among the dark branches and the green leaves heavy and wet with dew; a bird fluttered off its nest, and a red squirrel ran to and fro and scolded pettishly at the harmless housebreaker. Sylvia felt her way easily. She had often climbed there, and knew that higher still one of the oak's upper branches chafed against the pine trunk, just where its lower boughs were set close together. There, when she made the dangerous pass from one tree to the other, the great enterprise would really begin.

She crept out along the swaying oak limb at last, and took the daring step across into the old pine-tree. The way was harder than she thought; she must reach far and hold fast, the sharp dry twigs caught and held her and scratched her like angry talons, the pitch made her thin little fingers clumsy and stiff as she went round and round the tree's great stem, higher and higher upward. The sparrows and robins in the woods below were beginning to wake and twitter to the dawn, yet it seemed much lighter there aloft in the pine-tree, and the child knew that she must hurry if her project were to be of any use.

The tree seemed to lengthen itself out as she went up, and to reach farther and farther upward. It was like a great main-mast to the voyaging earth; it must truly have been amazed that morning through all its ponderous frame as it felt this determined spark of human spirit creeping and climbing from higher branch to branch. Who knows how steadily the least twigs held themselves to advantage this light, weak creature on her way! The old pine must have loved his new dependent. More than all the hawks, and bats, and moths, and even the sweet-voiced thrushes, was the brave, beating heart of the solitary gray-eyed child. And the tree stood still and held away the winds that June morning while the dawn grew bright in the east.

Sylvia's face was like a pale star, if one had seen it from the ground, when the last thorny bough was past, and she stood trembling and tired but wholly triumphant, high in the tree-top. Yes, there was the sea with the dawning sun making a golden dazzle over it, and toward that glorious east flew two hawks with slow-moving pinions. How low they looked in the air from that height when before one had only seen them far up, and dark against the blue sky. Their gray feathers were as soft as moths; they seemed only a little way from the tree, and Sylvia felt as if she too could go flying away among the clouds. Westward, the woodlands and farms reached miles and miles into the distance; here and there were church steeples, and white villages; truly it was a vast and awesome world.

The birds sang louder and louder. At last the sun came up bewilderingly bright. Sylvia could see the white sails of ships out at sea, and the clouds that were purple and rose-colored and yellow at first began to fade away. Where was the white heron's nest in the sea of green branches, and was this wonderful sight and pageant of the world the only reward for having climbed to such a giddy height? Now look down again, Sylvia, where the green marsh is set among the shining birches and dark hemlocks; there where you saw the white heron once you will see him again; look, look! a white spot of him like a single floating feather comes up from the dead hemlock and grows larger, and rises, and comes close at last, and goes by the landmark pine with steady sweep of wing and outstretched slender neck and crested head. And wait! wait! do not move a foot or a finger, little girl, do not send an arrow of light and consciousness from your two eager eyes, for the heron has perched on a pine bough not far beyond yours, and cries back to his mate on the nest, and plumes his feathers for the new day!

The child gives a long sigh a minute later when a company of shouting catbirds comes also to the tree, and vexed by their fluttering and lawlessness the solemn heron goes away. She knows his secret now, the wild, light, slender bird that floats and wavers, and goes back like an arrow presently to his home in the green world beneath. Then Sylvia, well satisfied, makes her perilous way down again, not daring to look far below the branch she stands on, ready to cry sometimes because her fingers ache and her lamed feet slip. Wondering over and over again what the stranger would say to her, and what he would think when she told him how to find his way straight to the heron's nest.

10. Describe how you visualized Sylvia and her search for the white heron. What is your reaction to her as a character? Predict how the experience will create a crisis of events in the conflict.

____

____

____

____

____

____

What questions occurred to you while you were reading?

____

____

____

____

11. Read the next few paragraphs that present the climax of the story. Why does Sylvia ultimately decide to keep the secret? How would you have decided in this situation? Why?

> "Sylvy, Sylvy!" called the busy old grandmother again and again, but nobody answered, and the small husk bed was empty, and Sylvia had disappeared.
>
> The guest waked from a dream, and remembering his day's pleasure hurried to dress himself that it might sooner begin. He was sure from the way the shy little girl looked once or twice yesterday that she had at least seen the white heron, and now she must really be persuaded to tell. Here she comes now, paler than ever, and her worn old frock is torn and tattered, and smeared with pine pitch. The grandmother and the sportsman stand in the door together and question her, and the splendid moment has come to speak of the dead hemlock-tree by the green marsh.
>
> But Sylvia does not speak after all, though the old grandmother fretfully rebukes her, and the young man's kind appealing eyes are looking straight in her own. He can make them rich with money; he has promised it, and they are poor now. He is so well worth making happy, and he waits to hear the story she can tell.
>
> No, she must keep silence! What is it that suddenly forbids her and makes her dumb? Has she been nine years growing, and now, when the great world for the first time puts out a hand to her, must she thrust it aside for a bird's sake? The murmur of the pine's green branches is in her ears, she remembers how the white heron came flying through the golden air and how they watched the sea and the morning together, and Sylvia cannot speak; she cannot tell the heron's secret and give its life away.

12. Identify the climax and discuss Sylvia's reason for keeping the secret. Is her position foreshadowed—suggested beforehand—in the story?

____

____

13. Read the final paragraph.

> Dear loyalty, that suffered a sharp pang as the guest went away disappointed later in the day, that could have served and followed him and loved him as a dog loves! Many a night Sylvia heard the echo of his whistle haunting the pasture path as she came home with the loitering cow. She forgot even her sorrow at the sharp report of his gun and the piteous sight of thrushes and sparrows dropping silent to the ground, their songs hushed and their pretty feathers stained and wet with blood. Were the birds better friends than their hunter might have been,—who can tell? Whatever treasures were lost to her, woodlands and summer-time, remember! Bring your gifts and graces and tell your secrets to this lonely country child!

14. From Sylvia's perspective, what has she lost and what has been gained? Why is the conflict resolved in the particular manner? What theme can be derived from the story? How did this theme develop over the course of the story?

15. On a separate sheet of paper, organize the information gained from your reading by (a) summarizing the plot, (b) describing the characters, (c) identifying the setting, and (d) stating the theme.

16. Finally review your efforts with the self-monitoring checklist. Compare your responses with the sample in the appendix.

EVALUATING YOUR SUCCESS

Learning is very much a cyclical process. As an active learner, you are constantly introduced to new ideas. These new ideas combine with prior knowledge and experience in ways that deepen your understanding. Applying strategies to do this consciously provides you with feedback about your success—active reading fosters greater understanding, information is easier to organize and remember, test results bring satisfaction to the experience. Sometimes, though, the process is more difficult. Whatever the case, this feedback becomes an evaluation that determines how you approach your next task, what strategies need revision, and which strengths should be emphasized.

Evaluating your progress in the study of fiction should not only inform you of how you are doing thus far but also suggest how you approach your next reading. Use the insight gained from this process and success will follow.

Review Questions

1. Identify the four major elements of fiction and explain their importance to understanding fiction.
2. What reading strategies are especially useful for reading fiction?
3. Describe the organizing strategies used to analyze fiction and aid memory.
4. What questions are most useful for monitoring the process of understanding fiction?

CHAPTER REVIEW

To complete this chapter, answer the following questions. When you are finished, review the chapter to check your answers.

1. True or False: Asking specific questions while reading stories is likely to increase your memory of the material.
2. True or False: Plot can best be defined as the descriptive aspect of a story.
3. True or False: Understanding literature is partially a consequence of visualizing characters and events.
4. True or False: Interpreting the theme of a story is something of a guessing game.
5. To understand characters in fiction, it is especially useful to
   a. make a careful interpretation of theme.
   b. analyze the impact of setting.
   c. use a thorough organizational strategy.
   d. consider how characters are understood in real life.

6. Personal involvement is crucial to the study of fiction because
   a. it helps make the story more memorable.
   b. it helps develop the sequence of events.
   c. it is an alternative to asking questions.
   d. it identifies the logical divisions in the text.
7. Select an object (a ripe banana, for example), a scene (two students studying in the library), and a short story (any story you would like to read). Practice creating mental images of each. Describe your experience and discuss how visualizing characters and events might help you better understand fiction.

____

____

____

____

____

____

8. List the four components of the organizing strategy for studying fiction, and explain their value in preparing for an exam.

____

____

____

____

9. Compare and contrast the use of general and specific questions in the study of fiction.

____

____

____

____

10. Describe your reaction to Sarah Orne Jewett's "A White Heron" and suggest how this nineteenth-century work is relevant to today's world.

____

____

____

____

NOTES

1. Saul Bellow, "Leaving the Yellow House," in the *Norton Anthology of Short Fiction*, edited by R. V. Cassill (New York: W. W. Norton, 1978), p. 77.
2. Shirley Jackson, "The Lottery," in the *Norton Anthology of Short Fiction*, edited by R. V. Cassill (New York: W. W. Norton, 1978), pp. 636–637.
3. Herman Melville, "Bartleby, the Scrivener," in *American Short Stories*, 4th ed., edited by Eugene Current-Garcia and Walton R. Patrick (Glenview, Ill.: Scott, Foresman, 1982), pp. 99–131.
4. Washington Irving, "Rip Van Winkle," in *American Short Stories*, 4th ed., edited by Eugene Current-Garcia and Walton R. Patrick (Glenview, Ill.: Scott, Foresman, 1982), pp. 18–33.
5. Mary E. Wilkins Freeman, "The Revolt of Mother," in *The Story and Its Writer*, 2nd ed., edited by Ann Charters (New York: St. Martin's Press, 1987), pp. 249–261.
6. Sarah Orne Jewett, *A White Heron and Other Stories* (Boston: Houghton Mifflin, 1886).

13

Writing Papers

Preview Exercise

Preview the chapter. Notice the various topics. Notice how the discussion focuses on writing as a process. Compare your approach to writing papers with the suggested approach.

Purpose for Reading ______________________________

____

____

Rare is the college course that does not require writing. A short essay, a research paper, perhaps an essay exam may be part of the course requirements. Written reports are an excellent way for instructors to involve students in some particular aspect of a subject. An American history instructor may require a report investigating, for instance, various interpretations of the Reconstruction period that followed the Civil War. In addition, writing assignments provide students with the opportunity to sharpen their reasoning skills by analyzing a subject in detail and creating a well-organized presentation.

A prime benefit of writing is that it promotes critical thinking. Throughout the process of creating a written report, students make decisions about what to say, how to say it, whether the presentation is clearly organized and carefully developed, when an argument is complete or whether it requires further support, and so on. The writing process not only promotes a fuller experience of a subject but also fosters a clearer understanding of how to communicate the insight gained from the experience.

Writing a report or paper can best be viewed as a series of events. The first stage is planning, exploring and organizing information. The second stage is drafting, composing the information into written form. The third stage is revising, reworking the composition into a finished presentation. And the final stage is the self-monitoring check, reviewing the success of the process.

Guiding Questions

1. How is planning best accomplished?
2. What is the central feature of the drafting stage?
3. How can revising improve the quality of writing?
4. What questions help to monitor the writing process?

PLANNING A PAPER

Effective planning is one key to good writing. Papers that are carefully planned have a clearer focus, are more fully developed, and provide more supporting evidence. Planning is the necessary beginning for any written assignment.

Selecting a Topic

Consider first the importance of selecting a topic. Instructors frequently give some general direction such as, "Write a five-page paper on the problem of drugs in American society." The instruction establishes the general focus of your efforts: the subject is drugs. But the subject is much too large for a five-page paper, so you need to limit the topic.

Some instructors leave even the general focus open-ended. An instructor may simply indicate that you are to "write a five-page paper relating to some aspect of this course." In this case, you must establish the general focus before proceeding to a more limited topic. However, some direction is suggested by the instructor's assignment. Decide what topics might be considered. Pick one that has some interest for you; then consider how to limit it.

Limiting the topic requires you to look at the larger subject from different perspectives. If the subject is drug abuse, for example, some aspect of problems street drugs cause might be explored: the relationship between drugs and crime, the educational consequences of drug use among teenagers, the impact of recreational drug use on work habits, and so forth. There are many ways to examine the drug problem, and each must be limited for the discussion to be meaningful. A more limited topic focuses your examination of a subject and makes it easier to organize the necessary information.

Limiting a topic can be accomplished in two steps: (1) identify the topic in a more specific way, and (2) decide what you want to say about the topic. Consider the subject of drugs again. If you are especially concerned about the relationship between drugs and crime, you might consider writing about how illegal drugs cause an increase in crime. First, identify a limited topic, how drugs affect the crime rate. Second, decide what you want to say about that influence, that drug use causes an increase in crime rates. The limited topic is: "The widespread use of illegal drugs has caused an increase in crime rates." Your responsibility in writing the paper becomes clearer, to provide an explanation for and examples of drug use causing increased crime rates. Writing is made easier by limiting the topic.

A Brief Exercise

For each of the following general subjects, create two limited topics. The first is done for you.

Drugs

1. Drug use among pregnant women can have disastrous effects on the child.
2. Criminal penalties for drug use should consider the type of drug and the frequency of its use.

Education

1. ______________________________________

____

2. ______________________________________

____

Job Hunting

1. ______________________________________

____

2. ______________________________________

____

Transportation

1. ______________________________________

____

2. ______________________________________

____

Making a List

Having chosen a limited topic, a writer must decide what information to use to support and explain it. In this case, a useful approach is to make a list of supporting ideas. Take a common statement: "I had a terrible day in school." The question is, What made it such a terrible day? What evidence is there to support that statement?

Here is a list of events that may be part of a terrible day at school.

1. Babysitter was sick.
2. Late for 9 o'clock class and missed surprise quiz.
3. Pen ran out of ink during biology lecture.
4. Missed appointment with adviser.

5. Couldn't find references in library.
6. Nobody showed for the study group.
7. Received a D on my economics paper.
8. Had to skip guest lecture in history because I was called to work second shift.

Notice how each item in the list can be used as evidence of a terrible day in school. As you explore any subject, think of as many supporting points as you can. Then select the best points to use for planning an outline of the paper you will write.

A Brief Exercise

For practice making a list of supporting points, select one of the following topics and create a list of at least ten supporting points: (1) hazards of missing class, (2) values of discussion groups, (3) tips for taking lecture notes, (4) reasons for using the library, (5) benefits of planned study. Use a separate sheet of paper to complete this exercise.

Planning an Outline

The next step, once the list of supporting points is complete, is to create an outline of the information. It is not necessary to include all supporting points in the outline. In fact, it's important to be more selective, to pick those points that provide the best support for the limited topic. Consider the example of a terrible day at school. Discussing all eight supporting points would probably lead to a laundry list of problems, whereas a few selected points developed in detail may be much more interesting.

Take the points of "missing the surprise quiz," "nobody for the study group," and "working second shift." Each problem is related to unexpected events caused by someone else. The end result suggested by the supporting points is that terrible days are sometimes beyond your control.

Look at how selecting certain supporting points leads to the organization of an outline.

I. I had a terrible day at school.
    A. First I missed a surprise quiz.
        1. My babysitter called in sick.
        2. I had to make other arrangements.
        3. So I was late for class and missed the quiz.

B. Next, nobody showed up for study group.
   1. Every Wednesday I meet with three other people to study for biology.
   2. This is my review for Friday exams.
   3. This week nobody showed and I was hoping for help with a couple of real problems.

C. Finally, I was called in to work second shift.
   1. I had planned to hear a guest lecturer in history.
   2. The instructor thought it would help on the next exam.
   3. But I had to go to work.

Each point in the outline becomes more fully developed and ultimately leads to a possible conclusion: "I had a terrible day in school, but there's not much I can do about it. Sometimes events are beyond my control. Maybe tomorrow will be better."

An outline helps organize supporting points, identify further points of explanation and illustration, and suggest a conclusion for the topic. The basic organization is simple.

I. Limited topic
   A. Supporting point
      1. Explanation and illustration
      2. Explanation and illustration
      3. Explanation and illustration
   B. Supporting point
      1. Explanation and illustration
      2. Explanation and illustration
   C. Supporting point
      1. Explanation and illustration
      2. Explanation and illustration
      3. Explanation and illustration
   D. Conclusion

Remember that the outline is an aid to organization and a method of planning. Use it accordingly.

A Brief Exercise

To practice creating an outline, review your list of supporting points in the previous exercise and create an outline of selected points. Decide on an appropriate conclusion. Use a separate sheet of paper to complete the assignment.

The planning stage is a preparatory activity. Each step—selecting a topic, making a list, organizing an outline—contributes to an organized process and lays the groundwork for drafting a paper.

Summary and Prediction Questions

1. Summary: How is planning best accomplished?
2. Prediction: What is the central feature of the drafting stage?

DRAFTING A PAPER

The planning stage only provides an outline of important information. The drafting stage is the composition—the putting together—of the writing process. It's the point where you decide not so much what to say, as how to say it. This stage is referred to as a "draft" because you create a working paper (a draft) not a final product.

A number of issues are considered during this stage. Most important is the issue of how to organize the paper. There are various ways to accomplish the task, but the most common form, the informative essay, includes three major parts: introduction, development, and conclusion.

Introduction

The easiest way to think about this form is in terms of paragraphs within the essay. The first paragraph is an introduction to the essay. Frequently it sets the stage for introducing the topic and is designed to spark the reader's interest.

Imagine, for instance, an essay on the hazards of buying a used car. The introductory paragraph might begin:

"Well, it won't start again. That's the second time this week. And I bought the car so I wouldn't have problems getting to school. My instructors are never going to believe I had car trouble twice in one week. Why did I ever buy this thing?" Does this story sound familiar? A lot of students wonder why their cars fail them at just the wrong time. Maybe there's an answer. Most students buy used cars, and they typically make three common mistakes. They rely on a salesperson for information about the car. They seem to think that appearance is more important than mechanical condition. And they tend to make decisions much too quickly.

Notice how the introduction first presents a situation to link together the experience of the writer and the experience of the reader. Virtually everyone has had car problems. Notice also how that situation leads to the limited topic: "Most students buy used cars and they typically make three common mistakes . . ." Each of the mistakes is identified as part of the topic.

Development

By identifying each of the three common mistakes as part of the topic, the introduction sets the stage for the development of the paper. Again, it is useful to think in terms of paragraphs. Developing the topic of "three common mistakes" requires at least three paragraphs. One paragraph discusses relying on a salesperson. Another discusses appearance versus mechanical condition. The third discusses snap decisions.

The writer's responsibility in each developmental paragraph is—as suggested in the discussion of outlines—to provide clear explanation and concrete examples for the main idea of the paragraph. Focusing on one main idea also gives attention to issues such as logical organization, unity, and coherence. To organize paragraphs when writing you can also use words such as "first," "next," "for example," "imagine," "consequently" and so forth to identify patterns in lectures and textbooks.

For instance, consider how one paragraph might be developed:

> Too often, students rely on a salesperson for important information about used cars. Imagine the typical sales pitch: "Here's a car for you. One owner. Low mileage. Nice clean look about it. Probably kept in a garage. Clean engine. Look at those tires. And priced right too." A ride around the block, some discussion of financing, and the car's purchased. Now consider the sales pitch again, in slightly different terms. "Here's a car you might look over. Most used cars have had one owner. 'Low mileage' is a relative term. For an older car, the mileage may not be very 'low' at all. No doubt it was waxed and polished before being put on the car lot, garage or not, so it looks attractive under the lights. The engine has been steam cleaned and the tires changed. If the price sounds fair, bring over your mechanic and a good friend to check things out. Give it a thorough test drive." Then you might discuss financing. Remember, it's the salesperson's job to sell a car, but it's the buyer's job to determine the quality of the car.

The purpose of the paragraph is to provide the reader with an understanding of why it's a mistake to rely solely on the salesperson. In this paragraph the writer suggests two approaches to the situation, the typical experience and an alternative. The paragraph is logically developed by example. It is unified because the details are clearly related to the main idea. And the paragraph has coherence; that is, it sticks together in its logical order and through its use of transitional words such as "Imagine . . .," "Now consider . . .," "Remember. . . ." Each developmental paragraph presents a fully developed idea.

Conclusion

Finally, a well-organized paper finishes with a concluding paragraph. In most instances this paragraph is a rather brief summary of important points, or perhaps a final judgment about the subject. In either case, the concluding paragraphs should bring the paper to a close.

A simple conclusion to the hazards of buying a new car might be:

> Mistakes are common when buying used cars. Relying on the salesperson, judging a car by appearance, and making snap judgments interfere with sensible buying practices. Think twice and think carefully the next time you enter a used car lot.

Most writing assignments are readily adaptable to the structure of the informative essay and it's an easy form of organization to practice. Simply remember that each essay has three major parts: introduction, development, and conclusion. First, the introduction creates a link between the reader and the writer and establishes the purpose of the essay, sometimes referred to as the thesis. Next the development includes the number of paragraphs necessary to fully develop the thesis. Each developmental paragraph contains a main idea or topic sentence that is fully supported with explanation and illustration. A good rule of thumb is that each point in the thesis equals at least one developmental paragraph. Finally, the conclusion is the summary of major points that brings the paper to a point of closure, a logical ending. (See Figure 13.1 for a graphic overview of the informative essay.)

A Brief Exercise

Select a writing assignment from one of your other classes, or create one of your own. Next, identify a limited topic, make a list of possible supporting points, and organize a clear outline. Then create a draft essay including an introduction, an appropriate number of developmental paragraphs, and a conclusion. Compare the overall form of your draft with Figure 13.1. Does your draft follow the basic organization of the informative essay? How can you improve your work?

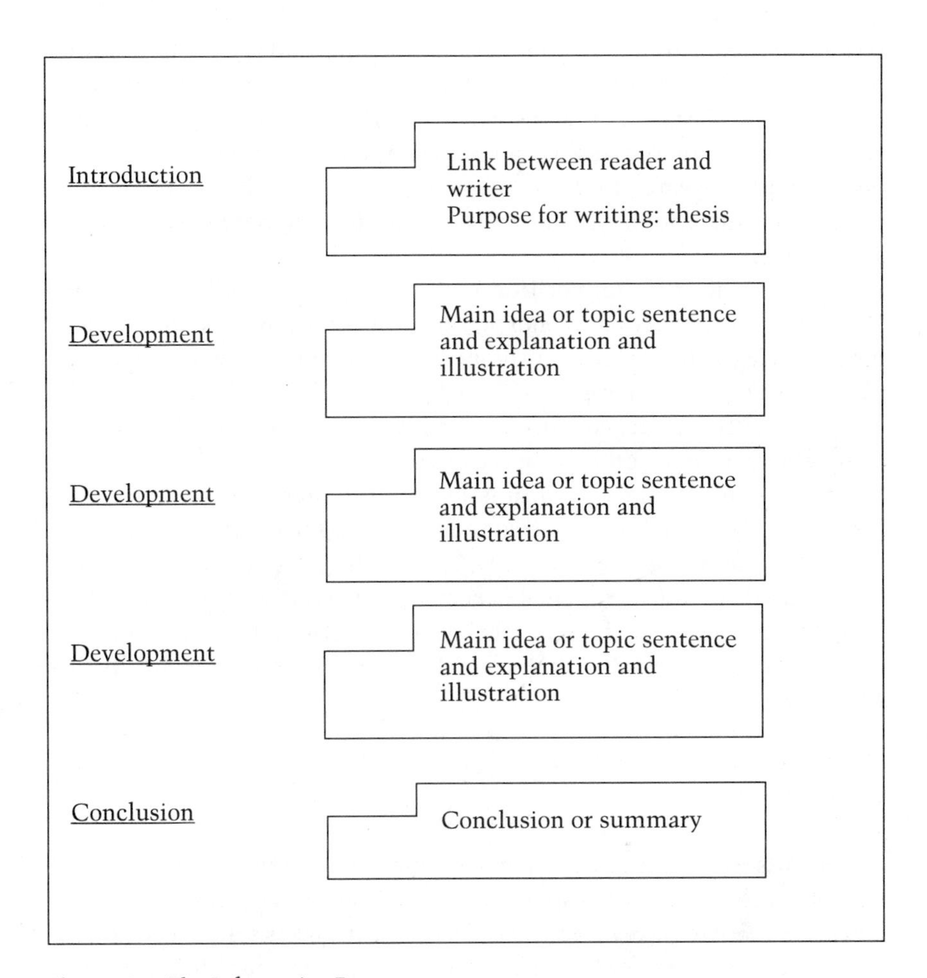

Figure 13.1 The Informative Essay

Summary and Prediction Questions

1. Summary: What is the central feature of the drafting stage?
2. Prediction: How can revising improve the quality of writing?

REVISING

Initial drafts always require revision. The purpose of the revision is twofold: to improve the paper's organization and development and to correct any faults in grammar, punctuation, spelling, and style. The best way to accomplish the revision is to carefully read the paper aloud to yourself or to a friend. Listen to how the paper sounds (for example, does it flow smoothly or are there awkward points?) and watch for technical problems (for example, beware of simple errors in punctuation that interfere with clear communication). Careful revision can turn an average paper into a superior one.

First, consider the composition of the essay. How well does it read? Does the introductory paragraph present a clear purpose? Do the developmental paragraphs include all the necessary support or evidence to explain and illustrate each point? Is each point fully developed? Does the essay end with a logical conclusion or restatement of purpose? Each question helps you focus on one aspect of composition.

Second, consider the technical issues of grammar, punctuation, spelling, and style. Is each sentence complete with appropriate punctuation? Are nouns and verbs in agreement? Are dangling and misplaced modifiers avoided? Are all words spelled correctly? Is your word choice appropriate to the meaning of a sentence? Many questions are necessary for a careful technical revision and several important resources aid in this revision.

Resources

Elements of grammar are partially a matter of previous learning and language sense. In most instances, you can judge whether or not a sentence is complete by reading it aloud to see if it makes sense. The same is true of noun-verb agreement or correct punctuation. Your lifetime experience with language guides you in careful revision. However, even if you have a very good "ear" for grammar, you will probably have to check some points of spelling, grammar, and usage.

A good writing handbook can be an excellent reference for resolving particular problems. Imagine, for example, you were having some difficulty with verb tense and punctuation. A handbook, such as the *Harbrace College Handbook*[1] may provide a quick answer to your problems. The table of contents indicates that the subject of "meaning and sequence of tenses" is discussed on page 79 under the general category "verb forms." The correct use of punctuation is considered under six general categories: "the comma" on page 116, "superfluous commas" on page 132, "the semicolon" on page 136, and so forth. The point is that any good writing handbook provides a wealth of technical information that can help you prevent errors in grammar.

Overcoming problems in spelling or deciding on a question of word choice suggests two additional resources, the dictionary and the thesaurus. A good dictionary such as *Webster's Ninth New Collegiate Dictionary*[2] should be the constant companion of any writer. You probably think of a dictionary as a source of definitions, or you may think of it as a source for checking correct pronunciations. Yet the dictionary is especially useful as a resource for correct spelling. Use it to your benefit.

Roget's College Thesaurus in Dictionary Form[3] is also a possible resource for checking spelling, but its primary value is in choosing the best word for a particular sentence. For instance, suppose you wanted to describe two different people "walking" down a street. One person is out for a leisurely walk, the other is in a hurry. A quick look under "walk" in the thesaurus suggests one good substitute for the leisurely walk is "stroll." The sentence might read, "It was a wonderful afternoon for a leisurely stroll through the neighborhood." For the person in a "hurry," you might look under "hurry" and find the word "scurry." And if "scurry" doesn't quite fit, you might look under "scurry" and find the word "dash." The sentence might read, "As it began to rain harder, my walk along the avenue became a dash to the corner store." In each case, the thesaurus helps you locate words that more precisely describe the meaning of the sentence.

Another aid to revision is "word-processing" on personal computers. Many word-processing programs are available that facilitate the writing process. Instead of pages of handwritten, or even typewritten, material the writing is done on a computer. Revisions can be made rapidly by deleting problem areas and substituting corrections or by reordering the sequence of paragraphs.

A word-processing program eliminates a great deal of rewriting or retyping because the program automatically eliminates deletions and integrates new additions in the revised composition, allowing for numerous changes at a very fast pace. Most useful, perhaps, are spell-check programs, which compare your words with a computer "dictionary." Such a program helps you check your work. Find out if your school offers short courses in word-processing and has computers available for word-processing. Then learn how to use this new resource.

Finally, if you find that your best efforts still leave you with some persistent problems, visit your campus writing center or learning lab. Explain your problem and find out what assistance they can provide. There are solutions to most problems if you just know where to find them.

A Brief Exercise

Take a few moments to think over past writing assignments. Then, on a separate sheet of paper, make a list of problems that appeared in those papers. Next, identify the steps in the revision process or the specific resources that might help resolve the problems. Finally, use this information the next time you revise a writing assignment.

It's important that revisions for both the composition and the technical errors be handled with care. Prior experience with the writing process will help alert you to common errors that require corrective action. A variety of resources for making corrections is readily available. Good judgment and wise decisions will make revision most successful.

Summary and Prediction Questions

1. Summary: How can revising improve the quality of writing?
2. Prediction: What questions help to monitor the writing process?

SELF-MONITORING

The writing process can be readily reviewed with a self-monitoring checklist. To begin with, there are three major categories of concern: planning, drafting, and revising. Each of these categories contains clearly identifiable subdivisions. Planning, for instance, includes selecting a topic, making a list, and organizing an outline. Judging the success of the revising stage virtually requires a self-monitoring approach. A good set of questions should direct your attention to each aspect of the writing process.

A Self-monitoring Checklist

_____ Have I selected a limited topic to focus my efforts?

_____ Am I able to create a thorough list of information to support and explain the limited topic?

_____ Do I create an outline of selected information that clearly organizes the supporting points for the essay?

_____ Does my draft essay follow my outline plan?

_____ Does the draft include an introduction, the necessary paragraphs for development, and a conclusion?

_____ Do I state my purpose in the introduction?

_____ Do my developmental paragraphs provide clear explanations and concrete examples for each main idea?

_____ Do I provide a logical conclusion to the essay?

_____ Am I reading my paper aloud to myself as a guide to the revising process?

_____ Am I revising the draft with attention to both the composition of ideas and the technical aspects of word choice, grammar, spelling, and punctuation?

_____ Do I use the necessary resources to expedite my revision such as a writing handbook, a dictionary, and a thesaurus?

_____ Am I experiencing any difficulties that suggest the need for a visit to the writing center or learning lab?

_____ How successful are my writing activities?

_____ What can I do to further improve my writing?

Summary Question

What questions help to monitor the writing process?

SUMMARY

Writing is an integral part of a college education. It is an activity that challenges your organizational ability and stimulates your analytical skills. Most of all, writing is a process of thinking from planning to drafting to revising. Learn to monitor your efforts and practice constantly to refine your skills. Master the writing process and you will succeed in the task of clear thinking and concise communication.

Review Questions

1. How is planning best accomplished?
2. What is the central feature of the drafting stage?
3. How can revising improve the quality of writing?
4. What questions help to monitor the writing process?

CHAPTER REVIEW

To complete this chapter, answer the following questions. When you are finished, review the chapter to check your answers.

1. True or False: Good writing begins with a focus on a limited subject.
2. True or False: *Roget's Thesaurus* is a good resource for correcting errors in grammar.
3. True or False: Word-processing skills can be an important resource for revisions.
4. True or False: Drafting a paper requires a good deal of careful planning.
5. The writer's responsibility in a developmental paragraph is to
   a. introduce the limited topic.
   b. provide a link to the reader's experience.
   c. offer an effective conclusion.
   d. provide clear explanation and concrete examples for the main idea.
6. An outline helps to
   a. stimulate thinking about a subject.
   b. organize information.
   c. overcome writer's block.
   d. guide the revision process.
7. How might a review of the patterns of organization in Chapter 5, "Taking Lecture Notes," be useful to a writer preparing a draft essay?

____

____

____

____

8. Select a recent writing assignment and check your efforts with the self-monitoring checklist. What did you learn about your strengths and weaknesses?

____

____

____

____

9. Make a list of resources that could prove beneficial to the revising process.

____

____

____

____

10. Describe your previous experience with writing and suggest ways you might improve your skills.

____

____

____

____

____

____

NOTES

1. John C. Hodges and Mary E. Whitten, with Suzanne S. Webb, *Harbrace College Handbook*, 10th ed. (San Diego: Harcourt Brace Jovanovich, 1986).

2. *Webster's Ninth New Collegiate Dictionary* (Springfield, Mass.: Merriam-Webster, 1987).
3. Philip D. Morehead, *The New American Roget's College Thesaurus in Dictionary Form* (New York: New American Library, 1978).

14

Using the Library

Preview Exercise:

Before previewing this chapter, take a few moments to think back over your experiences using libraries. What was your purpose? How frequently did you go? What sort of information were you after? Were you successful in your efforts? Now preview the chapter to compare the topics presented with your previous experience. What can you learn from this chapter?

PURPOSE FOR READING ______________________________

____

____

Libraries are vast repositories of information. Traditionally, libraries contained large collections of books, magazines, and newspapers. They were both a source of general information and a historical collection of "current affairs" that became "old news" with each new edition of the newspaper.

Today, libraries are changing at a dramatic pace. The so-called information explosion has inundated society with an array of new information brought about by changes in science, politics, and culture. Along with the rapid growth of information has come a change in the technology of communication. Besides being repositories of books and magazines, they are now a place of audio and video communication, microform storage and retrieval, and computer access to compact disc databases or to online database systems in remote locations. Libraries have become complete information resource centers.

How can you learn to use this modern library system? You learn, first, by investigating the library. You learn, second, by understanding how to access the information held by the library. And you learn, third, by making the library a central feature of your learning process.

Guiding Questions

1. How are the resources of a modern library best investigated?
2. What are the primary sources for accessing library information?
3. Why should the library play a central role in the learning process?
4. How can the library experience be monitored?

INVESTIGATING THE LIBRARY

The best way to learn how to use a library is to spend some time investigating its workings. Most college and university libraries offer an orientation program. Librarians recognize that a thorough understanding of the library is critical to your success in many classes, so they want to give you a head start on your research by giving you an orientation. Such programs introduce students to the basic organization of a library, from the card catalog to the special collections. They also offer suggestions for how to search out a particular item such as, for instance, a government document in the reference section. Many will provide practice in searching out information. Find out when and where library orientations are held and get yourself involved.

In addition to an orientation program, most libraries have informational brochures. Such brochures frequently offer quick assistance, even for problems as simple as "How to find a book in the library" or "How to find a journal." These brochures provide a step-by-step guide to solving a problem. They are easy to use, and they also save librarians' valuable time so that they can help students with more complicated tasks. See if your library has any helpful brochures, and remember that even if you don't need some of the information at the moment—such as how to use a microficheMARKER reader—you may be happy to know that information when you're working on some last-minute assignment.

Also keep in mind that librarians understand libraries better than anyone else, so they are an excellent source of assistance. Once you have been through an orientation and read available brochures, feel free to ask a librarian about how to locate a particular piece of information, how to investigate an uncommon subject, or how to use a computer-access database system. In fact, if you run up against a problem while doing some type of library research, it's probably time to ask a librarian.

Finally, don't forget the value of some personal investigation. No matter how thorough an orientation or how often you ask questions, the library will still contain some "secrets" that may help you. How do you find these secrets? Your best bet is to spend some time simply looking around. Rather than going to the library with a particular purpose in mind, take some time to browse through the library. Check out the periodicals, or serials, collection. Spend some time examining the range of information indexes, both book indexes and computer indexes. Wander through the reference collection and you'll probably be amazed at what you'll find. And if you've never used a microfilm or microfiche reader, give them a try. As you become more familiar with the library, you'll see it as a source of tremendous help, not a source of confusion.

A Brief Exercise

Visit your college library and answer the following questions:

1. When is the next library orientation program?
2. What informational brochures are available to help me learn my way around the library?
3. Where can I find a librarian if I need help?
4. How quickly can I find the card catalog or computer catalog, the *Readers' Guide to Periodical Literature,* the microfilm room, the periodical-serials room, and the U.S. Census reports?

Summary and Prediction Questions

1. Summary: How are the resources of a modern library best investigated?
2. Prediction: What are the primary sources for accessing library information?

PRIMARY SOURCES

The primary resource of any library is the card catalog. If you're looking for a particular book or for books by a certain author, or books about some special subject, the card catalog is the place to begin.

Card Catalog

Card catalogs are divided into two major parts: the author/title catalog and the subject catalog. The order of either catalog is alphabetical, so any search simply follows a natural alphabet sequence. Most catalog systems include books, periodicals (magazines, journals, and newspapers the library subscribes to), and media such as films or audiotapes.

Once you locate the appropriate card in the catalog, you'll need to understand the card. Most "main entry" cards are filed under the author's name, which is prominently displayed. (See Figure 14.1.) Other information includes the title, place of publication, date of publication, a physical description of the book; and in the case of the sample card, the date of original publication, an additional title head, and a note indicating that a separate card is listed under the editor's name. Perhaps most important is the number in the upper left-hand corner—the call number. It is the key to locating the book in the library.

Library books are classified by call numbers, using either the Dewey Decimal System or the Library of Congress system. The Dewey Decimal System is an older system that classifies books by ten general number classes. For instance, the numbers 300–399 would include works in social science. These general classes are divided into more specific number systems. Many libraries now use the Library of Congress system, which arranges books by capital letters and then subdivides by number. For instance, the letter H designates the broad category of social science in this system. (See Figure 14.2.)

Regardless of which system your library uses, it is the call number that will guide you to the location of the book in the library. The simplicity of the system is that you only need to follow an alphabetical or numerical sequence to locate your information. For instance, to locate the sample selection in Figure 14.1 by Sarah Orne Jewett, first locate the category of "PS" in the library. Then search for "2130" within the "PS" category, and finally "A2," "1965." At that point you either locate the book or discover that someone else already has it. In the latter case, then you might want to ask someone at the circulation desk when it's due back, or put a "hold" on it so you'll be contacted when it comes in.

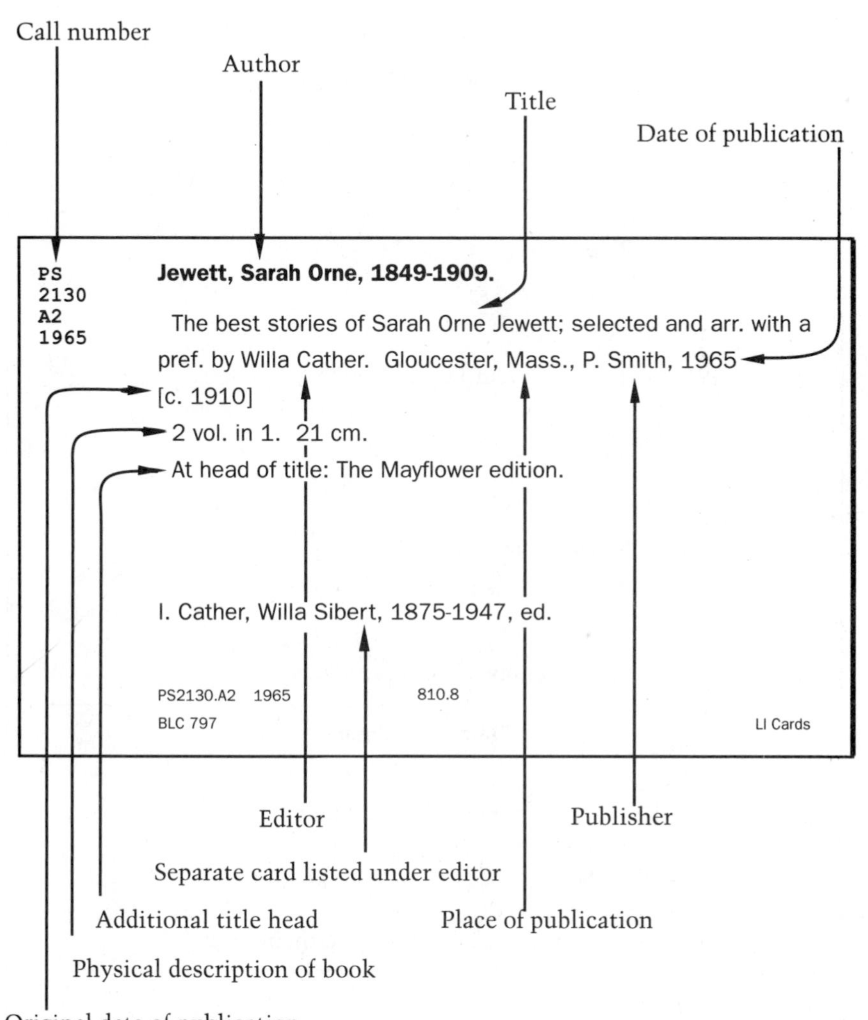

Figure 14.1 Main Entry—Catalog Card

Library of Congress	
A	General Works
B	Philosophy and Psychology
C–D	History and Topography (except America)
E–F	History, American
G	Geography and Anthropology
H	Social Sciences
J	Political Science
K	Law
L	Education
M	Music
N	Fine Arts
P	Language and Literature
Q	Science
R	Medicine
S	Agriculture
T	Engineering and Technology
U	Military Science
V	Naval Science
Z	Bibliography and Library Science

Dewey Decimal	
000–009	General Works
100–199	Philosophy and Psychology
200–299	Religion
300–399	Social Sciences
400–499	Language
500–599	Natural Sciences and Mathematics
600–699	Technology (Applied Sciences)
700–799	The Arts
800–899	Literature
900–999	Geography and History

Figure 14.2 Catalog Systems

Card catalogs are easy to use once you know the system. Computer catalog systems work in much the same way, except you begin at a computer terminal. Most computer access systems are extremely "user friendly," and provide you with easy directions to work with the systems.

Periodicals

The primary source for periodicals of general interest is the *Readers' Guide to Periodical Literature.*[1] Produced on a regular basis, this Guide arranges both authors and subjects under a single alphabet system. The periodicals indexed are listed at the beginning of the guide. Then specific references are in alphabetical order. The Guide is bound by year (1989, 1990, and so forth), so it is helpful for you to begin with some time frame in mind, although that's not necessary. (See Figure 14.3.)

Imagine you want to find some information concerning the European Economic Community. You merely search through the index of the Guide until you locate that subject heading. As you examine the articles listed, you notice an article titled "Reshaping Europe: 1992 and Beyond" with a notation that it's a cover story in *Business Week,* December 12, 1988. The title sounds interesting, so you write down the appropriate reference information—title, magazine, date, and page reference. Your next step is to determine where the library's periodicals, or serials, collection is kept. If the article is fairly recent, it is probably available in "hard copy"—the actual magazine or other periodical. If, though, it is an older piece, it is probably on microfilm.

Microfilm or microfiche, sometimes called "microform," merely refers to printed material that has been reduced in size and stored on film. In order to use this material, you'll need to learn how to use microfilm and microfiche readers. Don't be fearful of such machines. Machine readers basically take a reduced copy and enlarge it on a display screen in order to make it readable. With a microfilm reader, for instance, instructions are generally posted near the machine and the process is simply one of loading the film, viewing the appropriate article, copying information if necessary, and rewinding. It's just that simple. Remember to read the directions carefully or ask a librarian for help.

The *Book Review Index*[2] is another useful source of information. Frequently, you'll want to find out what the reviewers—"the critics"—have to say about important books. Or perhaps an instructor wants you to compare how different reviewers react to a controversial publication. The *Book Review Index* is the place to start (see Figure 14.4).

EUROPE, CENTRAL *See* Central Europe
EUROPE, EASTERN *See* Eastern Europe
EUROPE, WESTERN *See* Western Europe
EUROPE (MUSICAL GROUP)
Europe's Joey Tempest. E. Miller. il pors *Seventeen* 47:109-10+ My '88
EUROPE AND THE UNITED STATES
See also
United States—Foreign opinion—European
EUROPEAN COOKING *See* Cooking, European
EUROPEAN CURRENCY UNIT
Britain [sale of Treasurys denominated in European Currency Units] S. Miller. *Business Week* p59 Ag 15 '88
EUROPEAN ECONOMIC COMMUNITY
See also
ERASMUS (Organization)
British airline merger may provide test case for new pro-competition rules [EEC studying British Airways-British Caledonian Airways merger] *Aviation Week & Space Technology* 128:74 Ja 11 '88
Can Thatcher afford to be cool to the continent? S. Miller and others. por *Business Week* p55 Je 13 '88
Countdown to European unity. N. Gelb. il *The New Leader* 71:6-7 Mr 21 '88
EEC extracts concessions in approving airline merger [British Airways and British Caledonian] *Aviation Week & Space Technology* 128:253 Mr 14 '88
Europe seeks strategy for biology. D. Dickson. il *Science* 240:710-12 My 6 '88
The European Community: twelve becoming one. P.-H. Laurent. bibl f *Current History* 87:357-60+ N '88
European defense protectionism could weaken alliance with U.S. R. Burt. por *Aviation Week* &CF61 Space Technology 129:75+ N 7 '88
A European revolution. A. Phillips. il *Maclean's* 101:43-5 D 5 '88
Europe's East-West politics of trade [EC-Comecon agreement] P. Sherrid. il *U.S. News & World Report* 105:42 N 14 '88
Europhobia in Downing Street. B. Amiel. il *Maclean's* 101:7 My 30 '88
Loosening the restraints on Europe's merger mania. J. Kapstein. il *Business Week* p44-5 Je 13 '88
Mitterrand's new agenda: the United States of Europe. F. J. Comes and J. Rossant. por *Business Week* p57 Je 6 '88
New threat to the happy Lilliputs [Andorra, Liechtenstein, Monaco, San Marino, and the Vatican] *World Press Review* 35:36-7 D '88
No fences make good markets. R. Z. Chesnoff. il *U.S. News & World Report* 104:40-2 F 29 '88
Outsider's guide to Europe in 1992. R. I. Kirkland, Jr. il *Fortune* 118:121-2+ O 24 '88
The politics of acid rain control in Europe. Mr. Pallemaerts. bibl f *Environment* 30:42-4 Mr '88
Reshaping Europe: 1992 and beyond [cover story; special section] il map *Business Week* p48-51+ D 12 '88
Toward a unified Europe. P. Lewis. *Maclean's* 101:41 Je 6 '88
Toward real community? [1992 deadline for full integration of markets] F. Painton. il *Time* 131:54-5 Ap 18 '88
The U.S. should applaud the coming of Europe Inc. R. Kuttner. por *Business Week* p16 Jl 11 '88
A United States of Europe? *National Review* 40:18-19 Ag 19 '88
Western Europe. S. Luxenberg. il *Schlastic Update (Teacher's edition)* 121:19 S 9 '88
Who's afraid of 1992? S. Sullivan. il map *Newsweek* 112:32-4 O 31 '88
EUROPEAN HELICOPTER INDUSTRIES
Agusta, Westland develop recovery plan for EH101. J. M. Kenorovitz. *Aviation Week &* Space Technology 128:51+ Ja 11 '88
Canada may require more than 100 EH-101s for military, civil roles [helicopter] *Aviation Week* & Space Technology 129:30 Jl 11 '88
EUROPEAN ORGANIZATION FOR NUCLEAR RESEARCH
Britain decides to stay in CERN. D. Dickson. il *Science* 242:1629 D 23 '88
Britain to remain in CERN for now. D. Dickson. *Science* 239:16 Ja '88
EUROPEAN SOUTHERN OBSERVATORY (ORGANIZATION)
Beckers leaves NOAO for ESO project. *Physics Today* 41:72 Je '88
A European behemoth [Very Large Telescope] M. M. Waldrop. il *Science* 240:31 Ap 1 '88
Europe's astronomy machine [Very Large Telescope project in Chile] R. M. West. il *Sky and Telescope* 75:471-81 My '88

Figure 14.3 Reader's Guide to Periodical Literature

McNeely, Jeffrey A - *Soul of the Tiger*
KR - v56 - Ap 1 '88 - p518
LATBR - My 15 '88 - p4
LJ - v113 - Je 1 '88 - p124
NYTBR - v93 - S 11 '88 - p27
PW - v233 - Ap 22 '88 - p68
McNeil, Elisabeth - *The Shanghai Emerald*
Brit Bk N - S '87 - p612
McNeil, Helen - *Emily Dickinson*
AL - v59 - O '87 - p458
Lon R Bks - v9 - O 29 '87 - p22
McNeil, Linda M - *Contradictions of Control*
CS - v17 - Jl '88 - p549
McNeil, Maureen - *Gender and Expertise*
TES - Mr 18 '88 - p32
Under the Banner of Science
J Hist G - v14 - Ap '88 - p221
TLS - D 11 '87 - p1370
McNeil, W K - *Southern Folk Ballads, Vol. 1*
CAY - v8 - Winter '87 - p8
Choice - v25 - F '88 - p918
McNeil, William C - *American Money and the Weimar Republic*
AAPSS-A - v493 - S '87 - p198
BHR - v61 - Autumn '87 - p520
Historian - v50 - My '88 - p434
PHR - v57 - My '88 - p253
McNeile, H C - *Bulldog Drummond. Audio Version*
Lis - v121 - O 20 '88 - p36
McNeill, John J - *The Church and the Homosexual, 3rd ed.*
LATBR - Ap 24 '88 - p14
Taking a Chance on God
BL - v85 - S 15 '88 - p102
McNitt, Lawrence - *Invitation to APL for the IBM-PC*
CBR - v6 - S '88 - p51
McNulty, Faith - *Peeping in the Shell (Illus. by Irene Brady)*
c BL - v84 - D 1 '87 - p642
McPhail, Thomas L - *Electronic Colonialism. Rev. ed.*
JC - v38 - Spring '88 - p179
McPhee, John - *Coming into the Country*
Aud - v90 - My '88 - p22
Rising from the Plains
y Kliatt - v22 - Ap '88 - p48
NYTBR - v92 - N 29 '87 - p34
Trib Bks - N 22 '87 - p11
WAL - v22 - Fall '87 - p250
A Sense of Where You Are
y EJ - v77 - Ap '88 - p83
McPhee, Marnie - *Western Oregon*
R&R Bk N - v3 - Ap '88 - p6
McPherson, Aimee S - *This Is That*
Rel St Rev - v14 - Ap '88 - p177
McPherson, Andrew - *Governing Education*
TES - Je 10 '88 - p28
McPherson, Ann - *Women's Problems in General Practice, 2nd ed.*
Brit Bk N - N '87 - p743
McPherson, Bruce R - *Likely Stories*
R Contem Fic - v8 - Spring '88 - p196
McPherson, Harry - *A Political Education*
PW - v234 - 14 '88 - p69
McPherson, James M - *Battle Cry of Freedom*
AH - v39 - Jl '88 - p103
BL - v84 - Ja 15 '88 - p826
BW - v18 - Mr 13 '88 - p1
Choice - v25 - Jl '88 - p1745
Econ - v308 - Ag 20 '88 - p77
GW - v138 - Ap 3 '88 - p20
KR - v56 - Ja 1 '88 - p42
LATBR - Mr 20 '88 - p10
LJ - v113 - Mr 1 '88 - p65
NW - v111 - Ap 11 '88 - p77
NYRB - v35 - Je 2 '88 - p9
NYTBR - v93 - F 14 '88 - p1
SFRB - v13 - #1 '88 - p39
Trib Bks - Mr 20 '88 - p3
Wil Q - v12 - #4 '88 - p140
WSJ - v211 - Mr 30 '88 - p16
McPherson, Sandra - *Streamers*
PW - v234 - Ag 12 '88 - p434
McPherson, William - *To the Sargasso Sea*
Books - Mr '88 - p16
BW - v18 - S 4'88 - p12
HR - v40 - Winter '88 - p673
NYTBR - v93 - S 4 '88 - p24
PW - v234 - Jl 15 '88 - p62
McQuaid, Kim - *Big Business and Presidential Power*
Historian - v49 - Ag '87 - p584
McQuaig, Linda - *Behind Closed Doors*
BIC - v16 - D '87 - p22
Quill & Q - v53 - D '87 - p24
McQuail, Denis - *Mass Communication Theory*
JC - v37 - Summer '87 - p117
Mass Communication Theory, 2nd ed.
JC - v38 - Summer '88 - p191
New Media Politics
CS - v16 - S '87 - p722
JC - v37 - Summer '87 - p146
McQuarrie, Donald A - *General Chemistry, 2nd ed.*
y SB - v23 - Mr '88 - p223
McQuarrie, Jane - *Canadian Picture Books/Livres D'Images Canadiens*
r Lib Info Sci - v3 - '87 - p99
r RT - v41 - Ja '88 - p437
Index to Canadian Poetry in English
r Indexer - v15 - O '87 - p250

Figure 14.4 *Book Review Index*

Imagine that you are interested in reviews of James M. McPherson's study of the Civil War, *Battle Cry of Freedom.*[3] A search of the *Book Review Index* for 1988 indicates 16 entries—review references—for this book, including such publications as *American Heritage* and the *Wilson Quarterly.* With such information in hand, you can then proceed to locate those periodicals in your library and read the reviews.

College and university libraries also maintain a large number of specialized indexes such as the *Art Index* and the *Humanities Index.* These indexes focus on specific subject areas and are therefore especially helpful for particular fields of study. If, for instance, you were asked to do some research for your social science course, you might look to the *Social Science Index.*[4] This "cumulative index to English language periodicals" covers such fields as anthropology, political science, psychology, and urban studies. The index is also arranged alphabetically according to author and subject. (See Figure 14.5.)

Many book-type indexes are available to assist you in locating information in your library, so learn to use them.

Academic Index

A newer system for researching periodicals is the Academic Index.[5] This is a computer-based system called InfoTrac. It provides computer access to a periodicals index, including such areas as the humanities, the social sciences, and so forth, and is typical of how technology is influencing library research. It is a system that is quick and easy to use.

For instance, to begin your search of the system, you merely press "Enter." The next step, clearly presented on screen, is "Enter subject or name you wish to find." For example, you might want to find something about acid rain, so you enter that subject. Since this is a large subject area, the program will ask you for more specific information. Now you can narrow the subject of acid rain by typing "pollution." At this point the screen will begin to display references and you can "key down" to continue the list. At one point you will come to an entry for a book review titled "The Acid Rain Controversy." This article sounds interesting, so you follow the instruction to "press enter to view citation," which provides a more complete reference for the article. Then you may decide you want to locate that reference, so you enter "print" and the text of the reference is printed for you along with the notation that the "Library Subscribes to Journal." (See Figure 14.6.) Now you're ready to locate the journal and read the article.

APRIL 1988 TO MARCH 1989

Marsh loss in Nanticoke estuary, Chesapeake Bay. M. S. Kearney and others. bibl maps *Geogr Rev* 78:205–20 Ap '88

Marsiglio, William

Commitment to social fatherhood: predicting adolescent males' intentions to live with their child and partner. bibl *J Marriage Fam* 50:427–41 My '88

Marsiglio, William, and Mott, Frank L.

Does wanting to become pregnant with a first child affect subsequent maternal behaviors and infant birth weight? bibl *J Marriage Fam* 50:1023–36 N '88

Marson, Daniel C., and others

Psychiatric decision making in the emergency room: a research overview. *Am J Psychiatry* 145:918–25 Ag '88; Discussion. 146:291–2 F '89

Marston, Albert R., and others

Characteristics of adolescents at risk for compulsive overeating on a brief screening test. *Adolescence* 23:59–65 Spr '88

Martel, John S.

Lawyer burnout: it's causes - some thoughts on prevention. *Trial* 24:62–71 Jl '88

Martial Arts

Psychological aspects

Survival of the species. Y. Roberts. *New Statesman* 115:12–13 Mr 4 '88

China

Qigong - popularity is rising. Liu Zhuoye and Zhang Xingbo. *Beijing Rev* 31:32–5 N 14 '88

Martial law

See also

Courts-martial and courts of inquiry

Poland

The crushing of Solidarity [interview with R. Kuklinski] *Orbis* 32:6–31 Wint '88

Martin, A. Damien

(jt. auth) See Hetrick, Emery S., 1930–1987, and Martin, A. Damien

Martin, A. Damien, and Hetrick, Emery S., 1930–1987

The stigmatization of the gay and lesbian adolescent. bibl *J Homosex* 15 no1–2:163–83 '88

Martin, George M., and Turker, Mitchell S.

Minireview: model systems for the genetic analysis of mechanisms of aging. bibl *J Gerontol* 43:B33–9 Mr '88

Martin, Gillian

Harmony and discord: the relationship between Australian societies and their environment; review article. *J Hist Geogr* 14:420–4 O '88

Martin, Gordon A., Jr., and Lewis, David C.

Drug offenses and the probation system: a 17-year followup of probationer status. *Fed Probat* 52:17–27 Je '88

Martin, J. P. (John Powell)

The development of criminology in Britain 1948–60. *Br J. Criminol* 28:165–74 Spr '88

Martin, John D., and others

A study of the relationship between a personal philosophy of human nature (good or evil) and self-esteem. bibl *Psychol Rep* 61:447–51 O '87

Martin, John F., and Reddy, P. Govinda

Gidjingali and Yolngu polygyny: age structure and the control of marriage. bibl *Oceania* 57:243–60 Je '87; Discussion. 58:63–4 S '87

Martin, John Powell *See* Martin, J. P. (John Powell)

Martin, Julia Vitullo- *See* Vitullo-Martin, Julia

Martin, Lawrence L.

(jt. auth) See Berman, David R., and Martin, Lawrence L.

Martin, Linda G., 1947-

The aging of Asia. bibl *J Gerontol* 43:S99–113 Jl '88

Martin, M. J., and others

Comments on references to the American Board of Psychiatry and Neurology in an article. *Am J Psychiatry* 145:774–5 Je '88

Martin, Paul R., and others

Figure 14.5 Social Science Index

Academic Index

THE ACID RAIN CONTROVERSY.
-(book reviews)
The Acid Rain Controversy. (book reviews) by James L. Regens and Robert W. Rycroft rev by Jurgen Schmandt
A v244 Science April 14 '89 p234(2)
LIBRARY SUBSCRIBES TO JOURNAL

Figure 14.6 Academic Index

Learning to use the card catalog, the *Readers' Guide to Periodical Literature,* the Academic Index, and similar sources for locating information is critical to academic success. Moreover, these systems are extremely easy to use once you become familiar with them.

A Brief Exercise

Choose some subject of interest to you—medical care, urban pollution, agricultural policy, campaign financing. Then begin a search for information with the card catalog. Find references for at least two books and write down the author, the title, and the call number. Next go to the *Readers' Guide,* or one of the more specialized indexes appropriate to your subject, look up your subject, and locate at least two magazine or journal articles. Write down all necessary information such as author, title, name of magazine, date of publication, and page number. Try the same approach with the Academic Index or a similar system. Keep this information on a separate sheet of paper and use it to locate the information you need the next time you're asked to write a paper on a subject of your choice.

Summary and Prediction Questions

1. Summary: What are the primary sources for accessing library information?
2. Prediction: Why should the library play a central role in the learning process?

LIBRARIES AND LEARNING

The library plays a central role in learning simply because it is at the heart of the information explosion. While books are still the mainstay of the library, rapid changes in the availability of information require changes in how you obtain information. You can still read a Shakespearean play in your bed late at night. But if you want to see the play—and cannot attend a professional performance—many libraries contain video productions that are the next best thing to being there. Watching the video gives you an understanding of the performance that the text cannot.

Libraries also subscribe to hundreds, perhaps thousands, of periodicals, from *Newsweek* to *American Journal of Psychiatry* to the *Beijing Review.* In addition, they store past issues on microfilm and microfiche, creating a complete collection for each special subject. In this case, the library is the source of information and provides the means for obtaining the technology to access and retrieve the information.

Libraries provide further opportunities for learning through extensive reference sections. In most libraries, the reference section contains books that must be consulted *at* the library and cannot be taken out. Generally the material in reference is highly specialized, factual information that is used for quick reference rather than extensive study. Reference works range from the eight-volume *Critical Survey of Poetry*[6] to the twenty-volume *McGraw-Hill Encyclopedia of Science and Technology,*[7] and from *The Weather Almanac*[8] to *The New Grove Dictionary of Music and Musicians,*[9] another twenty-volume work. Reference materials are an important source of much specialized information.

Furthermore, college and university libraries have computer systems that allow users to search information stored on discs (called CD-ROM—compact disc read-only memory) or to use online search services of nationwide, remote databases, which provide fast and effective access to an extremely vast amount of information previously unavailable for practical use. The impact of computers on storage and retrieval of information has been phenomenal. As the link between information and technology grows, libraries continue to serve as a central force in coordinating attempts to offer students and others access to available information.

Finally, libraries play a central role in the learning process simply because professionally trained librarians can offer expert information to the novice researcher. Rare is the time that a librarian can't help you begin a search for the answer to a question that may seem baffling initially. Reference collections—which tend to remain unknown to, or unused by, all but the specialized researcher or librarian—can provide a vast array of information. Moreover, most libraries maintain special collections related to the school's areas of expertise; they also maintain historically valuable collections. Libraries play a central role in academic learning because librarians are the link between students and information. Without their knowledge and expertise much could be overlooked.

A Brief Exercise

Take time to sit down and chat with a librarian about the link between the information explosion and the new technologies available for accessing information. Find out what your library has available and how you might use it.

Summary and Prediction Questions

1. Summary: Why should the library play a central role in the learning process?
2. Prediction: How can the library experience be monitored?

MONITORING THE LIBRARY EXPERIENCE

Monitoring your library use means asking two main questions. The first is, "Am I aware of and familiar with the various resources of the library?" The second is, "Do I use these resources as necessary for active learning?" To be successful, make sure your response to these questions is yes. To monitor your library activities, consider these questions:

Self-monitoring Checklist

_____ Have I participated in a library orientation program?

_____ Do I have any of the library's informational brochures?

_____ Have I visited the library and talked with any of the librarians or made a personal investigation of the library to familiarize myself with what is available?

_____ Am I able to use the card catalog or computer catalog as a ready source of information?

_____ Am I familiar with and do I regularly use the *Readers' Guide to Periodical Literature,* the Academic Index, and similar indexes for locating information?

_____ Am I aware of the type of information available in the reference section of the library?

_____ Do I know how to use and do I make use of the microfilm and microfiche readers?

_____ Am I aware of the various computer resources available in the library?

_____ Do I ask for the help of a librarian if I have a special request or encounter a particular problem?

_____ How can I improve my use of the library?

Summary Question

How can the library experience be monitored?

SUMMARY

The theme of this chapter is that the library is of central importance in active learning. In order to use the library to the fullest extent, you must become familiar with its vast array of resources and learn how to use them to your benefit. Monitor your experience with the goal of continuous improvement in mind and success will be yours.

Review Questions

1. How are the resources of a modern library best investigated?
2. What are the primary sources for accessing library information?
3. Why should the library play a central role in the learning process?
4. How can the library experience be monitored?

CHAPTER REVIEW

To complete this chapter, answer the following questions. When you are finished, review the chapter to check your answers.

1. True or False: The card catalog or computer catalog is probably a useful place to begin a library search.
2. True or False: A microfiche reader is probably too complicated for most people to use.
3. True or False: Most libraries use the Dewey Decimal System or the Library of Congress system to catalog their book collections.
4. True or False: The Book Review Index provides specific information about where to locate reviews of a particular book.
5. An investigation of your library might follow which of the following strategies?
   a. Attend a library orientation.
   b. Read available informational brochures.

c. Ask a librarian for help.
d. All of the above.

6. A good place to begin searching for recent articles about a particular subject is
   a. the reference section of the library.
   b. the computer catalog.
   c. the *Readers' Guide to Periodical Literature.*
   d. the nearest bookstore.
7. Describe the process of locating a particular book in the card catalog and then locating that book in the library.

___

___

___

___

8. What information should you record from a periodical index so you can locate a particular article in a magazine?

___

___

___

___

9. Discuss how a librarian might help you solve a problem in locating a specific type of information.

___

___

___

___

10. In what ways are libraries central to active learning?

____

____

____

____

NOTES

1. Jean M. Marra (Ed.), *Readers' Guide to Periodical Literature: 1988* (New York: H. W. Wilson, 1989), p. 678.
2. Barbara Beach and Beverly Baer (Eds.), *Book Review Index: 1988 Cumulation* (Detroit: Gale Research, 1989), p. 550.
3. James E. McPherson, *Battle Cry of Freedom* (New York: Oxford University Press), 1988.
4. Cheryl Ehrens and Louis J. Hoffman (Eds.), *Social Science Index: April 1988 to March 1989* (New York: H. W. Wilson, 1989), p. 905.
5. Academic Index: "InfoTrac." Information Access Company, Belmont, Calif.
6. Frank N. Magill (Ed.), *Critical Survey of Poetry,* vols. 1–8 (Englewood Cliffs, N.J.: Salem Press, 1982).
7. Sybil P. Parker (Ed.), *McGraw-Hill Encyclopedia of Science and Technology,* 6th ed., vols. 1–20 (New York: McGraw-Hill, 1987).
8. James A. Ruffner and Frank E. Bair (Eds.), *The Weather Almanac,* 5th ed. (Detroit: Gale Research, 1987).
9. Stanley Sadie, *The New Grove Dictionary of Music and Musicians,* vols. 1–20 (London: Macmillan, 1980).

Post-assessment Questionnaire

When you began reading this book on active learning, you assessed your study behavior with a questionnaire. Since then, you have learned a great deal about how to learn, how to study, and how to improve your habits through your own efforts. Now it's time to take another look at how you assess your study habits. By comparing the results of your earlier assessment with this one, you have an opportunity to judge your progress in each area and to decide where further improvement may be necessary.

Self-assessment Form

Directions: For each of the statements below, circle the number most closely reflecting your behavior. Answer all statements and be honest about what you do even if you know you should use a different approach. Try to gain an accurate understanding of your actual study habits.

1 = Never
2 = Rarely
3 = Sometimes
4 = Frequently
5 = Always

Active Learning

1. I regularly prepare a plan of action to successfully complete my course requirements.	1 2 3 4 5
2. When preparing for any assignment, I have a clear purpose in mind.	1 2 3 4 5
3. I frequently summarize important information as I study.	1 2 3 4 5
4. I keep track of the progress of my studying by asking and answering questions about the material.	1 2 3 4 5
5. Continuous review is a regular part of my study schedule.	1 2 3 4 5

Managing Time Effectively

1. I prepare a general schedule of activities at the beginning of each semester.	1 2 3 4 5
2. As each assignment is given, I make a plan for completing the assignment and integrate it into my general schedule.	1 2 3 4 5
3. When I set up a study schedule, I also take into account my need for rest and relaxation.	1 2 3 4 5
4. As I plan a schedule, I allow enough flexibility to deal with unexpected events.	1 2 3 4 5
5. Whenever I organize a schedule, I keep in mind that some activities take priority over others.	1 2 3 4 5

Purposeful Study

1. I make sure I have a quiet place to work before I try to study.	1 2 3 4 5
2. I space my study periods so that I don't overload myself.	1 2 3 4 5
3. I establish goals for studying so that I know what I have to do and when I've completed the task.	1 2 3 4 5
4. I organize my time, place, and methods of study to make studying a habit.	1 2 3 4 5
5. Before I begin studying, I relax and clear my mind in order to concentrate on the task at hand.	1 2 3 4 5

Taking Lecture Notes

1. When I go to class, I make sure to take my notebook and a couple of pens or pencils.	1 2 3 4 5

2. As I listen to lectures, I pay close attention to the presentation and avoid daydreaming. 1 2 3 4 5
3. As I listen to lectures, I record important information as accurately as possible. 1 2 3 4 5
4. If necessary, I ask questions to fill any gaps that appear in my notes. 1 2 3 4 5
5. I review my notes as soon as possible after class and add anything I may have left out. 1 2 3 4 5

Reading Textbooks

1. Before reading a chapter, I take time to preview the material to prepare myself for reading. 1 2 3 4 5
2. As I read a chapter, I ask myself questions about the material and then read to answer those questions. 1 2 3 4 5
3. If the chapter is fairly long or contains a lot of new information, I divide it into manageable "chunks" in order to study it efficiently. 1 2 3 4 5
4. While reading I pay close attention to any charts, graphs, and illustrations that are presented. 1 2 3 4 5
5. I periodically review chapters until I am sure I know the information. 1 2 3 4 5

Marking Texts and Taking Notes

1. I underline important information as I read so that I can keep track of major points. 1 2 3 4 5
2. I use different methods for marking different types of information such as underlining important points and numbering supporting examples. 1 2 3 4 5
3. I make note of important information as I read by writing the ideas in my own words. 1 2 3 4 5
4. I periodically summarize important information while reading, especially following major subdivisions within a chapter. 1 2 3 4 5
5. I use text notes to organize a visual, or graphic, overview of my reading assignments, especially for chapter review. 1 2 3 4 5

Vocabulary and Concept Development

1. I actively seek the meaning of new words that I encounter. 1 2 3 4 5
2. If I encounter an unknown word while reading, I use the

context of the word and my knowledge of word parts to determine its meaning. 1 2 3 4 5

3. Because unfamiliar words in textbooks frequently represent new concepts, I read carefully for definitions and explanations. 1 2 3 4 5
4. I regularly devote extra attention to new concepts while studying, using special techniques—such as semantic mapping—when necessary. 1 2 3 4 5
5. I incorporate new words and concepts into my vocabulary by using them in my thinking, speaking, and writing. 1 2 3 4 5

Memory

1. With new information, I visualize the information mentally in order to remember it. 1 2 3 4 5
2. When I have a lot of information to memorize, I space the practice so I'm not trying to cover too much at one time. 1 2 3 4 5
3. In order to remember details, I rehearse the information by talking to myself. 1 2 3 4 5
4. I use mnemonic techniques (such as NATO = North Atlantic Treaty Organization) to aid my recall of information. 1 2 3 4 5
5. I organize information graphically in order to store it in my memory. 1 2 3 4 5

Taking Tests

1. As I prepare for exams, I make up sample questions based on the material I am studying. 1 2 3 4 5
2. When I begin a test, I read the directions twice and then survey the exam to make sure I know what to do. 1 2 3 4 5
3. When taking an essay test, I briefly outline my answer before I begin writing the essay. 1 2 3 4 5
4. Before answering any exam question, I read it carefully and completely. 1 2 3 4 5
5. On multiple choice and true-or-false tests I pay special attention to exact wording of the questions. 1 2 3 4 5

Studying Science and Math

1. I pay close attention to the pattern of organization used to present scientific information. 1 2 3 4 5

2. I regularly use the illustrations, graphs, and charts to better understand scientific explanations. 1 2 3 4 5
3. I apply a systematic approach to problem solving that emphasizes working practice problems. 1 2 3 4 5
4. I regularly use either the chapter's "discussion questions" or my own question-and-answer techniques to monitor my understanding of a textbook chapter. 1 2 3 4 5
5. I typically sketch drawings and graphs as a method for studying scientific information. 1 2 3 4 5

Reading Literature

1. When I read literature, I give special attention to plot, setting, character, and theme. 1 2 3 4 5
2. To read actively, I continually ask questions about elements like plot and character, and I read for answers. 1 2 3 4 5
3. After reading, I summarize the plot to gain an overview of events. 1 2 3 4 5
4. I mentally visualize characters and events in order to understand and remember them. 1 2 3 4 5
5. While reading I continually analyze situations to infer the meaning or theme of the story. 1 2 3 4 5

Writing Papers

1. When preparing a report or paper, I develop a plan before I begin writing the first draft. 1 2 3 4 5
2. Before any writing I make sure I have done enough research and have enough information. 1 2 3 4 5
3. I use an outline to organize the information for my paper. 1 2 3 4 5
4. After writing the first draft, I revise as necessary according to the purpose of my paper and the needs of the intended audience. 1 2 3 4 5
5. I proofread my final draft for any errors in spelling or sentence structure. 1 2 3 4 5

Using the Library

1. I use the library as an important source of information. 1 2 3 4 5
2. I start with the card catalog or a computer index when doing library research. 1 2 3 4 5

3. I use the *Readers' Guide to Periodical Literature* or similar guides when preparing research papers.	1	2	3	4	5
4. When in doubt about how to locate some specific type of information, I ask a librarian.	1	2	3	4	5
5. I visit the library to read periodicals relevant to my course work.	1	2	3	4	5

ANALYZING THE ASSESSMENT

Once you have finished the questionnaire, you need to analyze your responses for an overall assessment. Notice that each statement is presented positively. In fact, each item indicates an effective approach to each subject. So one way to judge your strengths and weaknesses is to see how often you do these things. Frequent performance of an action suggests you are on the right track. If you do other things less frequently, there's room for improvement. This approach to the questionnaire offers specific information.

Next notice that each response is followed by the numbers 1 2 3 4 5. These numbers allow you to rate your responses. "Always" gives you a high score of 5, and "Never" yields a low score of 1. Now for each category of five statements, you should add your scores together. Say you circled 4 (Frequently) for the first item in the category, Managing Time Effectively. Then if your response to the next three statements was "Sometimes," the score is 3 for each. And one "Never" equals 1. The total score for those five statements is 14. Next, mark the score of 14 on the chart that follows. Simply locate the study skill area and put an "X" on the chart according to the score received. The score numbers across the top of the chart will guide the placement of your score.

Once your scores are plotted on the chart, you can make a graph of the scores by connecting the X's with lines. For example, a score of 18 for Active Learning, 14 for Managing Time Effectively, 11 for Purposeful Study, and 20 for Taking Lecture Notes, gives you the sample graph shown in figure 1. The total graph will give you a clear visual image of your scores. The finished graph is one way for you to see your strengths and weaknesses. You can plot your own scores on the blank chart provided as figure 2.

As you study the graph, look at where your scores are generally high. These are areas of strength. Strategies learned in this book are working. You may want to continue improving these areas, but you have a good start. Notice where your scores seem lower. Here your self-assessment

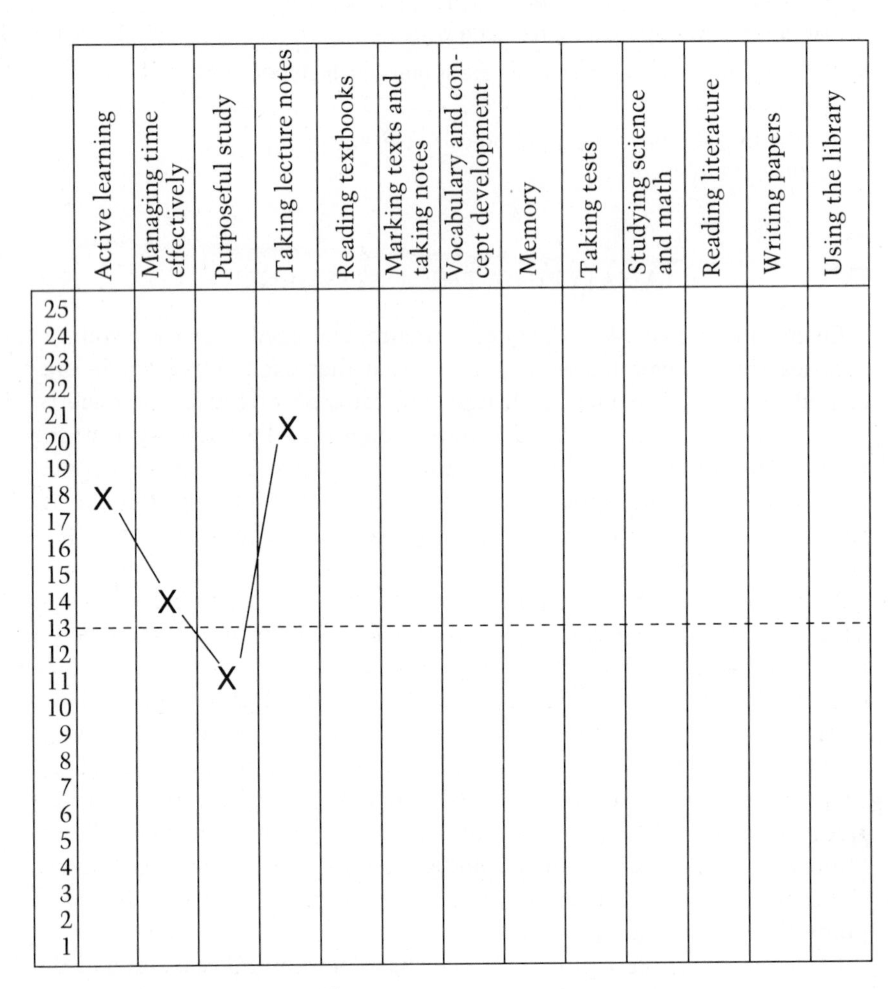

Figure 1 Sample Assessment Chart

alerts you to areas that still need attention. Problem areas usually require careful planning and extra effort. Your course instructor or a college counselor may have some good suggestions.

Finally, you may have some scores in the "Sometimes" category, around midpoint on the graph. The "Sometimes" response means you need a greater awareness of the topic and a more systematic approach to improvement. Consider reviewing specific chapters for additional guidance and apply strategies regularly.

	Active learning	Managing time effectively	Purposeful study	Taking lecture notes	Reading textbooks	Marking texts and taking notes	Vocabulary and concept development	Memory	Taking tests	Studying science and math	Reading literature	Writing papers	Using the library
25													
24													
23													
22													
21													
20													
19													
18													
17													
16													
15													
14													
13													
12													
11													
10													
9													
8													
7													
6													
5													
4													
3													
2													
1													

Figure 2 Self-assessment Chart

Remember that it's your responsibility to monitor your study habits. Stay alert to the need for improvement and work toward becoming an active learner.

Appendix to Chapter 5

BUSINESS 10/31

TOPIC: Marketing Research

Marketing res. to identify consumer need or problem

1ST clearly def. purpose

EX why a decline in sales

Exploratory res.

A. Internal inf.
1. sales inf.
2. marketing costs
3. financial records

B. External inf.
1. customer survey
2. retail mark. eval
3. govt. mark. data

↓

Information analyzed and interpreted

Figure 5.6 Sample Notes for Marketing Research

SHORT STORY 10/15

TOPIC: Plot str.

Plot = str. of events
= "What happens?"
(6 parts)

rising action ↗
5. Climax
falling action ↘
4. Crisis
3. Complication
6. Resolution (denouement)
2. Conflict
1. Intro.

Ex Richard Wright's "The Man Who Was Almost a Man"

1. Intro = Dave seeks manhood
2. Conflict = Prove manhood with a gun
3. Complication = Uses mother to get a gun
4. Crisis = Shoots wildly, kills a mule, lies about what happened;

Figure 5.7 Sample Notes for Understanding Plot Structure

SHORT STORY 10/15

Plot cont.

when truth known Dave laughed at, threatened, and in debt

5. Climax = Dave returns to shoot gun again, this time with control; tries to take control of his life

6. Resolution = Dave leaves on a train to find his future

Figure 5.7 *cont'd*

Define children's picture books?	CHILD. LIT. 9/25 TOPIC: Picture Books = a blend of text & illustration, each complements the other
List 4 values.	4 Values: 1) entertainment, 2) engagement, 3) lang. dev. & 4) visual imagination
How do picture books entertain? Give 2 ex.	1) entertainment - child immersed in illust. EX Spier's "The Fox Went Out..." EX Keats' "A Snowy Day" (child's play)
What do we mean by engagement?	2) egagement - draw child into story
Describe how Sendak's work creates engagement.	EX Sendak's "Where the Wild Things Are" — story of Max who behaves like wild thing and is punished, imagines going to where the wild things are, but returns home where someone loves him most of all. EX Zelinsky's "Hansel & Gretal" and Grifalconi's "Darkness & the Butterfly"

Figure 5.8 Sample Notes for "The Value of Children's Picture Books"

CHILD. LIT. 9/25

How do pict. books promote lang. dev.?

Give three different ex. of artistic technique in picture books.

Pict. Bks cont.

3) lang. dev. - lang experienced thru. books
EX Sendak - rhythmic
EX McCloskey - dialogue & narrative
helps child understand - interp.

4) visual imagination - images of lang. thru. artistic range of illus.
EX Haley's "A Story A Story" woodcut
EX Lionnie's "Swimmy" abstract watercolor-collage
EX Viorst "Alexander..." pen & ink

Figure 5.8 *cont'd*

Appendix to Chapter 6

AN EXERCISE IN PATTERNS

1. Major point
2. Sequence
3. Cause and effect
4. Comparison and contrast
5. Comparison and contrast
6. Enumeration
7. Example and illustration
8. Major point
9. Cause and effect
10. Example and illustration
11. Major point
12. Sequence
13. Major point
14. Sequence
15. Comparison and contrast
16. Enumeration
17. Sequence
18. Example and illustration

AN EXERCISE IN PREVIEWING

Sample Prediction

"The environment of the political system is the setting for politics. The attitudes people have and the way they behave is one part of that setting. Other parts include the cultural heritage, the natural environment, and the economy. Moreover, conditions, may change over time: rural to urban, agricultural to industrial."

Sample Purpose

"My purpose is to find out how the environment affects the politics of the country."

VISUALIZATION EXERCISE

The Almanac

- The first image that comes to mind is people reading, but not newspapers. Something else called an almanac.
- The next image is one of colonial New England with old salt box houses, a local "country" store, perhaps even an early harbor scene. Throughout people are standing around talking and reading and sharing articles in the almanac.
- A third image is of the almanac itself. Here's a little "pocket-sized and paper-bound" book, probably somewhat thinner than an actual book. Some people are using it to plan an event, others to prepare a meal, and still others to teach their children how to read or write. Some editions are quite nicer than others. But whatever edition, the almanac is everywhere.

Visual images of the almanac may be as simple as visualizing the almanac itself, or as complex as creating the total context in which the almanac is found. The important point is to understand the almanac through visual imagery.

AN EXERCISE ON READING TEXTBOOKS

"Public Opinion"

I. The preview clearly establishes the subject of public opinion and the focus on professional opinion makers. Television will be an important item and there is some discussion of philanthropic foundations.

- A good purpose for reading might be to find out who the professional opinion makers are and what sort of influence they have on the public's thinking.

II. A good question is, "Who are the professional opinion makers?"

- Important notes might include: Television has a major influence because so many people get their news from it. Major issues like Vietnam and civil rights were affected by TV coverage. And presidential elections become a focus of TV.
- Newspapers may not be as influential as TV, but they explore many issues in depth and many political leaders consider the coverage and commentary of newspapers.
- It is unclear here whether the mass media has a particular bias, but coverage is naturally selective and the preconceptions of some individuals must affect what information is presented.
- There are many smaller publications that actually promote a particular point of view such as the *Nation* and *The National Review.*
- Another source of opinion is the intellectuals, people who make their influence felt through research, writing, and teaching.
- Finally there are research centers like the Rand Corporation, groups like the Council on Foreign Relations, and philanthropic organizations like the Ford Foundation. Their research influences people.

Note that these items could be underlined in the text or written out in note form.

III. To answer the initial question: The professional opinion makers are television and newspapers, which have the most influence; smaller, yet significant, publications such as the *Nation;* the intellectuals; and various research and philanthropic organizations.

- The summary might look more like the notes in section II, or even the answer above, though perhaps with a bit more detail.

IV. The self-testing and review would continue until the material is mastered.

ANSWERS TO THE QUIZ

1. Television is preeminent simply because so many people get their news from television, and because presidential election campaigns increasingly focus on television, both news and advertising.

2. Television influenced public opinion during the war in Vietnam and the civil rights movement.
3. Newspapers generally go beyond TV in the depth of news coverage they provide and because they feature important columnists who influence political leaders.
4. A particular bias is unclear, but coverage is naturally selective and individual preconceptions surely affect decisions about what's important.
5. Intellectuals primarily influence public opinion through their research, writing, and teaching.
6. College faculty may be more liberal than the public at large, but there is no common point of view. The humanities faculty may be considered generally liberal, the business and engineering faculties more conservative.
7. Organizations like the Rand Corporation influence public opinion through their research; whereas organizations like the Council on Foreign Relations focus on educational activities.

Appendix to Chapter 7

SAMPLE RESPONSES

Small Groups

Triads at times can be more adaptable than dyads. However, on occasions they can be more unstable. "Two's company, three's a crowd" derived from this view. Triads are more stable in those situations when one member can help resolve quarrels between the other two. When three diplomats are negotiating offshore fishing rights, for example, one member of the triad may offer a concession that will break the deadlock between the other two. If that does not work, the third person may try to analyze the arguments of the other two in an effort to bring about a compromise. The formation of shifting pair-offs within triads can help stabilize the group. When it appears that one group member is weakening, one of the two paired members often will break the alliance and form a new one with the individual who had been isolated (Hare, 1976). This is often seen among groups of children engaged in games. In triads where there is no shifting of alliances and the configuration constantly breaks down into two against one, the group will become unstable and may eventually break up. In Aldous Huxley's novel *Brave New World* the political organization of the earth was organized into three eternally warring political powers. As one power seemed to be losing, one of the others would come to its aid in a temporary alliance, thereby assuring worldwide political stability while also making possible endless warfare. No power could risk the total defeat of another because the other surviving power might then become the stronger of the surviving dyad.

As a group gets larger, the number of relationships within it increases, which often leads to the formation of *subgroups*—splinter groups within the larger group. Once a group has more than five to seven members, spontaneous conversation becomes difficult for the group as a whole. Then there are two solutions available: the group can split into subgroups (as happens informally at parties), or it can adopt a formal means of controlling communication (use of *Robert's Rules of Order,* for instance). For these reasons small groups tend to resist the addition of new members because increasing size threatens the nature of the group. In addition there may be a fear that new members will resist socialization to group norms and thereby undermine group traditions and values. On the whole, small groups are much more vulnerable than large groups to disruption by new members, and the introduction of new members often leads to shifts in patterns of interaction and group norms.

Problems in Race and Ethnic Relations

As different kinds of people have come together, there have been difficulties between and among the various groups. People's suspicions and fears are often aroused by those whom they feel to be "different."

Prejudice

People, particularly those who have a strong sense of identity, often have feelings of prejudice toward others who are not like themselves. Literally, *prejudice* means "a prejudgment." According to Louis Wirth (1944) prejudice is "an attitude with an emotional bias." But there is a problem with this definition. All of us, through the process of socialization, acquire attitudes, which may not be in response only to racial and ethnic groups but toward many things in our environment. We come to have attitudes about cats, roses, blue eyes, chocolate cheesecake, television programs, and even ourselves. These attitudes run the gamut from love to hate, from esteem to contempt, from loyalty to indifference. How have we developed these attitudes? Has it been through the scientific evaluation of information, or by other, less logical means? For our purposes at this point we will need to define prejudice more precisely: *prejudice* is an attitude that predisposes a person to think, perceive, feel, and act in favorable or unfavorable ways toward a group or its individual members (Secord and Backman, 1974). In most cases prejudice takes a negative form.

What is the cause of prejudice? Although pursuing that question is beyond the scope of this book, we can list some of the uses to which prejudice is put, and the social functions it serves. First, a prejudice, simply because it is shared, helps draw together those who hold it. It promotes a feeling of "we-ness," of being part of an in-group—and it helps define such group boundaries. Especially in a complex world, belonging to an in-group and consequently feeling "special" or "superior" can be an important social identity for many people.

Second, when two or more groups are competing against each other for access to scarce resources (jobs, for example), it makes it easier if one can write off its competitors as somehow "less than human" or inherently unworthy. Nations at war consistently characterize each other negatively, using terms that seem to deprive the enemy of any humanity whatsoever.

Third, psychologists suggest that prejudice allows us to "project" onto others those parts of ourselves that we do not like and therefore try to avoid facing. For example, most of us feel stupid at one time or another. How comforting it is to know that we belong to a group that is inherently more intelligent than another group! Who does not feel lazy sometimes? But how good it is that we do not belong to that group—the one everybody knows is lazy!

Of course, prejudice also has many negative consequences, or dysfunctions, to use the sociological term. For one thing, it limits our vision of the world around us, reducing social complexities and richness to a sterile and empty caricature. But aside from this effect on us as individuals, prejudice also has negative consequences for the whole of society. Most notably it is the necessary basic ingredient of discrimination, a problem found in many societies—including our own.

SAMPLE RESPONSES FOR SENTENCE SUMMARY EXERCISE

1. People have a need for consistency in their everyday lives.
2. Self-concept influences the way people process information and may distort information to make it consistent with what they think.
3. In one experiment, students were grouped according to high, moderate, and low self-concept; then all were given the same personality test results.
4. Students in the experiment received the results in a manner consistent with their self-concepts; high emphasized positive feedback, low accepted interpretations emphasizing negative feedback.
5. The experiment demonstrates that self-concept determines how people view themselves and interpret feedback.
6. Self-concept also influences how people interpret their own behavior.
7. Unrealistically favorable self-concepts may cause some people to refuse responsibility for their failure.

8. High self-esteem individuals attribute success to their efforts and failure to external factors, for low self-esteem the opposite is true.
9. An experiment with students supports the view that low self-esteem people do not accept positive interpretations about themselves, while high self-esteem people do not accept negative views.

SAMPLE SUMMARY FOR "PROBLEMS IN RACE AND ETHNIC RELATIONS"

"Different kinds of people have difficulty with various other groups. A strong sense of identity suggests a possibility of prejudice toward others who are different. Prejudice is essentially a predisposition to view others either favorably or unfavorably. In some sense, prejudice is the natural consequence of shared attitudes, a defense against competing groups, and a projection of things we don't like about ourselves onto others. Prejudice can have clearly negative consequences, or dysfunctions."

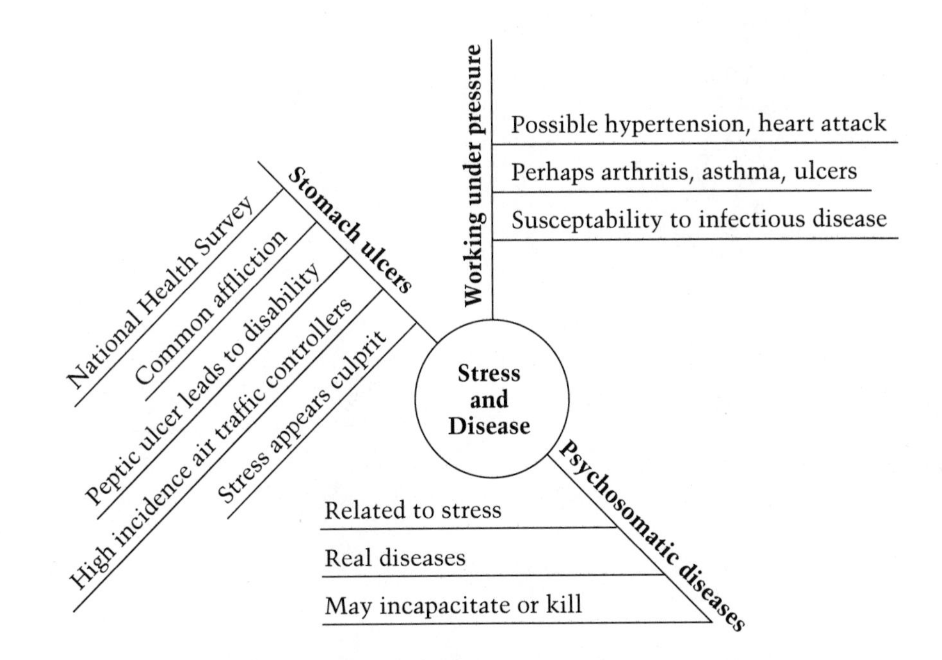

Figure 7.9 Sample Map of "Stress and Disease"

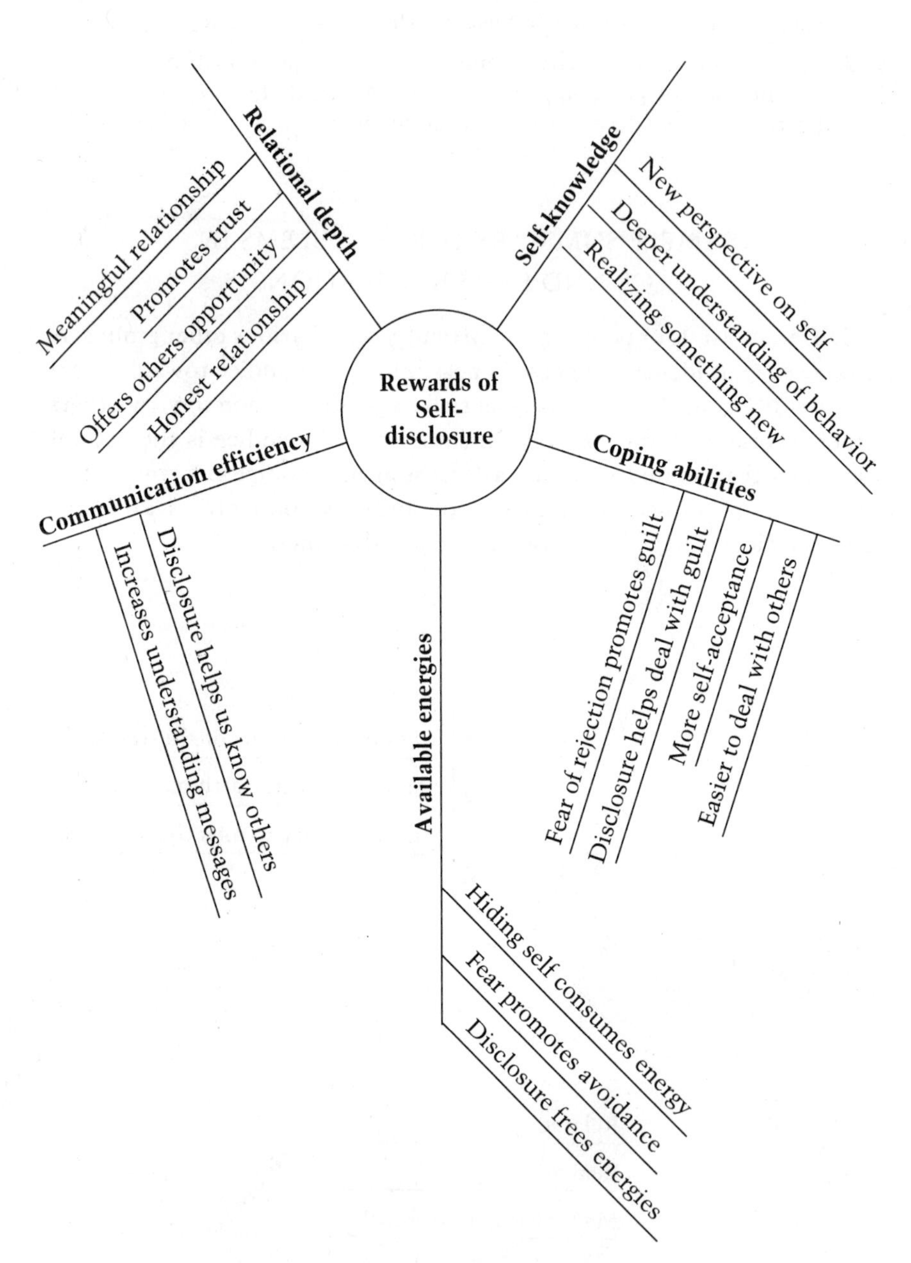

Figure 7.10 Sample Map for "Rewards of Self-disclosure"

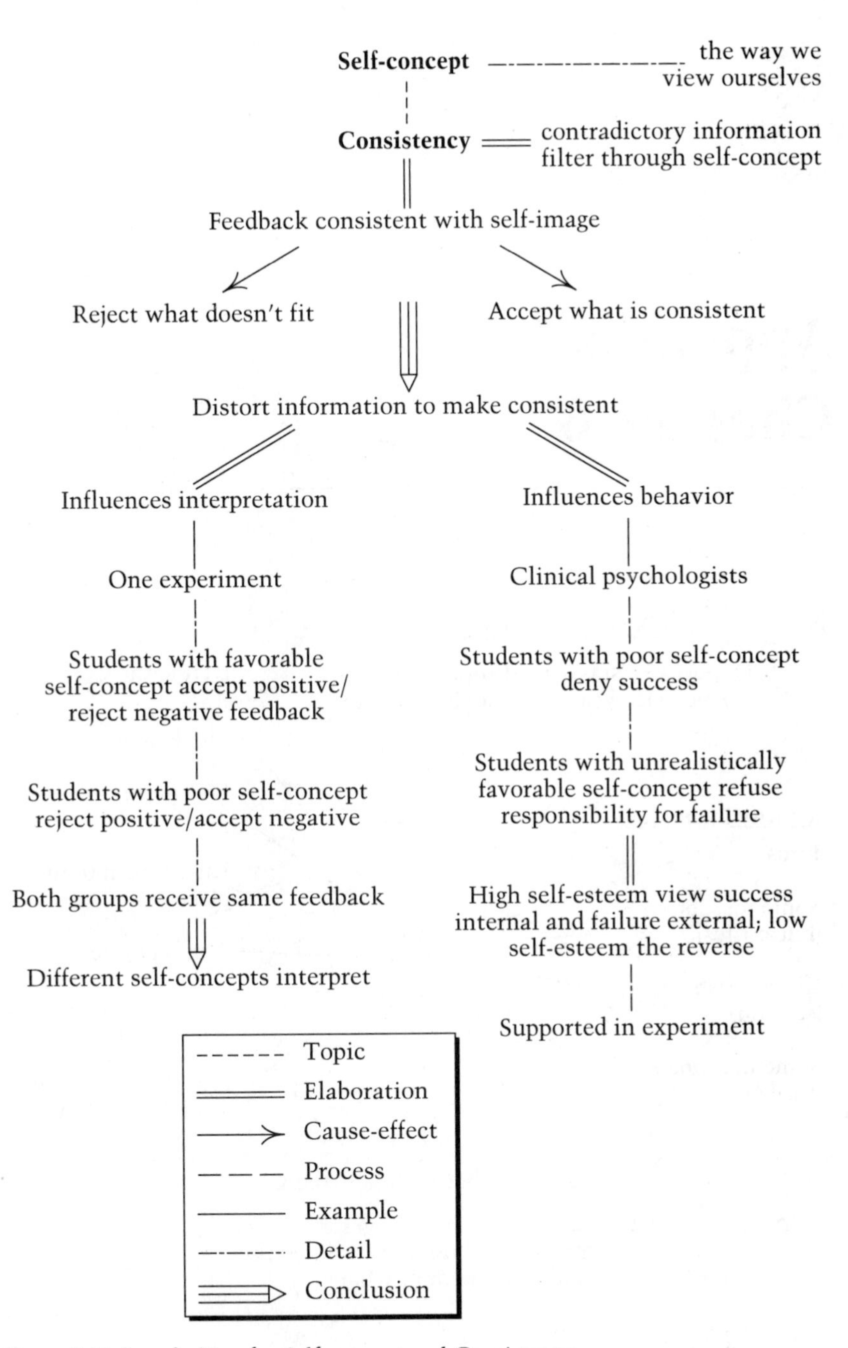

Figure 7.11 Sample Map for Self-concept and Consistency

Appendix to Chapter 8

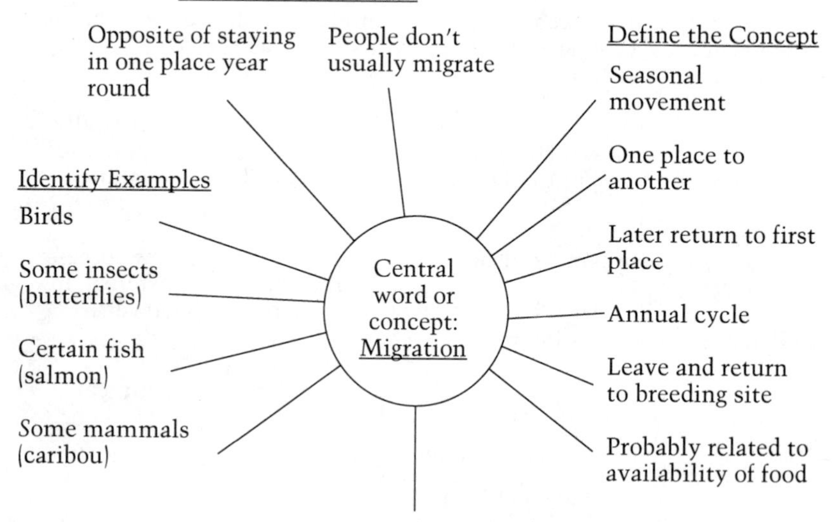

Figure 8.5 Sample Semantic Map: Migration

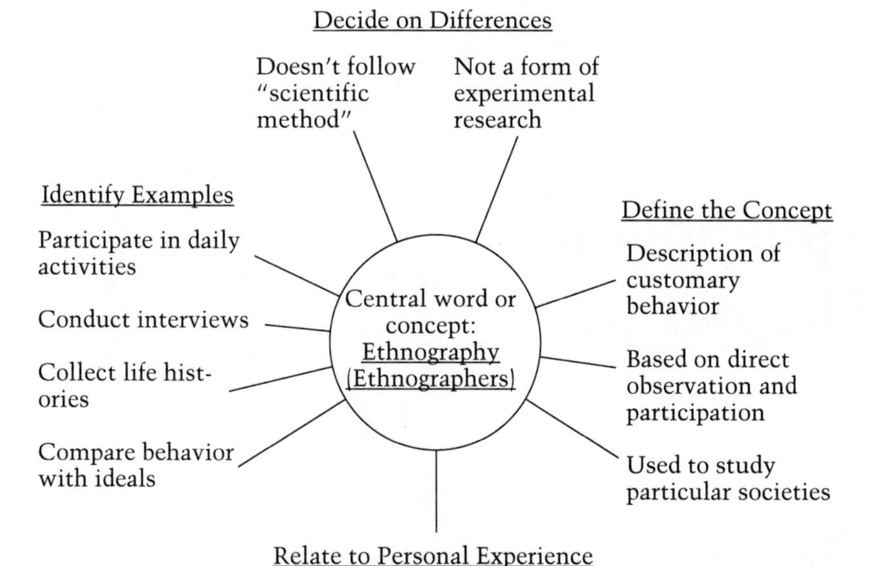

Figure 8.6 Sample Semantic Map: Ethnography

Appendix to Chapter 10

SAMPLE QUESTIONS ON MANAGEMENT OF SMALL BUSINESSES

1. True or False: Establishing standards for employee performance is necessary for the success of any small business.

2. True or False: Various alternatives are possible when a manager takes corrective action to solve a specific problem.

3. Which of the following is not a step discussed for directing employee activities?
   a. Establish standards of performance.
   b. Develop a training program.
   c. Compare performance with standards.
   d. Take any necessary corrective action.

4. Which of the following conditions indicates whether the manager's corrective action has worked?
   a. The employee feels less hassled by the schedule.
   b. The manager is confident that the correct action was taken.
   c. Customers seem satisfied with the store's service.
   d. An adequate supply of paint is on hand for each weekend.

5. Discuss what alternative courses of action a manager might take to correct the inventory problem.

6. Explain the value of establishing clear standards of performance for employee activities.

Appendix to Chapter 11

SAMPLE RESPONSES FOR THE EXERCISE ON "ELEMENTS"

1. The idea introduced is "elements."
2. It can be defined as "materials that cannot be decomposed in substances with different properties."
3. Examples are nitrogen and sodium.
4. The authors elaborate on the idea by discussing the difference between "compounds" and "mixtures."
5. For questions, an instructor might ask:
   a. Define the term "elements."
   b. True or False: An element cannot decompose into substances with different properties.
   c. What is the difference between a compound and a mixture?

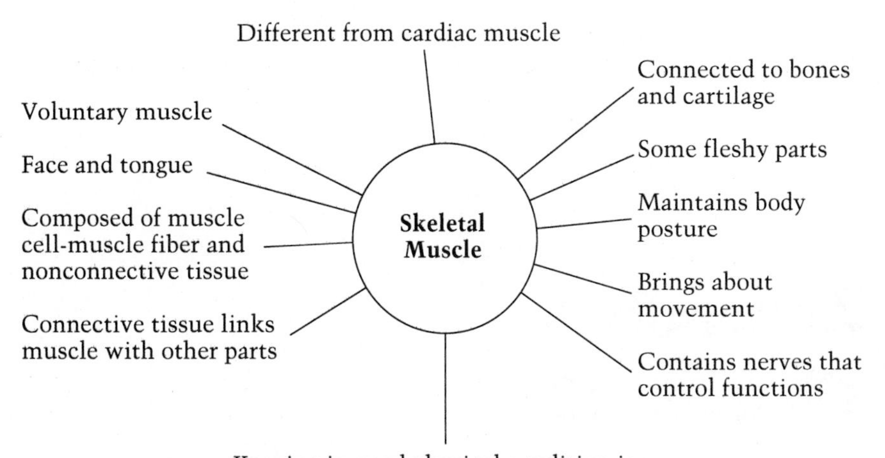

Figure 11.8 Sample Semantic Map: Skeletal Muscle

SAMPLE RESPONSES FOR THE EXERCISE ON SOLVING PROBLEMS

1. List important information:
   a. Empirical probability based on past experiences;
   b. Suggests what should happen on the basis of current knowledge;
   c. Is the relative frequency of an event.

2. Write the formula:

$$P'(E) = \frac{\text{number of times } E \text{ has occurred}}{\text{total number of times the experiment has been performed.}}$$

3. Sample Exercise Probability:

   0.67

4. Practice Exercise:

$$p'(\text{pitcher pitches a game}) = \frac{16}{50} = 0.32$$

Appendix to Chapter 12

SAMPLE RESPONSES TO "AN EXERCISE IN READING A SHORT STORY—SARAH ORNE JEWETT'S "A WHITE HERON"

1. Reading can be guided by questions relating to plot, setting, character, and theme. Examples are "Who are the characters?" and "Where does the story take place?"

2. Specific questions for character might include "Why does Sylvia adapt so well to her environment?" and "What motivated Mrs. Tilley to bring Sylvia to the farm?" Such questions involve you in the specifics of the story.

The setting is in the country, with images of a rural countryside with cows in the meadow. It's late in the afternoon, but the way through the woods is well known.

You may not have experienced the setting, but the carefree innocence of youth is a common experience. The character is realistically portrayed.

3. Additional questions are used by a diligent reader to sustain active involvement in the story. Can you think of some further questions?

4. Sylvia is especially happy to be with Mrs. Tilley because her life in the city was filled with fear, chaos, and confusion. This is a pleasant alternative.

The new young man is tall, "determined, and somewhat aggressive"—something of an opposite to Sylvia.

Sylvia's reaction is similar to her past fear and confusion. Mrs. Tilley is more accepting of the stranger. Differences in response are probably a consequence of differences in experience.

No doubt the next section will offer more insight into the connection between Sylvia and the young man.

5. Again, it's useful to continue reading with questions in mind.

6. Sylvia and the young ornithologist appear to have a love of nature in common, but their relationship to nature is quite different. Sylvia allows herself to become a part of that environment while the young man takes from the environment in the role of a collector. This difference is one potential for conflict. In addition, Sylvia is attracted to the young man as someone special and as someone who apparently has money, which her family does not.

Specific questions that occur to you may include reference to the "ideal setting," the "family history," or the "potential relationship" between Sylvia and the ornithologist.

A prediction of what may happen is somewhat obvious—a hunt for the white heron.

7. Any questions will follow from the previous assessment.

8. Sylvia and the ornithologist do go hunting, and Sylvia is attracted more to the man she sees as kind and sympathetic. Yet, she does not understand how he can kill the birds he likes. Her heart is drawn to this young man and she plans to bring him the white heron. Still, their approach to the woodlands is radically different. Sylvia may represent an accommodation with nature while the ornithologist may represent a desire to conquer nature.

9. Sylvia's search for the white heron is like an awakening to life, a realization that she can achieve what she desires with courage and determination. That search also presents her with an intimate awareness of the white heron's tender beauty and the secret of its nest. For a moment she has the sense of reward in the joy she will feel telling the young man. But is that telling a part of her character?

10. The climax comes with her decision not to reveal the locations of the heron, even in their awareness that she knows. That decision is foreshadowed by what you come to know about Sylvia, her accommodation with her environment, and the peace and security she finds in nature, a nature full of beauty of life.

11. The story now comes to a quick conclusion.

12. In the end, Sylvia wonders about the loss of her first feeling of love, when a young man first becomes meaningful to a young woman. Is the right decision ever made? Whatever, nature has won and a white heron has survived because of a choice by one young girl who understands the gifts and graces and secrets of this world.

The theme may be interpreted in many ways, but perhaps one is most obvious. There are difficult choices to be made in life when the appearance of immediate reward for oneself must be sacrificed for some more enduring value—in this case protecting the life of a white heron that represents the life and beauty of nature. Yet, the pain of such a choice is no less real.

Note that while this strategy is somewhat drawn out and involves a good deal of time, the process will eventually become a mental activity. Reading strategies, once learned, tend to move very smoothly and quickly. Detailed and lengthy analysis during reading is either a part of the learning process or used with especially difficult material. Written responses after reading for the organizational purposes are far more common.

13. The organization of "A White Heron" may look something like the following:

Summarize the plot:

"Sarah Orne Jewett's 'A White Heron' is about a lonely young girl, Sylvia, who struggles to find her place in a confusing world. Brought by her grandmother, Mrs. Tilley, from the crowded city to the rural countryside, Sylvia finds happiness in her new surroundings. Yet, this change quickly becomes unsettled with the appearance of a young ornithologist hunting a white heron. Sylvia has come to understand and appreciate nature in its natural surroundings and is saddened by the ornithologist's killing of birds to fill his collection. But Sylvia is young and her heart is attracted to this man. Perhaps she could lead him to the white heron.

"In her search, she climbs the highest tree deep in the forest at daybreak. There, among the woods and the sea and the rising sun, flies the white heron. This will be her triumph. But when it comes time, she keeps silent about the heron, and the young man leaves. She sacrifices her opportunity for love and appreciation to protect the nature of which the white heron is a part."

Describe the characters:

"Sylvia, the central character, is a young child who seeks security and peace in a rural environment, and finds herself forced to make one of the most important decisions in her life. Throughout the story she displays the traits of a dynamic character: insight, courage, love, understanding, and a struggling maturity. Her ability to make the right choice is further strengthened by the innocence of her nature.

"Mrs. Tilley is Sylvia's grandmother, who has rescued her from the city and brought her the pleasures of a rural lifestyle in which Sylvia learns the meaning of life, which serves as the basis for difficult choices.

"The young—unnamed—ornithologist is the essential source of conflict in the story. Though initially feared by Sylvia, he is seen as a kind and sympathetic person, merely desiring to add a white heron to his stuffed bird collection. That desire creates the conflict—a conflict of values—for Sylvia. On the one hand, Sylvia wishes to help him in his search and perhaps win his love. On the other hand, and ultimately, Sylvia wishes to leave the beauty of life as it is. Without the white heron, the young man will leave."

Identify the setting:

"The setting is clearly rural, a woodsy environment where Sylvia can learn about nature. In referring to the house, the text helps establish setting by noting, 'It was a surprise to find so clean and comfortable a little dwelling in this New England wilderness. And it's probably reasonable to assume that the time period is late nineteenth century, the story having been written in 1886."

State the theme:

"As Sylvia's experience suggests, there are difficult choices to be made in life when the appearance of immediate reward for oneself must be sacrificed for some more enduring value—in this case, protecting the life of a white heron that represents the life and beauty of nature. Yet the pain of such a choice is no less real."

Index

Acronyms, 136, 213, 218, 221–222, 269
Acrostics, 213–214, 217, 269
Association techniques, 216–217, 223–224
Attitude. *See* Positive attitude

Brainstorming, 223–224

College experience, 1–3, 18, 42
College resources, 3, 7. *See also* Library
Comprehension
  failure, 127–128
  note-taking for, 30
  questioning for, 31, 285
  self-monitoring, 30–32, 127–128
  summarizing for, 31–32
  think-aloud strategy, 79
  visual imagery and, 129–132
Computers, 319, 337
Concentration, 28, 71, 87–88
Concept development. *See* Vocabulary and concept development

Essay questions, 236, 242, 244–245
Essays, 314–316
Evaluating, 8–9. *See also* Self-monitoring; *specific topics*
Exams. *See* Test-taking; Tests
Exercise, physical, 68

Fiction, elements of, 277, 278–282. *See also* Literature, reading
Flash cards, 263–264
Flowcharts, 166, 173–176, 366

Goals
  flexible, 82
  immediate, 44–45
  long-term, 43–44
  setting, 43–44, 71–73
  short-term, 43–44
  specific, 43
  study, 71–73
  in time management, 41–45, 61
Grammar, 318–320
Graphic techniques, 166–176

Help, seeking, 82–83
Highlighting. *See* Marking texts

Illustrations
  in children's books, 104–106
  in remembering, 218
  in science and math study, 130, 259–260, 270
  textbook, 115, 130, 259–260, 270

Laboratory courses, 5
Laboratory manuals, 271–272
Learning, 23–36
  active, 23–36, 187, 203–204, 304
  cooperative, 80–81, 104, 199–200, 221
  evaluating, 25, 32–35
  incidental, 203–204
  intent and, 187–188
  libraries and, 336–338
  major stages in, 24–25
  planning and, 25, 26–29, 72
  self-assessment, 11, 343
  self-awareness and, 26–27
  self-monitoring, 25, 29–32
  strategies, 28, 29, 72
  taking responsibility, 24–25
Learning disability, 7
Lecture notes, 8, 87–108
  abbreviations and symbols, 96
  format, 94, 95–96
  organizing, 94–96
  outlining, 95–96
  reviewing and revising, 9, 100–107
  self-assessment, 12, 343–344
  self-monitoring, 107–108
  techniques for taking, 92–100
  see also Lectures; Note-taking
Lectures
  listening to, 87, 89–91
  organization of, 90–92
  preparation for, 89, 90–91, 92
  sample, 98–100, 104–106
Library, using the, 6, 325–339
  card catalog, 328–331
  computer systems, 337
  indexes, 331–336
  investigating resources of, 326–327
  and learning, 336–337
  microfilm, 331
  periodicals, 331–336, 337
  reference sections, 337
  self-assessment, 15, 346–347
  self-monitoring, 338–339
Listening
  active, 88–92
  inattentive, 88
  to lectures, 87, 89–90

in new situations, 5
in note-taking, 87
purpose in, 89
Literature, reading, 277–305
asking questions, 283–285
character, 278–279, 284–285, 289, 290
children's books, 104–106, 195
elements of fiction, 277, 278–282
narrator, 282–283
organizing strategies, 289–291
plot, 280–281, 284, 289, 290
self-assessment, 14, 346
self-monitoring questions, 291–304
setting, 279–280, 284, 289, 290
short stories, 292–304
strategies, 282–288
theme, 281–282, 284–285, 289–290, 291
understanding and interpreting, 288
visualizing, 285–288

Mapping, 166–170, 363–365. *See also* Semantic mapping
Marking texts, 147–154
highlighting, 28, 125, 148–149
identifying important information, 149
noting specialized vocabulary, 149–150
noting supporting points, 150–151
samples, 151–153, 360–362
self-assessment, 12–13, 344
self-monitoring, 176–177
see also Note-taking
Math study. *See* Science and math study
Memorizing, 133, 136, 262
Memory, 207–229
aids, 34–35, 270
chunking, 213–216
cognitive development, 215–216
comprehension and, 33–34
encoding, 210–212
evaluating progress, 227
forgetting, 33–34, 88, 136, 209, 220, 223–225
improving, 210–225
long-term, 194, 209
as a process, 208–209
rehearsal and, 136, 209, 211–213, 214
repetition and, 212–213
retrieval, 220–225, 234
review and, 33–34
self-assessment, 13, 346
self-monitoring, 227, 228
sensory register, 208
short-term, 193, 194, 209
storage, 212–220, 221–222
strategies for remembering, 225–227
strategies for science and math, 269–272
visual imagery and, 217–220, 222, 286
Monitoring. *See* Self-monitoring

Notebooks, 8
Note-taking, 154–177
for comprehension, 30
flowcharting, 166, 173–176
graphic techniques, 166–176
mapping, 166–170, 363–365
paraphrasing, 160–163
self-assessment, 12–13, 343–344
self-monitoring, 176–177
from texts, 125, 262
see also Lecture notes; Marking texts

Outlining
essay questions, 245–246
lecture notes, 95–96
papers, 312–313
Overlearning, 34–35, 222

Papers, writing, 308–321
conclusions, 316–317
developing, 315–316, 317, 318
drafting stage, 314–317
introduction, 314–315, 317, 318
listing information for, 312–313
outline, 312–314
planning, 309–314
revising, 317–320
resources of information, 318–320
selecting a topic, 309–311
self-assessment, 15, 346
self-monitoring, 320–321
time management, 83
Paragraph development, 315–316
Paraphrasing, 160–163
Planning
and learning, 25, 26–29, 72
papers, 309–314
and problem solving, 7–9
with purpose, 27
in purposeful study, 67–69
in test-taking, 242–243
in time management, 41, 45–51, 61
Positive attitude, 18–19
in listening, 88
and test-taking, 238
Practice. *See* Reviewing
Prefixes, 189–192
Previewing
at the beginning of lectures, 89–90
tests, 241–242

in textbook reading, 121–124
Problem solving
for memory retrieval, 223–225
plan of action for, 7–9
in science and math, 265–269
self-assessment, 10–18
self-awareness and, 4–10
in time management, 41, 58–60, 78
Punctuation, 318–320

Questioning
for comprehension, 31, 285
in listening to lectures, 90–91
in new situations, 5–6
in reading literature, 283–285
in self-monitoring, 29, 55–57
in textbook reading, 124
in time management, 55–57
Questions
discussion, 115–116, 134
essay, 236, 242, 244–245
multiple choice, 235, 243–244
subheading, 133–134
test, 233-237, 242, 256
true or false, 235, 244

Reading
literature, 277–305
passive, 71
for pleasure, 120, 277
textbooks, 112, 120–143
Reading comprehension. *See* Comprehension
Recitation, 34, 136, 269
Rehearsal
and learning, 34
and memory, 136, 209, 212–213, 214, 272
and vocabulary development, 198–200
Relaxation techniques, 68–70, 238–240
Relearning, 35, 222–223
Repetition, 212–213
Reports. *See* Papers, writing
Rereading, 136, 148
Reviewing
to evaluate learning, 33–34
lecture notes, 99–106
and memory, 33–34
in studying, 76
test answers, 243, 246–247
in textbook reading, 135, 137
Revising
lecture notes, 99–106
papers, 318–321
Root words, 189–190

Schedules
goals and, 73–74
organizing, 73–74
term/semester, 45–46
weekly, 46–55
Science and math study, 253–273
illustrations in, 130, 270
learning concepts, 260–265
remembering information, 269–272
self-assessment, 14, 345–346
self-monitoring, 272–273
solving problems, 265–269
studying textbooks, 254–260, 271
Self-assessment, 10–18
analyzing, 347–349
post-assessment, 342–347
questionnaire, 10–15, 342–347
Self-awareness, 1–19
college resources and, 3
and learning, 26–27
positive attitude and, 18–19
and problem solving, 4–18
self-assessment and, 10–18
of strengths and weaknesses, 6–7, 9
Self-concept, 66–67. *See also* Self-awareness
Self-monitoring, 8–9. *See also specific topics*
Self-talk, positive, 66–67
Self-testing
and cooperative learning, 221
to evaluate learning, 32–35
for improving retrieval, 221–223
in textbook reading, 133–134, 135–138
in vocabulary development, 199
Semantic mapping, 193–199, 264, 270, 272, 366–367, 371
Situations, new, 4–6, 7
Spaced study. *See* Study, purposeful
Spelling, 318–320
Strengths and weaknesses
analyzing, 15–18
self-awareness of, 6–7, 9, 10, 72, 134
Study, purposeful, 10, 12, 65–84
evaluating, 81–84
goals, 71–73
organizational strategies, 73–76
planning, 67–69
positive self-concept and, 66–67
preparing psychologically, 68–70
self-assessment, 12, 343
self-monitoring, 76–81
spacing for, 34, 75, 219–220
strategies, 65–66, 79–81
study materials and, 27–28

Study environment, 70–71
Study groups, 7, 80, 199–200
Success, identifying, 83
Suffixes, 189–192
Suggested readings, 89, 115–116
Summaries
  for comprehension, 31–32
  conclusions, in papers, 316–317
  in note-taking, 154–160
  periodic, in testbook reading, 134, 163–166
  plot, 289, 290
  writing, 31–32

Test-taking, 232–250
  evaluating text results, 9, 247–248, 249
  following directions, 240–241
  planning an approach, 242–243
  predicting questions, 233–237, 256
  preparation, 25, 238
  previewing the test, 241–242
  reviewing answers, 243–244, 246–247
  self-assessment, 14, 345
  self-monitoring, 248–249
  strategies, 240–248
  test-anxiety, 237–240
Tests
  chapter, 134
  essay, 236, 242, 244–245
  multiple choice, 235, 243–244
  true or false, 235, 244
  see also Self-testing; Test-taking
Textbook reading, 112–143
  basic steps in, 120
  cumulative process in, 132–133
  fix-up strategies for, 127–129
  identifying important information, 124
  note-taking and, 125
  periodic summaries in, 134
  previewing strategies for, 121–124
  review process, 135, 137
  self-assessment, 12, 344
  self-monitoring, 127, 142–143
  self-testing in, 133–134, 135–138
  systematic approach to, 121–142, 143
  using visual imagery in, 129–132
Textbooks
  chapter objective, 114
  chapter organization, 114, 143, 163, 255
  chapter outline, 114
  chapter previews, 254–257
  chapter subheadings, 115, 124–125, 133–134, 255
  chapter summaries, 134
  chapter tests, 134
  discussion questions, 115–116
  graphic overviews, 254–257
  illustrations, 115, 259–260, 270
  marking, 12–13, 28, 125
  organization, 27–28, 113–120, 254, 257–258
  patterns of chapter content, 114–115
  purpose, 113
  science and math, 254–260, 271
  suggested reading, 115–116
  word cues and phrase patterns, 116–117, 125
  writing patterns, 257–258
Think-aloud strategy
  for comprehension, 79
  for textbook reading, 125–127, 130–132
Time management, 40–61
  basic steps in, 41
  evaluating strategies for, 41, 60–61
  goals in, 41–45, 61
  planning in, 41, 45–51, 61
  problem solving techniques, 41, 58–60, 61, 78
  scheduling, 51–55
  self-assessment, 11, 343
  self-monitoring, 41, 55–57, 61
Tutoring, 7

Underlining. *See* Marking texts

Visual imagery
  and comprehension, 129–132
  exercises in, 68–70
  and memory, 217–218, 222, 270, 286
  and reading literature, 285–288
Vocabulary, specialized, 149
Vocabulary and concept development, 181–204, 260–265
  concept words, 184–187, 192–193
  defining words, 182–187, 191–192
  evaluating, 201–202
  and learning, 187–188, 203–204
  learning strategies for, 187–203
  prior knowledge and, 188, 193, 196, 261
  self-assessment, 13, 181–204, 344–345
  self-monitoring, 200–201
  specialized terminology, 187, 192–193
  systematic approach to, 201–202
  unfamiliar words, 186–187, 188–192, 198
  words in context, 183–184, 186, 188

Weaknesses. *See* Strengths and weaknesses
Weekly schedules, 46–55
Word collection, 199
Word definitions. *See* Vocabulary and concept development
Word-processing programs, 319
Writing
  essays, 314–317
  papers, 308–321
  summaries, 31–32

CREDITS

Continued from the copyright page

Chapter 7, notes 2, 3, and 4, excerpt from *Introduction to Sociology* by Henry L. Tischler, Phillip Whitten, and David E. K. Hunter, copyright © 1983 by Holt, Rinehart and Winston, Inc. Reprinted by permission of the publisher.

Chapter 7, note 7, from *Personal Adjustment: The Psychology of Everyday Life*, 2d ed., by Valerian J. Derlega and Louis H. Janda. Copyright © 1981 by Scott, Foresman and Company. Reprinted by permission.

Chapter 7, notes 8 and 10, from *Cultural Anthropology* by Serena Nanda, © 1980 by Litton Educational Publishing, Inc. Reprinted by permission of Wadsworth, Inc.

Chapter 7, notes 9 and 12, excerpts from *The Psychology of Being Human* by Zick Rubin and Marjorie McNeil. Copyright © 1977 by Marjorie McNeil and Zick Rubin. Reprinted by permission of Harper & Row, Publishers, Inc.

Chapter 7, note 13, excerpt from *Human Communication: The Basic Course*, 3rd ed., by Joseph A. DeVito. Copyright © 1985 by Harper & Row, Publishers, Inc. Reprinted by permission of the publisher.

Chapter 11, note 5, from *Earth* by Frank Press and Raymond Siever. Copyright © 1974, 1978, 1982 by W. H. Freeman and Company. Reprinted by permission.

Chapter 11, note 6, from *The Solar System* by Roman Smoluchowski. Copyright © 1983 by Scientific American Books, Inc. Reprinted by permission of W. H. Freeman and Company.

Chapter 11, note 10, from *A Survey of Mathematics*, 2d ed., by Allen R. Angel and Stuart R. Porter. Copyright © 1985 by Addison-Wesley Publishing Co. Reprinted by permission of Addison-Wesley Publishing Co., Inc. Reading, MA.

Chapter 14, note 1, from *Readers' Guide to Periodical Literature*, 1988, Vol. 48, page 678. Copyright © 1988, 1989 by The H. W. Wilson Company. Material reproduced by permission of the publisher.

Chapter 14, note 2, a selection from *Book Review Index*, 1988, edited by Barbara Beach and Beverly Baer. Copyright © 1989 by Gale Research Inc. All rights reserved. Reprinted by permission of the publisher.

Chapter 14, note 4, from *Social Science Index*, 1988–1989. Copyright © 1989 by the H. W. Wilson Company. Material reproduced by permission of the publisher.